T0355409

Child Psychology in Twelve Questions

Child Psychology in Twelve Questions

Paul L. Harris

OXFORD
UNIVERSITY PRESS

OXFORD
UNIVERSITY PRESS

Great Clarendon Street, Oxford, OX2 6DP,
United Kingdom

Oxford University Press is a department of the University of Oxford.
It furthers the University's objective of excellence in research, scholarship,
and education by publishing worldwide. Oxford is a registered trade mark of
Oxford University Press in the UK and in certain other countries

© Paul L. Harris 2022

The moral rights of the author have been asserted

Published in the United States of America by Oxford University Press
198 Madison Avenue, New York, NY 10016, United States of America

British Library Cataloguing in Publication Data
Data available

Library of Congress Control Number: 2022931966

ISBN 978-0-19-286650-9

DOI: 10.1093/oso/9780192866509.001.0001

Printed and bound by
CPI Group (UK) Ltd, Croydon, CR0 4YY

Links to third party websites are provided by Oxford in good faith and
for information only. Oxford disclaims any responsibility for the materials
contained in any third party website referenced in this work.

Contents

Acknowledgments

Given the protracted gestation of this book, it is hard to provide an exhaustive list of all the people who offered help, feedback, and encouragement along the way, but particular expressions of sincere gratitude are definitely in order. The course on which the book is based has been taken by nearly a thousand students. I thank them for their participation, enthusiasm, and questions. I especially thank those who have remained in touch or pursued some aspect of the topics that we discussed in class. I am also grateful to the many teaching fellows and doctoral students who, over the years, alerted me to lines of argument or enquiry that I had overlooked. Several people—Susan Engel, Vikram Jaswal, Carl Johnson, Bob Kavanaugh, Mark Meerum Terwogt, Frosso Motti-Stefanidi, Meredith Rowe, and Simon Torracinta—kindly provided comments on individual chapters. Finally, two anonymous reviewers read the entire manuscript. They responded with enough enthusiasm for me to stop my endless tinkering. I am especially grateful to them.

Introduction

Child psychology as a scientific enterprise is about a hundred years old—comparatively juvenile in comparison to other branches of science. Yet the reader who wants to learn what has been discovered so far faces an obstacle. There are plenty of textbooks offering an encyclopedic review. They are packed with recent research, aimed at the latest cohort of students, but such a welter of findings and mini controversies can obscure enduring questions as well as established answers. Admittedly, firmer guidance is on offer in books aiming to help parents and teachers. In these books, however, the more meditative and less practical questions about the nature of the child's mind are rarely asked.

I promise to be neither encyclopedic nor especially practical. Instead, I propose to discuss some of the enduring questions in developmental psychology. For example, how do children become attached to their caregivers? Are they confused or clear-sighted about the difference between fantasy and reality? When and how do they form a sense of right and wrong? How far do children construct their own basic ideas about the world or believe what other people tell them? Is it reasonable to conceive of children as budding scientists or should we think of them as theologians, or even as anthropologists? In each case, I try to give readers a sense of why these questions are important, the answers that have been proposed, and the uncertainties that persist.

The book has been written for the general reader who wants to learn about the field of developmental psychology. It is based on an introductory course in Developmental Psychology that I have taught and steadily honed since 2001 to students at the Harvard Graduate School of Education with little or no background in psychology. The students come from a wide range of disciplines, from many different countries, and from a considerable age range (about 22–70 years). Most take the course for credit, but none is obliged to take it. Over the years, there has also been a succession of auditors who have taken the course out of curiosity or based on a personal or professional interest in children.

The structure of the book is simple. Each chapter takes up a distinct topic—for example, the development of attachment or morality or memory—and describes the central questions and findings for that topic. Although there is attention to historical shifts in research, the focus is primarily on what has endured. Where relevant, readers are introduced to influential researchers, with appropriate biographical material.

In the concluding chapter, I highlight three recurrent themes. First, no matter where they are born on the habitable planet, children's biological endowment enables them to rapidly make sense of, and internalize, the surrounding culture—its social mores, its language(s), and its belief system. Second, young children display a complicated mix of deference and independent-mindedness; they seek information from others, but they can also set that information aside, come to their own conclusions, and act on them. Finally, children's judgments and their behavior are not always coherent; like the adults they will grow into, they can be disconcertingly inconsistent.

So, this is a somewhat idiosyncratic introduction to the psychology of the child, not an exhaustive overview: *Rough Guide* rather than *Michelin*. But I hope to give readers a sense of the important landmarks, both well known and neglected, and to show that understanding the minds of children is not an enterprise for the impatient or the fast moving. It calls for a willingness to linger.

1
Where does love come from?

Attachment theory

Do children's early relationships, especially with caregivers, have an enduring impact on their emotional life? Thanks to the research program set in motion by the English psychiatrist John Bowlby, we have persuasive evidence for such a long-term influence. Born in 1907 into a wealthy, upper-class, English family, Bowlby was sent to a boarding school at the age of 10. His later comment on that experience was caustic. He told his wife that he: "would not send a dog to boarding school". With a view to following in his father's footsteps, Bowlby went on to study medicine at Trinity College, Cambridge, but he also looked further afield, taking courses in philosophy and psychology.

A critical interlude followed. Bowlby took temporary positions as a teacher at two special schools. One was Bedales, a progressive, co-educational boarding school that must have differed sharply from the Spartan boarding school he had attended. The other was Priory Gate, a small residential school catering for "difficult" or "maladjusted" children that emphasized accommodation, wherever possible, to the child's curiosity and natural impulses. Two children made a lasting impression on Bowlby: a 7-year-old boy, who spent the whole day trailing after him and came to be known as Bowlby's "shadow", and a 16-year-old boy, the illegitimate son of wealthy parents, emotionally deprived as a child and expelled from his previous school for persistent stealing. Many years later, Bowlby wrote about these encounters: "I was alerted to a possible connection between prolonged deprivation and the development of a personality apparently incapable of making affectional bonds, and because immune to praise and blame, prone to repeated delinquencies."

These experiences consolidated Bowlby's decision to pursue a career in psychiatry. He completed his training in medicine and psychiatry and concurrently entered into a training analysis in order to become a psychoanalyst. His supervisor was Melanie Klein, but their relationship was conflictual. She stressed the impact of children's early fantasies on their psychological development, whereas Bowlby was keen to study the impact of real emotional deprivation of the kind he had glimpsed at Priory Gate.

After World War II, when many children had been orphaned and displaced, Bowlby had an unexpected opportunity. He was invited by the World Health Authority to write a review of research on the effects of early maternal deprivation and loss. His report—"Child Care and the Growth of Love"—was eventually published in 1953 and became a bestseller (Bowlby, 1953). Using a medical analogy, Bowlby concluded that just as a child's physical growth requires nourishment from vitamins, so a child's emotional development requires nourishment from love. In the decades that followed, drawing on ideas from psychoanalysis, ethology, and psychology, Bowlby set out a magisterial account of emotional development in a highly influential trilogy: "Attachment" (1969), "Separation" (1973), and "Loss" (1980).

Bowlby emphasized that the young of many species rapidly form an attachment to a caregiver. This attachment is not based on any genetic connection to the mother but rather on a biological program for developing an attachment. Newborns are equipped to seek out and identify an attachment figure. Goslings, for example, become attached to the first figure that appears before them after birth. Normally, this is the mother goose, but, as the ethologist Konrad Lorenz discovered, if a human adult looms over a newborn gosling instead, he will become an attachment figure instead. A famous photograph of Lorenz shows him swimming across a lake followed by a small flotilla of goslings.

Do human infants have such an attachment program? At first sight, this seems unlikely. After all, babies are scarcely able to swim or even waddle after an attachment figure. Still, as Bowlby pointed out, they have a repertoire of signals and behaviors that make it highly probable, if not certain, that a caregiver will be close by. Babies can vocalize and cry to summon a caregiver, and as they get older they can crawl and toddle in pursuit. Bowlby thought of this attachment repertoire as a system organized like a thermostat. The baby has a target level of desired closeness to the caregiver, much as a thermostat can be set to a desired temperature. If this target is not reached—if the caregiver is too far away—the attachment system gets switched on, and the baby draws on its repertoire to get closer to the caregiver—the baby will cry, vocalize, crawl, etc., depending on its age and on where the caregiver is situated. So long as the attachment system is switched on, it takes control, overriding other behavioral systems in the baby's repertoire. For example, the various activities involved in play and exploration are put on hold. But once the desired level of proximity to the caregiver is reached, the attachment system is switched off, the baby settles down again, and other systems of behavior, including play and exploration, can be reactivated. The target level of proximity to the caregiver is not necessarily constant. A tired or sick baby will want to be closer to a caregiver and so the attachment system is likely to be switched on more often and to be more difficult to deactivate. In common parlance, a sleepy or sick baby will become "clingy".

Bowlby argued that, at first, babies are indiscriminate in their attachment seeking. They are likely to send out their "come hither" signals—gurgles and smiles—to all-comers, but from around 6 months, they become more selective. They seek out and become preferentially attached to a person who has reliably responded to their past signals. That person may or may not be the biological mother or even the person who looks after the baby's physical needs. Just like goslings, the tie between a human baby and an attachment figure is not based on a genetic connection. Rather, the baby's brain is programed to be opportunistic—it is on the lookout for a caregiver who is responsive and available, whoever that might be.

What happens when an attachment is formed but subsequently disrupted? For example, what happens if the mother is absent or unavailable for a prolonged period of days or weeks? Initially—and this is what we would expect in terms of attachment theory—there is an intense activation of the attachment system. The baby cries passionately and searches for the loved one. But if she does not return, despair and listlessness set in, although these reactions are sharply reduced if another attentive caregiver is available, especially someone who is already familiar to the baby (Robertson & Robertson, 1971). If the absence is prolonged, the baby starts to emotionally detach him- or herself from the lost caregiver. If the caregiver does return, the baby may look or turn away or resist being picked up and cuddled. If the absence is permanent and no alternative caregiver is available—if, for example, the infant ends up in an orphanage with no personalized care over a sustained period—long-term problems in the formation of selective emotional ties may ensue. We will discuss those problems in due course.

Looking back at Bowlby's trilogy, we can see that it is a three-way synthesis. From psychoanalysis, he took the idea that early experience has enduring effects, although unlike Melanie Klein, he insisted on the impact of actual caregiving as opposed to fantasized experience. From ethology, he took the idea that the human baby, like the young of many species, is born with an innate repertoire aimed at establishing an attachment with an available and responsive caregiver. Finally, from experimental psychology, he derived a fuller appreciation of the devastating effects of prolonged social deprivation. The work of Harry Harlow was especially influential in this respect (Harlow, 1958).

Harlow set out to discredit the prevailing assumption in learning theory that any attachment between child and mother was ultimately grounded in the satisfaction of basic physical needs, notably hunger and thirst. His classic experiment on this issue was conducted with baby rhesus monkeys raised with two artificial "mothers". One mother, fashioned from wire, offered a source of milk. The other, roughly similar in size and shape, offered no milk but provided what came to be known as contact comfort; this mother was covered in a soft-textured cloth and was, therefore, more gratifying to cuddle and cling to. Harlow observed that it was the cloth rather than the wire mother who came to serve as an attachment figure—not just because the baby monkey nestled up to her more often, but also because, at moments of anxiety or distress, the monkey would run back to her rather than the wire mother. Indeed, the cloth mother became a kind of haven or secure base to which the monkey could retreat in search of comfort and, once calmed, venture forth to explore the wider environment.

Still, a cloth mother proved to be no substitute for a real mother. Harlow's larger body of research went on to show that monkeys deprived of access to flesh and blood interaction exhibited problems in later life. They were rebuffed by peers who had been raised under normal rearing conditions; they were ineffectual sexual partners; and if they did eventually deliver children of their own, they displayed little caregiving competence, sometimes trampling on and mistreating their own infants. Harlow and his colleagues effectively demonstrated that prolonged maternal and social deprivation in early childhood can have effects not just on emotional development in childhood but on relationships during adolescence and adulthood (Ruppenthal et al., 1976).

Patterns of attachment

Attachment theory took a new turn when Mary Ainsworth, an American developmental psychologist, began to collaborate with Bowlby. Ainsworth did not study the effects of severe deprivation— the gross and unremitting deprivation that Harlow had focused on with rhesus monkeys or the distress caused by prolonged separation from an attachment figure. Instead, she was interested in the more subtle forms of "unavailability" that human mothers might show. Effectively, she prompted Bowlby, as well as subsequent generations of attachment researchers, to focus on variation in patterns of caregiving that fall within the normal range. She argued that mothers who respond to a baby's signals, and who thereby foster an attachment, will nonetheless vary in the way they respond. Some will be good at noting and interpreting the baby's signals of distress and prompt in offering comfort. Some might have worries or dispositions that make it harder for them to focus on the baby. Given these sources of variation, it is likely that babies will differ in what they expect of their mothers. Some mothers will come to be seen as reliable and sensitive in their responses to signals of discomfort and distress, whereas others will not.

Building on the findings of an earlier study conducted with mothers and infants in Uganda, Ainsworth and her colleagues (Ainsworth et al., 1978) devised a test to put these potential differences under a psychological microscope. The basic idea was disarmingly simple: find a way to switch on the attachment system, make a close-range, observational analysis of how infants cope, note individual variation in their patterns of responding, and group together those who show similar patterns. To activate the attachment system, Ainsworth brought mothers and their 12-month-old infants into an unfamiliar sitting-room with plenty of toys. The successive episodes of this so-called Strange Situation procedure included an opportunity for the baby to play with the toys alongside their mother, to respond to a stranger who came into the room, to cope with being left with the stranger for a brief period, and also to cope with being left completely alone for a short period before a reunion with the mother.

Ainsworth and her colleagues identified three different patterns of responding: secure, avoidant, and resistant. Secure babies willingly went to the mother on her return. If they had been upset by her departure, they were soon reassured when she came back. More generally, in the presence of the mother, these babies played happily. This secure pattern was displayed by the majority of the babies. The remaining minority was split between two different subgroups: avoidant and resistant. On reunion with the mother, avoidant babies did not actively approach her. They often continued playing with the toys in the room. Even if they had been upset at the mother's initial departure, they showed no definite inclination to approach her. Resistant babies were generally upset when the mother left and, like secure babies, they approached her on her return, but they were less easily comforted. Indeed, they often displayed an ambivalent pattern toward the mother, approaching her for comfort but then scrambling away from her.

Ainsworth interpreted these patterns of behavior as reflecting different strategies that babies learn to adopt in dealing with their mother's perceived availability. Secure babies are confident. They have learned that their caregiver can be counted on as a source of reassurance. When she is there, she serves as a secure base for play and exploration, and when she returns after an absence, she is an immediately reassuring presence. Avoidant babies, by contrast, have come to expect that their caregiver will be unavailable, either literally or at a psychological level. Convinced that they will not obtain comfort from her, they give up and turn away. So, when she returns, they do not actively approach her. Resistant babies have conflicting hopes and expectations. They seek reassurance from their caregiver, but they have learned that she is sometimes unavailable or unresponsive. So, they approach her with misgivings, sometimes backing off after a bid for comfort.

There is considerable support for the claim that these different patterns of attachment reflect the way that the caregiver thinks about and responds to the baby. First, over many studies, measures of the mother's responsiveness predict the kind of attachment that the baby shows toward her (De Wolff & van IJzendoorn, 1997). Indeed, interviews that focus on how the mother thinks about her baby, particularly the extent to which she regards her baby as a distinct person with individual thoughts and feelings, are, if anything, better predictors of later attachment than observations of her overt mothering (Meins et al., 2001). Second, infants often show distinct but nevertheless stable patterns of attachment with different caregivers. For example, they might show a secure pattern with their father but a resistant pattern with their mother. Some have argued that a baby's personality, and especially his or her emotional temperament, is primarily responsible for the type of attachment that he or she displays (Kagan, 1995). But if temperament were the determining factor, we would expect a baby to respond similarly to different caregivers. Finally, intervention studies directed at helping mothers to interpret and respond to their baby's signals increase the likelihood of a secure attachment (Bakermans-Kranenburg et al., 2003).

Patterns of early attachment are also useful predictors of how infants will subsequently behave in other domains. As we will discuss in Chapter 4, pretend play starts to emerge in the second year of life. Toddlers "feed" their dolls, "answer" a pretend telephone, orchestrate make-believe tea parties, or flee from imaginary monsters. When they play together with their mother, securely attached toddlers are more likely to engage in longer and richer bouts of such fantasy play than their resistant or avoidant peers (Slade, 1987). When these secure toddlers are older and go off to kindergarten or school, they display more curiosity, are better able to make and retain friendships, and are less dependent on teachers (Arend et al., 1979; Schneider et al., 2001; Sroufe, 1983).

Can attachment theory, with its emphasis on the well-being of a securely attached child, be extended to children growing up in different cultures? A host of investigators—in the USA, the UK, Germany, Israel, China, Japan, Indonesia, Mexico, South Africa, Kenya, Mali, and many other countries—would say yes. If children from different cultures are tested in the Strange Situation, the majority typically shows a secure attachment, as would be expected, and the remaining minority can generally be allocated to either the insecure avoidant or resistant categories (Mesman et al., 2016).

By implication, attachment theory travels well: all babies have an innate repertoire for forming attachments, and most end up displaying one of the three basic patterns of attachment to a primary caregiver, be it secure, avoidant, or resistant. Still, it is possible to launch a more radical critique. Arguably, the emphasis in attachment theory on maternal sensitivity to infant signals betrays a Western bias. More specifically, in line with the Western valuation of personal autonomy, it presumes that individual caregivers should be sensitively attuned to infants' needs with the longer-term goal of nurturing their self-expression and emotional independence. However, researchers with a more anthropological orientation have emphasized that outside the Western industrialized world, many communities have a radically different child-rearing agenda. First, the care of babies and toddlers rarely falls on the shoulders of a single person. Instead, a flexible network of parents, grandparents, older siblings, and neighbors looks after them. Second, such communities do not prioritize the sensitivity of a lone caregiver to a particular infant's needs. Rather, they expect children, even infants, to accommodate to the agenda of the family and the larger caregiving community (Keller, 2018). Still, it is worth remembering that the Strange Situation and its diagnostic significance had been inspired by Ainsworth's earlier findings in Uganda.

Aiming to bridge this alleged divide, Judi Mesman and her colleagues looked for episodes of sensitive caregiving in three non-Western rural communities: a coastal community in the northeastern Philippines, a foraging pygmy community in the Republic of Congo, and a small-scale agrarian community in central Mali (Mesman et al., 2018). In each site, they observed episodes of prompt responding to infant signals by caregivers other than the mother. For example, an aunt oriented her 7-month-old niece to look at some passing children, but when her niece started to fuss, she promptly handed her back to her mother, who in turn offered the breast. A father interrupted his work on a fishing instrument to respond to the vocal bids of his 18-month-old daughter; he fetched a packet of crackers, opened them for her when she could not manage with her teeth, and eventually got a cup of water when she made further bids for his care. An uncle noticed that his 13-month-old niece, having been frightened by something, had started to cry. He took her in his arms, whereupon she immediately stopped crying. The uncle in this episode was 3 years old, underlining the way that caregiving is widely distributed. In the context of such distributed caregiving, it is reasonable to ask if attachment theory, with its primary focus on the infant's relationship with a single caregiver, can be applied to such settings. Contrary to critics of attachment theory (e.g., Keller et al., 2018), I am cautiously optimistic that such an extension is feasible, especially if we focus on infants' competence and flexibility. In these non-Western settings, we continue to see infants deploying a variety of signals to elicit the care they need. Admittedly, the responses they receive may come from a wider range of caregivers, but even in these settings, infants still differentiate among those potential caregivers and produce their bids selectively (Meehan & Hawks, 2013). I return to this theme of infant selectivity at the end of the chapter.

New ideas in attachment theory

In the hands of Bowlby and Ainsworth, the focus of attachment theory was on the infant and young child. To be sure, they also observed the mother, but primarily in order to understand her impact on the developing child. Mary Main, a former student and collaborator of Ainsworth, expanded that focus. She devised the Adult Attachment Interview (AAI) to uncover adults' tacit or unconscious notions of how close attachments work (Main et al., 1985). In this interview, adults are asked to think back to their childhood, to recall emotionally charged episodes with their parents, and to describe and interpret their parents' behavior and feelings. The interview transcript is then coded along various dimensions, especially the "coherence" with which episodes are remembered and narrated, as well as the presence of any unrealistic idealization of the parents. Main ended up identifying three different patterns of response to the AAI. Adults characterized as "autonomous" describe their childhood in an accepting, coherent, and internally consistent fashion. Adults characterized as "dismissing" give brief, incomplete accounts, profess to have few childhood memories, and tend to idealize the past and their parents. Finally, "preoccupied" adults give inconsistent, rambling accounts in which they appear to be still struggling with past conflicts.

In various ways, these adult patterns echo what is found in infancy. The autonomous, dismissive, or preoccupied stance of the adult resembles the secure, avoidant, or resistant stance of the infant. Does this mean that such patterns can be transmitted across generations? Analyzing a large number of independent studies, van IJzendoorn (1995) found that mothers classified as autonomous on the basis of the AAI interview were indeed more likely to have a securely attached infant. In one especially compelling study, the mothers were interviewed when they were pregnant. Months later, when their infants were 1-year-olds, they were observed in the Strange Situation procedure. The expected connections emerged—with autonomous mothers especially likely to have an infant with a secure attachment (Fonagy et al., 1991). By implication, caregivers' distilled memories—or reconstructions—of the care that they received as children tacitly guide, or at least foretell, the type of attachment they will have with their own children. For better or worse, when they become parents, adults often end up recreating with their own children the pattern that they recount about their own childhood.

Does the three-way classification created by Ainsworth truly exhaust all the configurations that exist between child and caregiver? For many years, researchers had occasionally noted hard-to-classify infants who showed puzzling signs of more than one attachment category, or showed unexpected and odd behaviors such as abrupt immobility or "freezing", together with signs of apprehension toward their caregiver. Main and Solomon (1990) proposed that a fourth category be created for these so-called disorganized infants. They suggested that these infants had not settled on a stable strategy for coping with distress—hence the difficulty in assigning them to one of the classic trio of attachment patterns.

Subsequent research has suggested that the D or "disorganized" pattern, despite its unsettled character, can be reliably identified and remains stable during the infancy period (van IJzendoorn et al., 1999). Its frequency does not vary with the baby's gender or temperament, or with the mother's mental health. Nevertheless, family background factors appear to play a key role. In a representative sample of infants across the USA, the incidence of the disorganized pattern was around 15%, but that figure climbed to 25% in a sample with a low socioeconomic status (SES) and to just under 50% in a sample of maltreated infants. Accordingly, investigators have concluded that the disorganized pattern can be a response to maltreatment. That said, it is important to caution that maltreatment by a caregiver does not invariably lead to a disorganized pattern of attachment. In addition, the disorganized pattern can be found in the absence of any clear evidence for maltreatment (Granqvist et al., 2017). For example, the disorganized pattern is frequent among children raised in institutional settings, but the potential contribution of maltreatment in those settings remains unclear (Lionetti et al., 2015).

Pending further analysis of the exact causes of the disorganized pattern, researchers underline the following plausible paradox, well captured by attachment theory. Suppose that the infant ordinarily turns to a familiar caregiver for comfort at times of distress or fear—one of the fundamental attachment responses according to Bowlby and Ainsworth. But suppose further that an infant also reacts with distress or fear to angry or alarming behavior on the part of the caregiver, and indeed becomes wary of a caregiver who is prone to such behavior. It is not hard to see that such an infant might then display a conflicted or paradoxical reaction. The caregiver who is the source of the infant's distress or alarm is also a potential source of reassurance and comfort. But to seek reassurance from him or her is to approach a source of distress and alarm. Under these circumstances, the infant might well show a conflicted or disorganized pattern of behavior.

Romantic relationships

So far, we have seen that attachment theory can be applied to both sides of the parent–child relationship. It helps make sense of the behavior of the infant as well as the pattern of caregiving shown by a parent. What about romantic relationships between adults? Is there any kind of parallel between romantic love and the patterns of attachment we see between parent and child? To start to explore this question, Hazan and Shaver (1987) distributed a questionnaire in their local newspaper—*The Rocky Mountain News*—and analyzed the replies from several hundred respondents ranging from 14 to 92 years. They also followed up with a sample of college students—mostly in their late teens. Participants were asked to say which of the following three options best applied to them:

1. *I am somewhat uncomfortable being close to others; I find it difficult to trust them completely, difficult to allow myself to depend on them. I am nervous when anyone gets too close, and often love*

partners want me to be more intimate than I feel comfortable being.

2. *I find it relatively easy to get close to others and am comfortable depending on them and having them depend on me. I don't often worry about being abandoned or about someone getting too close to me.*

3. *I find that others are reluctant to get as close as I would like. I often worry that my partner doesn't really love me or won't want to stay with me. I want to merge completely with another person, and this desire sometimes scares people away.*

The studies of the two different samples produced almost identical results. The majority of respondents judged that option 2 applied to them, and around 20% judged that one of the other two options applied to them. Option 2 is not hard to recognize as the "secure" option, with options 1 and 3 being the avoidant and resistant options, respectively. Participants' self-assessments turned out to predict their replies to further questions about love and romance. For example, secure participants were more likely than either of the other two groups to agree that: "In some relationships, romantic love really lasts; it doesn't fade with time." On the other hand, resistant participants were quite likely to agree that: "It's easy to fall in love. I feel myself beginning to fall in love often", whereas avoidant participants almost never endorsed that option.

These findings suggested that in terms of emotional dynamics, there are intriguing parallels between parenting and romance. In both cases, the relationship settles into a recognizable pattern, even if debate continues about how best to characterize those parallels (Fraley & Shaver, 2000). There is also some evidence that early attachment patterns predict how people behave within a romantic relationship. For example, in a longitudinal study carried out at the University of Minnesota, 20-year-olds who had shown more consistent signs of a secure attachment when they had been observed as toddlers were less prone to get enmeshed in disagreement with their romantic partners. They were better able to move on to a more positive discussion following a conflictual exchange. Indeed, their partners showed the same ability to tamp down conflict (Salvatore et al., 2011).

Impressive continuity in close relationships was reported by Waldinger and Schulz (2016). They interviewed 80-year-old men about their relationship with their partner—with these relationships averaging 40 years in length. The interview was modeled on the AAI described earlier and provided a composite index of the extent to which the men described—in a credible and coherent fashion—a loving, secure relationship with their partner. The men had been recruited into the study decades earlier when they were adolescents. At that point, the quality of their relationships with their parents had been assessed via lengthy interviews lasting 10–12 hours. Again, a composite index was derived, indicating the overall warmth of these family relationships. Waldinger and Schulz (2016) found that there was a modest link between the two measures: adolescents with warmer family relationships ended up as octogenarians with more secure and loving relationships with their partners—arguably, a connection that was carried forward over the years by the ways in which the men coped with emotionally challenging episodes, as assessed in mid-life, when they were between 45 and 50 years of age. Moreover, similar findings emerged for each of the two cohorts in the study— men who had attended Harvard as undergraduates and men from disadvantaged families in low-income Boston neighborhoods.

Religion and attachment

Granted that Bowlby's ideas are helpful in conceptualizing adults' romantic relationships, some researchers have pushed even further. They have asked if attachment theory can help us to think about religious beliefs and religious practices. A central tenet of Christianity is that it is appropriate to turn to God for reassurance and comfort, especially at times of loss or grief. In that sense, it is not unreasonable to think of God as an attachment figure, albeit with divine attributes. With this in mind, attachment researchers have emphasized intriguing parallels between ordinary attachments and the way that believers represent their relationship to God. First, God is often seen not as a remote, otherworldly figure but as someone who is ever present and available. Designated modes of communication, notably prayer or ritual, as well as dedicated places of worship typically serve to enhance the sense of proximity to God or communion with Him. In addition, as attachment theorists would expect, there is evidence that anxiety and distress are likely to increase the likelihood of such proximity seeking. For example, Brown and colleagues (2004) found that widows, as compared to women who had not lost their spouse, showed an increase in the importance they attached to their religious beliefs, and the greater that perceived importance, the greater the reduction in their grief.

Does the particular type of attachment an individual has acquired in the context of their family relationships influence the way that they conceive of their relationship to God? As explained by Granqvist and Kirkpatrick (2016), two different possibilities seem feasible. On the one hand, there might be a close correspondence between the two types of attachment. For example, adults who have a mental model of family attachment figures as reliable and trustworthy might have a similar conception of God. On the other hand, some form of compensation might also be feasible. Adults who have come to think of other people as unreliable and inconstant might find it especially comforting and reassuring to turn to God instead. After all, God might be seen as providing the type of security and constancy that ordinary human relationships cannot provide. Recent studies provide some evidence for both the correspondence and the compensation pathways (Granqvist et al., 2020). Individuals who have stable attachment relationships are likely to conceive of God in similar terms—as a stable and beneficent figure. Individuals with less secure relationships are more likely to report experiencing a sudden conversion, especially in a period of emotional turmoil.

The research just described focuses on individual differences among adults. In that respect it echoes the line of research initiated by Ainsworth—who stressed individual differences among children in their attachment to a caregiver. Still, it is worth underlining an important paradox that emerges when we extend attachment theory to religion, especially to Abrahamic religions such as Christianity, Judaism, and Islam in which a patriarchal figure plays a central role. For Bowlby and his associates, the physical presence of an attachment figure was seen as vital for emotional well-being, with separation or prolonged loss detrimental to that well-being. Yet God is not ordinarily present in any physical sense. How then do believers take comfort in him? Attachment theory offers the beginnings of an answer. As Bowlby argued, older infants and children construct a so-called working model—a mental representation of how a close relationship works. It is this mental model that comes to guide their behavior to an attachment figure and their expectations about how responsive the attachment figure will be. It is a short additional step to suppose that, eventually, it is the working model itself, and especially the ease with which it can be brought to mind, rather than the physical presence of the attachment figure that provides reassurance. In concrete terms, children might console themselves by mentally activating the working model of their attachment relationship, even when the attachment figure is physically absent. This seems plausible enough. After all, as they get older, young children do accept separations more easily. Similarly, it seems feasible that adults can gain consolation by bringing to mind the working model that they have of their relationship to God. That mental act would in itself provide solace.

Severe deprivation—Bowlby revisited

Bowlby's encounters as a teacher at Priory Gate, as well as the many studies that he reviewed in the aftermath of World War II, had suggested that early emotional deprivation has an impact on development not just in the short term but also in the long term, leaving a permanent mark on the child's developing mind and brain. The research carried out by Harlow with rhesus monkeys lent support to that possibility. Systematic maternal deprivation in childhood led to persistent social and emotional problems well into adulthood.

On the other hand, some later studies, many of them carried out in the UK, offered a more optimistic picture of early deprivation. When children were moved from poor institutional care to adoptive or foster homes, they often displayed a remarkable recovery. Two influential overviews of these findings, one by Ann and Alan Clarke and one by Michael Rutter, encouraged a belief in the plasticity of the developing brain, and more broadly in the beneficial effects that adoption can offer to children who have suffered early social and emotional deprivation (Clarke & Clarke, 1976; Rutter, 1972).

The fall of the Ceausescu regime in Romania in 1989 unexpectedly reopened the question of whether all forms of early deprivation can be resolved. Researchers had already studied children in poor-quality orphanages, but those discovered in Romania came appallingly close to the conditions that Harlow had engineered for monkeys. Babies were left for long hours in cots. There was very little personalized care of individual infants. After the fall of the regime, international agencies facilitated the adoption of thousands of children to Western Europe and North America, thereby setting in motion a grim, natural experiment.

Follow-up studies of Romanian children who were adopted revealed a persistent and distinctive pattern, especially among those who spent years rather than months in the orphanages prior to adoption. Their adoptive parents often reported an unusual lack of restraint in the way their children approached unfamiliar adults. Indeed, the children reacted in approximately the same way to complete strangers and familiar adults. They were prepared to go off with strangers and failed to show the type of checking back behavior that children would ordinarily show in such an unusual situation. Among 6-year-olds, this lack of restraint was associated with restlessness and inattention, as well as problems in social relationships with peers (O'Connor & Rutter, 2000). At 11 years of age, the lack of restraint was still observable. Some children violated social boundaries with an interviewer by talking a great deal or sitting too close, whispering in the interviewer's ear, or touching the interviewer (Rutter et al., 2007).

It is important to stress that this pattern is not found in all adopted children. Even among those who had spent more than 2 years in a Romanian orphanage, only about one-third were affected. For this minority, however, the absence of any opportunity to form a stable attachment in early childhood clearly had enduring consequences, consequences that persisted even when the children had the benefit of living with carefully screened and benign adoptive families for most of their subsequent childhood. It looks as if the brain's plasticity has its limits. Some early experiences can shape the brain in unalterable ways or in ways that remain impervious to ordinary love and kindness. Still, it remains an open question as to how that shaping should be interpreted.

One plausible interpretation is that the human brain naturally "expects" some type of stable, selective attachment to be formed in early childhood. This is the interpretation that Bowlby might favor. In the complete absence of such an early attachment, children retain a maladaptive and indiscriminate approach to strangers despite adoption into a loving family. However, another interpretation is that the human brain is designed to adapt to a disconcertingly wide range of child-rearing patterns: ordinarily, it develops the form of selectivity—a preference for known and reliable caregivers—that most communities regard as normal and healthy; but it can also develop a less selective form of interaction—one directed indiscriminately at all sorts of potential caregivers. More graphically, maybe the human brain can adapt itself to the nuclear family with a single, primary caregiver or to a communitarian arrangement, with an ever-changing rota of caregivers. If the Romanian children brought to the UK have difficulties in later life, is it because they lack the type of attachment that is critical for normal development? Alternatively, were they transplanted from an impersonal, communitarian arrangement, for which they developed an adaptive strategy, to an environment where such indiscriminate sociability is regarded as inappropriate and even risky?

Conclusions

Psychology, and developmental psychology is no exception, has had its fair share of faddish research programs: narrow, often scientistic lines of investigation that seem out of touch with human life as it is lived in the family, the classroom, or the workplace. Attachment theory cannot be criticized on that score. Its inception—Bowlby's observations of emotionally deprived children—has more or less guaranteed that its findings tell us something important about how children relate to their caregivers and how they flourish thereafter.

Two findings strike me as especially compelling within this enduring and expanding research program. Even outside of the orphanage, in ordinary families, children experience a range of care. Some have loving and responsive caregivers, and some do not. Not only do children enter into the caregiving relationship with a set of behaviors designed to signal their needs, but also they are surprisingly good at figuring out and remembering who it is that takes good care of those needs, not just the need for physical nourishment but also the need for emotional and psychological nourishment. In other words, within the context of the caregiving relationship, babies are good judges of character. They take note of who looks after them and who does not. Indeed, they can make up their mind about people very early—in the course of the first year of life—a remarkable psychological accomplishment. As I will show in later chapters, children bring this psychological acumen to bear in other domains. For example, when children are given opportunities to learn from other people, it is not the case that every pedagogically inclined adult or peer receives their blessing and attention. As readers will know intuitively from recollections of their own school days, potential teachers are likely to be briskly assessed.

The second finding is, in some ways, the obverse of the first. I have just emphasized the remarkable selectivity that babies typically show as they navigate among potential caregivers, accepting comfort and reassurance from one person, but being more hesitant toward another. However, when we look at gross emotional deprivation—of the kind experienced by infants spending months or years in an orphanage—we see that such selectivity can be impaired. One of the most striking long-term features of a minority of the Romanian orphans is their indiscriminate approach to adults, even those that they have only just met. By implication, we human beings are not born with an immediate sense of who our nearest and dearest should be. Yet in the absence of gross neglect, we are able to make that determination within a few short months. In the first year or so of our lives, most of us have the chance to learn that some people love and take care of us more than others and we respond to those that do. But some children never learn to be so selective. Deprived of love and affection, they are prone to look for it indiscriminately.

2
How do children learn words?

Universality and variation

Did Shakespeare have an exceptionally large vocabulary? It would seem easy to answer this question. Especially these days, with the help of a computer, we can scan his plays and poems, identify each instance of a new word, and arrive at a total. However, we will encounter some problems. Some words are homographs. Take "stage" as an example. It can mean the stage of a theater or one stage in a sequence. So, in this case, a computer count, based on spelling alone, would lead to an underestimate of Shakespeare's vocabulary. Another problem is that many words differ only in terms of a morpheme. If we gave Shakespeare separate credit for "strut", "struts", and "strutted" we might be accused of overestimating his vocabulary. And how do we deal with Shakespeare's inventiveness? Should we think of his coinages as part of his vocabulary or not? Despite these niceties, it is reasonably safe to conclude that Shakespeare's vocabulary was exceptionally large, even if we compare him to fellow writers such as Milton. However, as David Crystal (2008) points out, when we compare Shakespeare to contemporary speakers, we need to keep in mind the fact that today's English is extremely rich and diverse, so that many speakers have a vocabulary that compares well with Shakespeare's in terms of size—even if they lack his genius.

If we look from a developmental perspective at how a large vocabulary is acquired, two points stand out. First, judging by the number of words they know when they enter school, children must expand their vocabulary extremely quickly, and yet, at first sight, it is not obvious how they manage to do so. Even learning the names for common objects is more complicated than it looks. Second, despite such rapid acquisition, there are huge disparities among children in the pace of that expansion and in the ultimate size of their vocabulary. Not everyone is destined to compete with Shakespeare. I first discuss vocabulary growth in early childhood and then turn to the evidence for individual differences in that growth.

In the normal course of development, children start to produce words in the second year of life, typically around 12 to 18 months. Four or five years later—at the age of 6—they know the meaning of somewhere between 2000 and 14,000 words. Given this rapid growth in vocabulary, it follows that children must be adding—as a very rough average—about five new words to their vocabulary each day, although the pace of addition likely varies in the course of development, being somewhat slower in the first months of acquisition and gathering speed thereafter. The addition of any particular new word might extend over several encounters. But for some items it is likely to be a rapid, one-off process—what Susan Carey called "fast mapping". She introduced 4- and 5-year-olds to a new word—"chromium"—for the color olive, by making the following simple request at an opportune moment in the school day: "You see the two trays over there: bring me the chromium one, not the red one." A week later, she asked children to give her the chromium object from an array of nine differently colored objects. Many were able to do so on the basis of the single, brief exposure they had received a week earlier (Carey, 1988).

Carey speculated that this very rapid learning and stable retention might be peculiar to language. Perhaps the brain has some specialized machinery dedicated to the business of taking in and remembering new vocabulary items. To check out this idea, Lori Markson and Paul Bloom (1997) introduced 3- and 4-year-olds to either a new name or a new fact. In the name condition, the experimenter told the children a name for an unfamiliar object: "This is a koba." In the fact condition, the experimenter told them a fact about the unfamiliar object: "This came from a place called Koba." The experimenter came back a month later, showed the children an array of objects, and, depending on the condition, asked them to point to "the koba" or to the object that "came from Koba". Children did remarkably well in either condition, correctly identifying the object about 70% of the time. Apparently, "fast mapping" can extend to new facts as well as new names. So, this study provides no evidence that vocabulary learning calls on some special or dedicated learning ability. Instead, it shows that young children are very good at building up their knowledge base, rapidly adding facts as well as names.

This rapid learning of new names is especially remarkable in light of a puzzle first spelled out by the philosopher Quine—the problem of reference (Quine, 1960). Consider a linguist doing fieldwork, taking notes on some hitherto undocumented language. A helpful local informant points to a passing rabbit and says, "Gavagai!" The linguist makes a new entry in her notebook: Gavagai = rabbit. But how can the linguist be sure that this is what her informant meant? Gavagai could mean "rabbit" but it could mean "animal" or "running" or "four-legged" or "bob-tailed". This problem of indeterminacy also confronts the young child. For example, when the experimenter pointed to one of the unfamiliar objects and said, "This is a koba", how did the child know that the experimenter meant the object itself rather than the shape of the object—or a corner of the object? Of course, these interpretations might be odd, but there's nothing illogical about them. To the extent that they cannot be ruled out, we might expect children to be prone to error and misinterpretation when they learn new vocabulary items. Yet most investigators agree that such mapping errors are rare.

How do children solve Quine's problem? It seems likely that they use various heuristics and cues to help pinpoint the intended referent. For example, it is plausible that children make the working assumption that the speaker is referring to a whole object of a given shape that belongs to a given category (Markman, 1990). So, hearing the word "rabbit" for the first time, the child assumes that it refers to the whole animal (not to its tail) and also that other animals with the same shape will be called "rabbit". In fact, there is a good deal of evidence that, long before they learn to talk, babies naturally divide the world up into objects. They think of a given object as a set of coherently moving parts, so that when fragments move together in space, they realize that those fragments belong to a single object.

A clever experiment by Phil Kellman and Elizabeth Spelke drove this point home (Kellman & Spelke, 1983). They showed 4-month-old babies a vertical rod that moved from side to side while partially hidden behind a block. The babies could not see the middle section of the moving rod, but they could see its two ends protruding above and below the block and moving in synchrony from side to side. After the babies had watched this display and become familiar—and somewhat bored—with it, they were shown a new display: on one side of the display, the complete rod was now visible rather than just two parts of it; on the other side, only the two parts were visible one above the other, spaced just like the parts that babies had seen earlier. We know that babies generally prefer to look at a novel rather than a familiar display. So, which side of the new display did babies regard as familiar? If they had previously assumed that the two visible parts of the moving rod were connected so as to form a complete rod, they should now prefer, in the interests of novelty, to look at the two separate parts rather than the all too "familiar" complete rod. This was what was found. Apparently, even in a cluttered environment in which many objects are not fully visible, babies have a natural disposition to see complete rather than fragmentary objects, especially when they are helped to that conclusion by the fact that those parts suffer a "common fate"—by moving in the same direction at the same time. It is plausible that toddlers bring this "whole object bias" to the task of word learning. Their default assumption is that an informant is not calling attention to a part of the object, or to a collection of objects, but to a single, whole object.

Speakers can also provide helpful cues. Recall Quine's hypothetical example in which the native informant looks at and points to a rabbit. The linguist who understands those non-verbal, indicative gestures realizes what direction he or she should look. She can rule out many potential referents because they are not in the direction indicated by the pointing gesture. Dare Baldwin (1991; 1993) probed toddler's sensitivity to such non-verbal cues. Eighteen-month-olds were given an object to play with, but as they did so an adult looked at a different, novel object nearby and said, "It's a modi!" The toddlers typically stopped playing, looked up at the speaker, followed her gaze, and looked at the novel object. In subsequent comprehension tests, it was evident that they correctly realized which object was the modi, even though when they had first heard the word, their attention had been directed at a different object, namely the one they were playing with. Note that this sensitivity to a speaker's gaze is not universal. When children with autism were tested in the same situation, they often failed to shift their attention away from the object that they were playing with and, as a result, made the mistake of thinking that the new name applied to that object and not to the one the speaker was looking at (Baron-Cohen et al., 1997a).

In fact, typically developing children not only make use of nonverbal cues such as direction of gaze or pointing, but also keep track of a speaker's current goals in figuring out what object he or she is referring to. For example, Tomasello and Barton (1994) had 24-month-olds watch a speaker who said, "Let's find the toma. Where's the toma?" and then proceeded to search in five buckets for the missing toma. In one condition, the speaker immediately found the toma in the first bucket and said "Ah!" gleefully. In a second condition, the speaker found other objects in the first two buckets but then found the toma in the third, and again said "Ah!" gleefully. Children who were relying only on the speaker's direction of gaze would have been flummoxed in this latter condition because the speaker effectively looked at different objects before finding the toma. Yet children figured out which object was the toma and did so equally well in both conditions. By implication, they were monitoring the speaker's goal—to find the toma—as well as his declaration of success—"Ah!"—so as to identify which particular object he intended.

Children also use syntactic cues to help identify a referent (Katz et al., 1974). Suppose that we show toddlers a doll and say either "This is a zav" or "This is Zav." We refer to the same doll in either case, but the likely meaning is different. Two-year-olds appear to grasp this. Without the indefinite article—"This is Zav"—they don't make the mistake of extending the name to other dolls. They effectively treat it as a proper name for the doll: "Zav". With the indefinite article—"This is a zav"—they realize that they are being given the name for a member of a category, and they extend the name "zav" to other, similar-looking dolls falling into that same category.

Summing up these various studies, it is clear that toddlers do not find Quine's problem insoluble. They attend to the speaker's current gaze and goals to help them decide which particular object he or she is referring to. They assume, reasonably enough, that the speaker is probably referring to the entire object, not to some fraction of it. They also use syntactic clues to infer whether they should then treat the name as a proper noun or a common noun. Granted that children can get off to an early start in building their vocabulary with the help of these heuristics and cues, how rapidly do they make progress?

Larry Fenson and his colleagues took advantage of parents' interest in their children's language development to answer this question (Fenson et al., 1994). They gave several hundred parents a list of target words to look through and asked them to pick out words that their children ranging from 8 to 30 months produced. From these parental reports, it was possible to get a reasonable estimate of children's vocabulary size at different ages—as well as the variation among children at a given age. For 30-month-olds who were at the 90th percentile in terms of overall vocabulary size, their initial "lift-off" had started at around 12–14 months, and by 30 months they had built up a productive vocabulary of nearly 700 words. So, they were adding around 40 words to their vocabulary each month. By contrast, for 30-month-olds at the 10th percentile, their "lift-off" had started some months later—at around 18–20 months. When these children were 30 months, they had a vocabulary of about 350 words. So, they were adding words at the slower rate of about 30 words each month. Indeed, Rowe and her colleagues (2012) were able to confirm that the "pace" of vocabulary growth at 30 months predicts vocabulary size later on. Extrapolating from these findings, we can guess that children will arrive at school when they are 5 or 6 years old with marked differences in their vocabulary size. Not surprisingly, differences in vocabulary size are likely to have implications for children's performance in school because they are closely related to variation in reading comprehension (Pace et al., 2019; Snow et al., 1998).

Individual differences in vocabulary

What brings about these early individual differences in initial lift-off and subsequent vocabulary growth? I will first discuss the role of parental input and then ask about the potential existence of innate "capacity" differences in language learning. In a pioneering study, Janellen Huttenlocher and her colleagues recorded conversations between mothers and their young children at regular intervals (Huttenlocher et al., 1991). An important feature of the study was that all the mothers were full-time caregivers in a relatively educated, middle-class, urban community. In other words, this was a homogeneous sample in terms of socio-economic status.

When the children were 16 months, Huttenlocher and her colleagues carried out a 3-hour-long observation of an interaction between mother and child. It turned out that the mothers differed dramatically in how talkative they were: some were garrulous and some were taciturn. At one extreme, a mother produced a total of 7000 words in the course of the 3 hours and at the other extreme a total of 700 words. Still, within any given fixed sample of say 100 words, the mothers were quite similar in terms of the variety of words that they produced. They were also quite similar in terms of the relative frequency with which they produced particular words. Not surprisingly, "cat" was more frequent than "elephant" for garrulous and taciturn mothers alike. In other words, the mothers—in this fairly homogeneous sample, at any rate—differed mainly in how talkative they were rather than in the breadth of their vocabulary, although of course how much any given mother talks in any given time period would have an impact on the total number of different words that she might produce in that period and also on the frequency with which any particular word—especially common words—is produced.

Was the mothers' degree of talkativeness a response to the type of child that they had? In principle, mothers might talk more in response to talkative children. Probably not—mothers tend to be quite stable in how talkative they are—irrespective of whether they are talking to their own child or another child (Smolak & Weinraub, 1983). Turning the question the other way around, did the talkativeness of the mother have any impact on the child? Here, Huttenlocher and her colleagues made a provocative observation. At 16 months, the children of talkative and taciturn mothers sounded quite similar—they typically had a fairly small vocabulary of about 25 words. Four months later, however, when the children were 20 months, they were starting to sound different. Children of talkative mothers had a vocabulary of about 125 words, whereas children of taciturn mothers had a vocabulary of about 75 words—a gap of 50 words. Later, when the children were 24 months the gap was even bigger. Children with talkative mothers had a vocabulary of about 375 words as compared to 250 words for children of taciturn mothers—a gap of 125 words.

A plausible implication of these findings is that a lot of talk from a caregiver helps children to expand their vocabulary, presumably because the more talk a child hears, the greater the chances of hearing a given word at all and, indeed, the greater the chances of hearing that word repeated more than once, if need be. So, in principle, we can think of most children—aside from children with a developmental pathology, such as autism—as well equipped to benefit from word learning opportunities—as described in the previous section—but differing considerably in the number of word-learning opportunities they are offered by their caregivers. Consistent with this emphasis on the sheer quantity of input to children, the relative frequency of individual words (when averaged across all the mothers) proved to be a good predictor of the age at which children would acquire those words, especially with respect to simple object words, like cup, bottle, cat, and elephant. So, words like cat with a very good chance of being produced and repeated by a caregiver were likely to enter children's vocabulary at an early point. Infrequent words like elephant entered later than more common words like cat.

As mentioned earlier, the sample of mothers in this study was quite homogeneous. All the mothers were relatively educated, middle-class, and full-time caregivers. So, is variation among mothers in their talkativeness mostly a matter of personality? Arguably yes, in this rather homogeneous sample. However, variation among mothers is also likely to be affected by demographic factors, including level of education. To examine this possibility,

Huttenlocher and her colleagues subsequently studied a more diverse sample: 50 families from the greater Chicago area, with the families chosen so as to reflect as closely as possible the variation found in the 2000 US census data on income and ethnicity for the area (Huttenlocher et al., 2007).

The families received five successive visits when children were 14, 18, 22, 26, and 30 months. During each of these five visits, the child and the caregiver (in almost all cases this was the mother) were video-recorded for 90 minutes as they engaged in regular home activities. The findings speak both to stable characteristics on the part of the caregivers—characteristics that were more or less invariant across all five visits—and to adjustments on their part to the increasing age and language competence of the children that they were looking after.

Consider first those characteristics that were stable. There was sharp variation among the caregivers in the number of words that they produced in any given 90-minute observation period. Nevertheless, that number tended to remain stable no matter what the age of the child. In other words, talkative mothers were equally talkative whether their children were just starting to talk—at the age of 14 months—or modest conversationalists—at the age of 30 months. This fits the suggestion made earlier. The talkativeness of the caregiver is probably a stable trait and not just a fluctuating response to characteristics of the child.

When the caregivers were divided into four groups by education, ranging from those who never went to college through to those with an advanced, graduate degree, there was a marked connection with talkativeness. Caregivers who had never attended college produced between 700 and 1700 words per session—depending on whether or not other siblings were present (in general, siblings took up "airtime" and reduced the caregivers' opportunities to speak to the target child). At the other extreme, those with an advanced degree produced more than twice as many words, between 3000 and 4000 per session, again depending on whether other siblings were present. The same pattern emerged for the number of utterances and the number of sentences. Whatever index was used, educated caregivers talked more to their children and continued to do so at the same rate, irrespective of the child's age.

This variation in talkativeness among the caregivers meant that they offered a more or less diverse speech sample to their children in any given session. More talkative caregivers produced a larger array of different words and sentence types than did their quieter counterparts. For example, when the children were 2½ years old, caregivers who had completed college introduced approximately 425 words during the 90-minute session, whereas caregivers who had never been to college introduced approximately 265.

Education was also linked to the way that caregivers talked and not just to how much they talked. More educated caregivers typically produced sentences with more words in them and a larger proportion of their sentences had a more complex grammatical structure—containing two or more clauses. This stylistic variation was not simply due to differences in how much they talked in the course of a given session. Instead, it was detectable more or less straightaway, thereby exemplifying the notion of "thin slicing"—the idea that a brief segment ("a thin slice") of a person's behavior can carry their personal signature (Ambady & Rosenthal, 1992; Gladwell, 2005). In the case of speech, the relative length and complexity of a person's sentences is likely to be immediately apparent. We ordinarily need to listen to only a short stretch of a person's speech to detect their speech style and this proved true for the caregivers in this study.

As noted, Huttenlocher and her colleagues found that any given caregiver's particular speech signature remained stable across the successive sessions. So, when caregivers were rank-ordered in terms of their sentence length or sentence complexity, those who came out on top were likely to do so throughout all five sessions. Moreover, this stable rank-ordering emerged even when the investigators looked within a particular educational group. For example, even when they restricted attention to the 17 caregivers with an advanced degree or alternatively the 6 caregivers who had completed high school but never attended college, the rank-order within these subgroups also proved stable. This pattern fits the findings in the earlier study by Huttenlocher and her colleagues (1991). Even if education is a strong predictor of how much caregivers talk to their young children, there are also stable individual differences among caregivers with a similar background.

Summing up the findings reported by Huttenlocher and her colleagues, parents vary dramatically in how much they talk and also in the complexity with which they talk. These characteristics are a stable part of their communication style. In general, better-educated parents talk more and with greater complexity, but even within a given level of education, personality leaves its imprint. This makes intuitive sense. Consider two men with an advanced degree from Harvard: George W. Bush and Barack Obama. Despite their similarity in terms of years of education, the two men differ in terms of their characteristic speech profile.

Individual differences in comprehension

How early does a caregiver's speech profile start to have an influence on his or her child's vocabulary growth? The initial study carried out by Huttenlocher and her colleagues studied this impact in terms of children's productive vocabulary and found few differences at 16 months, modest differences at 20 months, and more noticeable differences at 24 months. But at this early stage in their language career, children's ability to understand words typically exceeds their ability to produce them. So, we can imagine that a caregiver's impact on comprehension might be quite marked, even early on. Fernald and her colleagues (2013) tested this idea by showing toddlers two pictures, for example a picture of a dog and a cat, and prompting them to look at one of them: "Where's the doggy? Do you like it?" The experimenters then measured how quickly toddlers turned to look at the picture of the dog and how long they spent looking at it. The results were dramatic. Between 18 months and 24 months all the children got quicker in turning to look at the target picture and spent more time looking at it. But there were also marked differences between the children depending on their family background.

The 18-month-old children of upper-class mothers (almost all had completed 4 years of college and more than half had completed a master's or doctoral degree) behaved like the 24-month-old children of lower-class mothers (only a third had finished college). Indeed, if anything, they were somewhat quicker to look at the target picture and spent just as long looking at it. In other words, by 18 months, toddlers with highly educated mothers had a head start: their language processing was about 6 months ahead of toddlers from less-privileged backgrounds.

Two further studies by Fernald and her colleagues have consolidated the claim that maternal input is important not just for children's production but also for their comprehension of words. Weisleder and Fernald (2013) studied a group of children growing up in low-income homes where most of the mothers had not completed high school. Even within this relatively homogeneous group, mothers varied dramatically in the amount of talk directed at 19-month-olds in the course of an average day—from 670 words to more than 12,000 words. This variation in input was associated with variation in children's language processing. Children who had received more maternal speech spent more time looking at a named picture. Moreover, this responsiveness predicted the amount of vocabulary growth that children displayed over the next half-year. Effectively, there appears to be a virtuous circle, at least for some fortunate children: a rich linguistic input helps those children to process language more effectively, which in turn is likely to help them take even greater advantage of the input they receive by learning new words more effectively.

How exactly might a talkative caregiver have an impact on a child's language processing? So far, I have focused on the simple idea that parents are providers of word-learning opportunities. Parents who shower their children with words are likely to have a big impact by giving their children more opportunities to learn new words. But is that all there is to it? Surely, other skills and sensitivities are likely to play a role in helping children to acquire language. Hirsh-Pasek and her colleagues (2015) studied the development of children growing up in low-income families, asking if either the quantity or the quality of the mother's input at 24 months was a better predictor of children's expressive language 1 year later at 36 months. Quantity was indexed by the mother's talkativeness—by how many words she produced per minute. Quality was primarily indexed by the connectedness of the dialogue between mother and child—by the degree to which each of them made a coordinated contribution to their ongoing conversation. Overall, quality, as indexed by connectedness, proved a better predictor of children's language production at 36 months than did quantity. A plausible implication of these findings is that interventions that seek to boost children's vocabulary by encouraging mothers to talk more may not be very effective if that extra input does not lead to a balanced conversational exchange between mother and child.

Strong support for this emphasis on parent–child dialogue, rather than the sheer amount of parental input, was reported by Romeo and her colleagues (2018). They recorded the conversations that took place between 4-, 5-, and 6-year-olds and their parents at home during the waking hours of a single weekend. Analysis of these conversations showed that children's performance on a composite measure of verbal ability was especially closely linked to the number of conversational turns that had occurred between adult and child rather than to the number of words produced by an adult. Moreover, when they listened to short stories while lying in a scanner, children who had engaged in more conversational turns with an adult displayed more activity in Broca's area, a part of the brain closely linked to language processing. In turn, the amount of activity in this area of the brain was correlated with children's performance on the composite measure of verbal ability. By implication, young children's involvement in conversation is changing their neural response to language and those neural changes are linked to verbal ability as indexed by psychometric tests.

Is this focus on conversation with primary caregivers warranted? After all, grandparents, siblings, and family visitors will also talk to the child. A child might also overhear a lot of conversation that is not directed at them, especially in a large, extended family. Indeed, ethnographic studies of language acquisition in a wide range of communities confirm—not surprisingly—that the number of word-learning opportunities open to children expands markedly once we take this broader language environment into account (Rowe & Weisleder, 2020; Sperry et al., 2019). Still, for the time being, there is little evidence that children benefit from these wider opportunities in the same way that they do from conversations with caregivers. Admittedly, children can learn new words when they overhear them in a sheltered laboratory environment, but we do not know how easily they do so amid the more complicated hubbub of family talk (Golinkoff et al., 2019).

Taken together, the evidence shows that caregivers are markedly and consistently different in the amount of language data that they provide for their children but also in the way that they provide it. Not only are some caregivers more talkative, but also they present their children with longer and more complex sentences, and they do so fairly consistently, within any given slice of their verbal input. In addition, caregivers vary in the extent to which they "connect" with their children by engaging in the to-and-fro of a balanced conversational exchange. These characteristics of the caregiver predict how rapidly their children's vocabulary increases in size, how rapidly a child responds to a verbal prompt such as "Look at the doggie", how the speech area of the child's brain responds when listening, and how the child performs on a test of verbal ability.

Earlier, I emphasized the link between a caregiver's education and the way that they talk to their child. But why exactly might that link exist? One possibility is that better-educated mothers have greater expectations of their children and of themselves. They are more sanguine than mothers with less education about what their children can learn and understand at any given age and more optimistic about how much of a difference their own input can make to their children's progress. Meredith Rowe (2008) gathered some support for this idea. When she measured mothers' knowledge of child development, it proved to be a relatively strong predictor of the way that they talked to their children.

Consistent with this line of thinking, mothers can adjust their conversational style if they are told that their children might benefit.

Weber and colleagues (2017) evaluated a relevant intervention study in rural Senegal. In villages targeted for the intervention, mothers received information about cognitive development and the potential impact of parenting practices on young children's language and cognitive growth. At the start of the study, mother–child pairs about to receive the intervention talked as much as pairs in a control group who would only receive the intervention later on. Following the intervention, mother–child pairs in the intervention group talked more. Moreover, there was evidence that the boost in child talk was not simply due to the increase in talk by the mother—change in the mother's knowledge of child development was also a contributing factor.

Findings supporting the role of mothers' knowledge also emerged in a US study targeting mothers of 10-month-olds (Rowe & Leech, 2019). Mothers who received the intervention watched a 5-minute video about the benefits of pointing at objects for babies to look at, especially for their future language development. At 18 months, the children of these mothers produced and understood more words than the children of control mothers who did not see the video. Importantly, this difference in language development was only found among mothers who initially thought of children's abilities as fixed and hard to change—rather than malleable. This selective impact of the intervention makes sense. Presumably, some mothers assumed, without needing to see the video, that their input might help their children's language. So, the video did not alter how they talked to their children.

In the future, we are likely to see more such interventions, as well as debate about which are effective, which have long-term effects, and which are justifiable—given that they may radically change parents' norms about how to talk to their children (Morelli et al., 2018; Rowe & Weisleder, 2020).

Genetic variation?

It would be very tempting, especially for those invested in the benefits of early childhood education, to conclude at this point that there is a straightforward causal connection between caregiver input and child vocabulary growth. Some parents offer their children more or better opportunities to learn the meanings of words and their children learn faster as a result. Perhaps Shakespeare's mother was an especially energetic conversationalist with young William. There is, however, an important interpretive problem that should not be ignored. Parents can transmit characteristics to their children in two different ways, either via the genes that they pass on or via the environment that they provide. So far, I have focused on the possibility that caregivers vary in the language-learning environment that they provide for their children, but another possibility is that caregivers vary in the genes they pass on.

Consider the following hypothetical causal story. Parents might differ from one another in their innate language ability. That variation might be responsible for the fact that parents have their own distinctive language profile—a characteristic and stable tendency to talk a given amount and in a more or less complex fashion. Their children will be exposed to that distinctive profile, but they will also share genes with their parents. That genetic variation among the children might determine the ease with which the children learn and use new words. So, according to this account the main impact of parents on their children's language development depends on the genes that they pass on and not on the language data they offer their children. Indeed, it could be argued that most parents, even those who do not talk a great deal and typically use shorter or less complex sentences, offer their children enough data to learn from. The relative rate with which children learn is determined by children themselves, by their own learning capacity, and not by the learning environment provided by their parents. Interventions with parents, encouraging them to engage in more active conversation with their children, might, as we have seen, yield a short-term boost, but ultimately children will pursue their own linguistic trajectory no matter what input parents provide.

Research on behavioral genetics allows us to assess the plausibility of this idea. In the Colorado Adoption project, Robert Plomin and his colleagues studied parents with three different types of relationship to their child (Plomin et al., 1997). They looked at parents who had only a biological relationship to their child—they had given their child up for adoption and so they did not provide a long-term, learning environment for the child. Second, they looked at adoptive parents who were providing a long-term learning environment for their adopted child but had no genetic relationship to that child. Finally, they looked at regular parents who were raising their own children and therefore might have both a genetic and an environmental impact on them. The verbal IQ of the parents was measured. In addition, repeated assessments of the children's IQ were made as they got older. When the children reached the age of 16, there was a fairly strong correlation between their verbal ability as indexed by the IQ battery and the verbal ability of biological parents as well as regular parents. By contrast, there was no relationship between children's verbal ability and that of their adoptive parents. By implication, much of the variation among adolescents in their verbal ability was attributable to their genes and not to the linguistic environment that their parents had provided.

The picture was different for the period of early childhood. The correlations between parent and child were quite modest for all three groups of parents. Nevertheless, they were slightly higher for regular and adoptive parents—especially when children were 4 years old—than for biological parents, making it feasible that, at this early time-point, it was the language environment being provided for the child that was important rather than the child's native endowment. However, it is important to emphasize that this study of links between parental IQ and child IQ is not the optimal way to assess variation among parents in the language environment that they provide and its potential impact on their children. That is best studied by measuring what parents actually say to their children. The way that parents perform on paper-and-pencil tests of verbal IQ is, at best, a very indirect guide to the way that they talk to their children. In the longer term then, we need data, especially from adoptive parents, on how they talk to their adopted children. If we find a correlation between the adopted children's vocabulary and the language data provided by their parents, we cannot explain such a correlation in terms of genetic transmission. That would considerably strengthen the argument that language input matters for children's language development.

But there is a developmental puzzle that calls for further discussion. Why is the verbal ability of children more closely related to that of their biological parents when the children are 16 years of age than when they are 4 years of age? We cannot dismiss this result as the lone outcome of a single study. In a study of the relative similarity of monozygotic and dizygotic twins in language skills, the data again showed that the amount of variation attributable to genetic, as opposed to environmental, factors increased as children got older (Hayiou-Thomas et al., 2012). Intuitively, we might have expected just the opposite. We might have expected that the effect of genetic variation would be especially obvious in early childhood and taper off as children get older. Why do we see the reverse pattern? Why is genetic variation more evident among adolescents as compared to preschoolers?

One possible explanation for the delayed but increasing influence of genetic variation is as follows. Suppose that families differ considerably in the linguistic environment that they offer to a child. As we have seen, there is plenty of evidence for such variation. So long as children are mostly learning to talk in the context of the home, their rate of progress is likely to be measurably affected by the particular learning opportunities provided in that environment. Eventually, however, children go off to school and for several hours each day they will encounter the same teachers and the same way of speaking as many other children. No doubt particular schools and particular teachers differ from each other, but they may ultimately be more similar to one another than are families. After all, virtually all schoolteachers have college degrees. So, the range of educational attainment among teachers is probably narrower than it is among families at large. As a result, across a large population of children, their opportunities for learning language might become less divergent when they enter school. Under these conditions of relative environmental equality, we can reasonably expect that genetic variation among children will become more evident.

Here is a different explanation of the puzzle, however. Arguably, young children can exercise little control over whom they talk to, or the types of books that they engage with, because their linguistic environment is primarily governed by their family. However, older children, and adolescents, can exercise more control. To take a concrete example, depending on their verbal ability, older children can choose more or less challenging books to borrow from the library. According to this explanation, older children have more opportunities to engage in personalized "niche-picking"—to pick the linguistic niche that suits their verbal ability (Scarr & McCartney, 1983). According to this scenario, the genetic impact of niche-selection might become more evident with age.

Finally, here is yet a third explanation. Let us suppose that most children, aside from those with a developmental psychopathology, have the genetic capacity to acquire the basics of language in their early years. Therefore, any variation between young children is governed primarily by their learning environment rather than by genetic ability. Caregivers who communicate a lot with their children provide a rich, language environment in which children can make rapid progress. Caregivers who communicate less provide a less-conducive language environment so that their children make slower progress. However, as they get older, genetic variation among children might play an increasingly important role—there might even be particular combinations of genes dedicated to the more advanced or complex aspects of language—that are only switched on in later childhood. On this account, Shakespeare's linguistic genius might not have been so evident when he was a young schoolboy "with his satchel", but it might have become increasingly apparent as he moved toward adulthood.

The key differences among these three explanations are as follows. The first implies that genetic variation becomes more apparent because the amount of environmental variation declines with age. The second implies that genetic variation becomes more apparent because it increasingly determines the kind of linguistic niche or environment that children expose themselves to. The third implies that the degree of genetic variation actually increases with age. Future research is likely to help adjudicate among these accounts—to indicate whether, in the course of development, children's linguistic environments do indeed become more homogeneous, or more individualized—or whether children's inherited linguistic competence becomes more diverse. Whatever the best explanation, we need to keep in mind the possibility that although early intervention might limit the amount of variation we see among young children—by leveling the early playing field—it may not suppress the variation that we eventually see when children become adults. We do not all end up like Shakespeare.

Conclusions

There is plenty of evidence that acquiring language comes "naturally" to the human species. Children do not need to be taught to speak. They acquire language as part of their everyday social interactions within their family and beyond. Furthermore, they acquire language despite the diversity of caregiving arrangements that we see across the globe. Some children often receive the undivided and sustained attention of one or two adults, whereas other children grow up in a multigenerational family where they are frequent bystanders to the ongoing conversation (Brown & Gaskins, 2014). Yet, in each case, children master the surrounding language and pass through similar milestones (Casillas et al., 2020).

However, even if language is "naturally" acquired by the vast majority of children, there are marked individual differences among them, as indexed by the growth of their vocabulary. These differences are consequential. Children who enter school with greater language skills than their peers tend to maintain that educational advantage. There is no persuasive evidence of any catch-up by those who lag behind. An increasing body of evidence highlights the impact of environmental factors on children's early language development. Children who are engaged in a lot of conversation with their caregiver tend to build their vocabulary more quickly, and they effectively enter school with an advantage. That said, an important caveat is needed. There is persuasive evidence that genetic factors come to the fore as children get older. Research in the coming years will—hopefully—face and resolve this fascinating tension.

3

Does language change how children think?

The contested relation between language and thought

1896 was a good year for developmental psychology. Jean Piaget was born in Switzerland and Lev Vygotsky in Russia. Each came to offer a deep, powerful way of thinking about cognitive development. Piaget, trained in biology, logic, and the history of science, grew up in the well-ordered and stable milieu of Neuchâtel. He assumed that the infant starts out with the minimum of cognitive equipment. Yet by dint of active observation of, and experimentation on, the surrounding world, the child gradually constructs his or her own intellectual framework and principles. The direction of that development is toward greater and greater intellectual equilibrium and objectivity. In particular, the child gradually comes to understand the stability that lies behind the flux of appearances: the enduring nature of physical objects and physical quantities. Piaget believed that this path toward an enlightened, intellectual stability is open to all children provided they have the opportunity to actively explore the world and to generate their own autonomous but rational hypotheses about its workings.

Vygotsky's vision of development is very different. A student of the humanities, and especially the theatre, he conducted his research amid the upheavals of post-revolutionary Russia. Unlike Piaget, he was convinced that the nature of the child's cognitive development is radically contingent on the surrounding culture. Vygotsky's child belongs to a particular moment of history, not to a timeless, invariant world. In particular, a child's mental world is amplified by the cultural tools placed at his or her disposal: language for al-most all children, the printed word for many, and increasingly in this century, we might add the computer, the internet, and social media.

One way to highlight the difference between Piaget and Vygot-sky is to look back at their discussion of number understanding in children. Piaget (1965a) claimed that a genuine understanding of number will arise from children's everyday experiences with objects—experiences in which they gradually discover, for example, that five egg cups do not change their quantity if each one is placed side-by-side or spread out in a much longer line; in either case, they can hold five eggs in total. Piaget doubted that simply being able to count contributed anything to this grasp of the invariance of num-ber across all sorts of different physical and spatial arrangements. Counting, he assumed, was all too often just a verbal recitation, unsupported by any deeper understanding. Vygotsky, by contrast, discussed the way that thinking is amplified by cultural tools, of which counting is an excellent example. Together with his close col-league Alexander Luria, he speculated that the counting system in a given language might help its user to conceive of numbers in an abstract fashion, freed from any concrete exemplars (Luria & Vy-gotsky, 1992). We return to this speculation about the development of number understanding later in the chapter.

Egocentric speech and its fate

Even though they were exact contemporaries, there was no direct communication between Piaget and Vygotsky. That said, Vygotsky evidently studied Piaget's writings during the 1920s and early 1930s and was skeptical of some of his claims. His doubts are eloquently expressed in his masterpiece *Thought and Language*, published in Russian in 1934, the year of his premature death at the age of 38 (Vygotsky, 1986). But, for his part, Piaget only became aware of that critique when the book was translated from the Russian nearly 30 years later. The profound divisions between them are highlighted by their views on language.

In his early observational work on preschool children, Piaget had identified and analyzed the phenomenon of what he called "ego-centric" speech: children's alleged tendency to talk to no one in particular while playing alongside their peers. According to Piaget, this a-social speech directed at no specific interlocutor was indica-tive of the young child's social and intellectual limitations. Although children's utterances may have some of the outward forms of mature communication, they are not properly tailored to the needs of a given listener, and in that sense, they can best be characterized as egocen-tric. In the course of development, children become more sensitive to their audience and their language gradually becomes more at-tuned to their listener's needs. Egocentric speech slowly disappears, Piaget argued, as genuinely social communication emerges.

Vygotsky assumed, contrary to Piaget, that the young child is a so-cial creature from the start. He emphasized that most of children's early remarks are directed expectantly at a comprehending listener. To prove the point, he placed young children in a room where the other children were speaking a foreign language or were deaf. Lack-ing any sign of comprehension from their interlocutors, children fell silent. By implication, children speak to enter into communication with others; they are not simply talking to or for themselves.

Vygotsky acknowledged that Piaget had observed a genuine phenomenon—something like egocentric speech does exist. Still, he argued that its function is different from what Piaget had proposed. It is best seen as a form of thinking aloud. At first, children are poor at differentiating thinking aloud from ordinary communication di-rected at other people, but as that differentiation is gradually made, speech-for-the-self, or what Piaget had called egocentric speech, does not stop. Instead, it goes underground. It is formulated silently and not vocalized. So, although egocentric speech ceases to be heard, it is not suppressed by more social speech. It splits off from social speech to become inaudible, private speech. As evidence for his in-terpretation, Vygotsky showed that as children get older, egocentric speech actually becomes less and less easy for listeners to understand and decode, as would be expected if it were increasingly used not as a mode of communication but as a tool for private thinking. Piaget would have expected the opposite, namely that the child's egocentric speech becomes more rather than less understandable in the course of development if its root cause were the young child's insensitivity to the needs of a listener.

Vygotsky further proposed that language, once it gets internalized as private speech, helps children's thinking, especially when they are planning what to do next. In support of this functional role, Vygotsky observed that when children were frustrated in their activities by a practical obstacle (e.g., when they set about doing a drawing but discovered that there was no paper to draw on or pencil to draw with), the proportion of egocentric speech almost doubled. This fits the idea that private, inner speech is used as a medium for directing and redirecting the future actions of the self.

Experimental work supports Vygotsky's developmental claims. Winsler and Naglieri (2003) gave more than 2000 children a paper-and-pencil task in which they were given sheets of paper on which letters and numbers were distributed. They had to connect up successive numbers, successive letters, or letters and numbers in alternation, by drawing a line from one to the next. The interviewer recorded audible utterances in which children named one of the letters or numbers aloud. Children were also asked immediately afterwards how they had worked on the task and credited with using private speech if they reported talking to themselves (e.g., "said the numbers to myself in my head"). Audible naming of the letters or numbers steadily declined with age. Whereas almost half the 5-year-olds were heard to say a letter or a number, this figure dropped to 10% among 17-year-olds. Conversely, reports of private speech were rare among 5-year-olds but frequent among 17-year-olds. In sum, this study supports Vygotsky's developmental claim: as children get older, overt, private speech wanes but inner, private speech waxes.

Time for questions

Language serves not just as a tool for private planning and thinking, it is also a major tool for gathering information—not from direct observation of the world but from other people. For many years, this important function of children's questions was overlooked, partly because psychologists and educators, from Rousseau onward, doubted whether it was good for children to have their questions answered rather than figuring things out for themselves.

Early research on children's questions typically involved keeping a log of the questions asked by a given child or gathering together records from several such children. Not surprisingly, this method tended to focus on children's more interesting or exotic queries. For example, Sully (2000) reports on a child (probably his own son) who asked: "Who made God?" and "Why does the wind blow?" Sully does not tell us the answers the boy received. Instead, he analyzes the questions in order to infer the kind of mental framework that prompted them in the first place. Sully concludes that young children conceive of the world as "a sort of big house where everything has been made by someone, or at least fetched from somewhere" (Sully, 2000, p. 79). In this view, children's questions are premised on design-based thinking. They want to know how a given entity was brought into existence ("Who made God?") or what purpose it serves ("Why does the wind blow?"). There is likely some truth to this characterization. After all, many of the objects that surround children, the houses, chairs, cars, cups, soap, and towels, actually are human-made artefacts, intended for human use.

However, such collections of questions have various limitations. First, investigators are unlikely to record more practical or prosaic questions. So, the sample of questions is biased. Second, the sample of children is also biased. They are being raised by parents who have the time and inclination to note down their questions, and that is not standard parental practice. Finally, a given question is typically part of a longer dialogue. It is important to look at the replies that children receive as well as the follow-up questions that they might go on to produce afterwards.

To study the acquisition of language, the psycholinguist Roger Brown and his students (Brown, 1973) pioneered the intensive, naturalistic recording of young children's conversations at home. Michele Chouinard (2007) used the resultant database to carry out a comprehensive analysis of the questions asked by four preschool children. She found that when they were talking with a familiar adult at home, they asked between one and three questions each minute. They requested help ("Can you fix this for me?"); permission ("Can I go outside?"); or clarification ("What did you say?"). But, importantly, about two-thirds of the children's questions were aimed at obtaining information.

Simple, factual questions ("What's that?", "What does it do?", "Where is my ball?") predominated until children were approximately 30 months. But then they began to ask *how* and *why* questions. Among 3-year-olds, explanation-seeking questions accounted for about one-quarter of the total. They asked about matters ranging far and wide, from the practical to the metaphysical: "Why you put some water in there, Mom?", "How come I cannot go outside?", "Why doesn't the butter stay on top of hot toast?", and "How did God put flesh on us and make what's inside us?".

Note that if we make the conservative assumption that these four preschoolers spent, on average, 1 hour at home each day with a familiar caregiver, that caregiver would have the opportunity to answer more than 20,000 explanation-seeking questions before the child reached his or her 5th birthday. Given these huge numbers, it is likely that children can learn a lot by asking questions, despite the misgivings of psychologists and educators noted earlier (Harris, 2012). Of course, exactly what they learn depends on how their questions are answered.

Not surprisingly, children do not always obtain satisfactory answers. Sometimes, parents simply say that they don't know the answer. Sometimes, they think the question is misplaced. Still, children typically receive an informative reply to about one-third of their explanation-seeking questions (Frazier et al., 2009). How children respond to the answers they receive tells us something about why they ask questions in the first place. If they receive an informative answer, children often express agreement or follow up with another question on the same topic. But if they receive an uninformative answer, they are more likely to offer their own explanation or to repeat their question. By implication, when children ask a *why* or *how* question, they are genuinely seeking information. They like an adult to be informative, not just attentive or responsive.

The young children discussed so far were recorded in their own homes, talking to a familiar adult, often their mother. What happens when children go to school? Do they ask lots of questions there as well? In a study of English preschoolers, Tizard and Hughes (1984) recorded the conversations of 4-year-olds both at home with their mothers and in nursery school. The children behaved quite differently in the two settings. They asked many more questions at home; indeed, they often asked a series of interconnected questions, all probing the same topic. By contrast, in nursery school, this kind of tenacious, information-seeking dialogue almost never occurred.

Obviously, the home setting and the school setting are different social contexts. A teacher surrounded by a dozen or more children might have few practical opportunities to engage in a long dialogue with a single child. Also, a teacher is less likely than a parent to have a detailed knowledge of an individual child's knowledge base, idiosyncratic preferences, and family history, thereby making appropriate answers to a child's questions more challenging. But beyond these practical considerations, a pedagogic assumption is likely to be at work. Tizard and Hughes noticed not only that children had fewer and shorter conversations with their teachers than with their mothers, but also that the tenor of those conversations was different. Teachers tended to talk more than the child, whereas conversations in the home were more evenly balanced. Also, teachers characteristically asked a series of questions, and the child's primary role was to answer them. These exchanges often involved teachers probing for a specific answer, sometimes in vain, but sometimes needlessly. For example, 4-year-old June asked her teacher: "Can you cut that in half?" Having obliged, the teacher spotted a teaching moment and asked: "How many pieces of paper have you got?" "Two", replied June. The teacher continued: "Two. What have I done if I've cut it down the middle?" "Two pieces", persisted June. After four such attempts to extract the answer she had in mind, the teacher supplied it herself: "I've cut it . . . *in half*", ignoring the fact that June had already introduced this concept with her initial request.

Yet in the context of preschool, there are still opportunities to observe the quizzical mind of the young child at work. In an intriguing study conducted in a large city in eastern Turkey, Ramazan Sak (2020) asked more than 300 teachers trained in preschool education to "share the questions you have been asked by preschoolers in your classroom that were difficult to answer". Children's difficult questions could be sorted into four main themes—science and nature (e.g., "How do fish breathe in water?"), religion and mortality (e.g., "Where do dead people go?"), sex and fertility (e.g., "Why do men not have babies?"), and daily life (e.g., "Why am I not as beautiful as my sister?").

The replies that teachers reported varied in informativeness—some were accurate (e.g., "Fish have gills. They can use the oxygen in the water with these gills. So, they can breathe through their gills"), but a considerable proportion were either misleading (e.g., "Your (deceased) father is on the moon right now, and he is watching us. When you grow up, you will go to your father and you will see him") or vague (e.g., "There are some situations where being pregnant is needed. These situations are found among women, not men"). Other difficult questions either went unanswered or received an unhelpful response (e.g., "Why is water wet?"—"Water is wet because the water itself is wet and water makes everything wet"). Clearly, young children do ask challenging questions—even in the classroom.

The Whorfian hypothesis

Recall that Vygotsky conceived of language as a social tool that children first use in the context of interpersonal communication and gradually internalize for more private and individual purposes, for thinking and planning. Benjamin Whorf, a linguist specializing in the study of Native American languages, also proposed an important connection between language and thinking. But instead of focusing on the impact of acquiring just any language, Whorf speculated about the impact of acquiring one language as compared to another, be it Russian, English, or Chinese. He argued that different languages cut up the world differently, so that the acquisition of any particular language is likely to influence our construal of the world. A person who acquires a given language comes to think about the world according to the grid imposed by that particular language. Ideas that lie outside the grid of that language become "unthinkable" or at least "difficult-to-think-about".

Take the example of time. In English, we speak of time as running from some point behind us to a point ahead of us. We look *forward* to events in the future and *back* to events in the past. We *face* the future and *turn our back* on the past. We forget events that happened *way back when* but worry about what lies *ahead*. The implication of Whorf's argument—the Whorfian hypothesis as it came to be known—is that English speakers not only talk about time in terms of this spatial metaphor, but also come to think about time in spatial terms.

Despite the intuitive appeal of this idea, there was a gap in Whorf's reasoning. Even if we express ourselves differently in one language as compared to another, that does not necessarily mean that we think differently as a result. Although English speakers adopt a spatial metaphor in talking about time, their silent thoughts about time might carry little trace of that audible metaphor. Indeed, their silent thoughts might be more or less identical to those of someone who speaks Mandarin or Navaho. To prove Whorf's point, we need to get into the speaker's mind—to show that the inaudible, mental processes of English speakers are influenced by their habitual means of overt expression.

Experiments on color

An early effort to get inside the speaker's mind was made by Roger Brown and Eric Lenneberg (1954). They argued that if Whorf's claim is correct, it ought to apply not just across languages but also to variation within languages. In particular, items that are readily named in English ought to be easier to think about than items that are hard to name. Take the domain of color. Some colors seem easy to name.

Blood is indisputably red, a well-tended English lawn is definitely green, and surely bananas are yellow. But should we call the ancient couch stored in our attic beige or brown? Building on this linguistic observation, Brown and Lenneberg showed Harvard students an array of color samples from the local paint store and pointed at a selection of them. After a short interval, the students were asked to remember which of the various colors had been pointed at. As predicted, they were more accurate in remembering some colors than others, and those that they remembered more accurately turned out to have a readily available name in English: red was more accurately remembered than beige. The plausible conclusion was that as they watched the experimenter point to any given color, the students did not store a purely visual impression of that color. They bolstered their memory with the help of a verbal label, provided English made one readily available: hence the variation in memory for particular colors.

An elegant experiment, conducted among the Dani of New Guinea, looked at first sight as if it might consolidate this conclusion. The Dani language is not blessed with many color terms. There is a word for dark colors, there is a word for light colors, and that is about it. So, when Eleanor Heider went to New Guinea to test Dani-speaking adults with the procedure used with the students in Massachusetts, it was reasonable to expect that they would not show much variation from one color to another—indeed, each color would be quite tricky for them to remember since there was no word with which to encode it in a distinctive fashion. Contrary to this expectation, the Dani showed the same pattern of variation as English speakers. Even though none of them spoke English, colors that are more easily named in English proved easier for the Dani to remember than colors that are harder to name in English (Heider, 1972). Given that the Dani spoke no English, this was, to say the least, a disconcerting result.

Heider came up with a powerful explanation that essentially turned Whorf's ideas on their head. She argued that when we survey the many colors of the spectrum, there are certain colors that serve as visual attractors or beacons. They stand out from the surrounding colors. We notice and remember these focal colors easily. So, for example, red and blue are focal colors, but hues that lie somewhere in between—mauve, purple, indigo, violet—are not focal colors. Heider further supposed that these hot spots in our perception of the color spectrum are universal. Blood red is focal for the Dani just as it is for speakers of English. On this hypothesis, the similarity between Harvard students and the Dani in their memory for colors is not language dependent. It is built into our human visual experience of color. So, why could the Harvard students easily name the colors they remembered best? A plausible explanation is that, contrary to Whorf, it is not language that influences our experience of color but rather it is our experience of color that influences our language. When a language adds color words to the lexicon, it is focal colors that take priority. Admittedly, the students could easily name the colors they remembered best, but that ease of naming was not critical for their memory, as demonstrated by the performance of the Dani. Easy naming was a correlate of the students' performance but not a cause.

Thinking about what is not the case

Defenders of Whorf's hypothesis that language shapes thought might reasonably console themselves with the following counter argument. Maybe language imposes a grid on the way that we construe the world, but it does so primarily in those domains that our perceptual system has not already colonized. In the case of colors, our perceptual system is likely to impose a grid, arguably even before we are old enough to name any colors; but perhaps in more abstract domains where the perceptual system can exercise little dominion, language has a decent chance of exerting some influence. Alfred Bloom, a psycholinguist sympathetic to Whorf's claims, seized on one such linguistic domain: the counterfactual conditional whereby we express thoughts about what might have happened if . . . .

In English, a counterfactual conditional is explicitly marked by the subjunctive mood. For example: "If you *had* set off earlier, you *would have* caught your train" (or, more aptly for long-suffering commuters: "If you *had* set off earlier, you *would have* waited even longer for your train"). In Mandarin Chinese, by contrast, there is no subjunctive mood, so that counterfactuals have to be expressed more circuitously. For example: "If X happened—it did not happen—but if it happened, Y happened." Bloom (1981) speculated that English speakers would, thanks to the clear syntactic marking of such contrary-to-fact thoughts via the subjunctive mood, differentiate sharply between a counterfactual assertion and a regular, factual assertion, whereas Chinese speakers would have more difficulty in keeping them apart. To test this idea, he gave students a passage containing such a contrary-to-fact assertion. For example:

> Bier was an eighteenth-century European philosopher. There was some contact between the West and China at that time but very few works of Chinese philosophy had been translated. Bier could not read Chinese but if he had been able to read Chinese, he would have discovered that those Chinese philosophical works were relevant to his own investigations. What would have most influenced him would have been the fact that Chinese philosophers, in describing natural phenomena, generally focused on the interrelationships between such phenomena, while Western philosophers by contrast generally focused on the description of such phenomena as distinct individual entities . . ..

After they had read the passage, students were posed various questions about what had and had not actually occurred. In line with Bloom's hypothesis, the Chinese students were more likely to confuse hypothetical assertions with assertions of fact—to claim, for example, that Bier had actually been influenced by Chinese philosophy, whereas, in the passage that they had read, this was only entertained as a possibility. On the strength of this and similar studies, Bloom made far-reaching claims about a fundamental difference between the habitual modes of thinking in China as compared to the English-speaking world.

Terry Au, a native speaker of Mandarin, looked at the passages that Bloom had used and noticed a problem. They were not written in idiomatic Chinese and sounded stilted to her native ear. Perhaps the Chinese students tested by Bloom had been misled by the awkwardness of the passages rather than by the Mandarin syntax. To check this possibility, she devised two new sets of test materials. One set was written in fluent, idiomatic Chinese and the other in stilted English. When these test materials were presented to Chinese and English speakers respectively, the pattern observed by Bloom was reversed. Now it was the English speakers who mistook the hypothetical for the factual and the Chinese speakers who kept them apart (Au, 1986).

Further evidence against Bloom's hypothesis has emerged in research with children. Three- and four-year-olds are quite good at thinking about counterfactual possibilities. For example, if they are shown a doll that is made to walk across the floor, leaving dirty footprints, and asked what would have happened if instead the doll had taken off her shoes at the door, children correctly claim that the floor would now be "clean" rather than "dirty" (Harris et al., 1986). At this age, preschoolers have rarely mastered the complicated syntax of the English counterfactual conditional. By implication, children can entertain thoughts about counterfactual possibilities, and answer questions about their consequences, before they are in a position to benefit from the distinctive way that English expresses such hypotheticals.

In short, even when we study a domain in which perception might loosen its grip and language might be expected to exert some influence on thinking, it does not appear to do so. Mastery of a language with explicit marking of the counterfactual does not appear to help thinkers differentiate the actual from the hypothetical, and children can entertain thoughts about contrary-to-fact possibilities before such mastery.

One reaction to this negative evidence is to retreat to the conclusion that language does little more than enable us to express our thoughts. It is an instrument of communication but not an instrument that has any impact on the way we think. In his influential book *The Language Instinct*, Stephen Pinker came to that conclusion (Pinker, 1994). He proposed that preverbal toddlers can certainly think but in a language that he dubs "Universal Mentalese"—a mental code that is more or less invariant across preverbal children and may even be shared, at least in part, by other creatures such as chimpanzees, but a code that operates antecedent to, and independent of, the acquisition of a spoken language such as English, Mandarin, or Apache. On this model of the relationship between thought and language, the causal action is unidirectional. The child thinking in Universal Mentalese gradually learns how to convert those thoughts into a particular spoken language for communication purposes, but the nature of that spoken language, even when mastered, does not have a retrospective impact on the thoughts that give rise to the words.

Language and number

Despite the appealing simplicity of Universal Mentalese, a surge of later studies from a different quarter has revitalized the Whorfian hypothesis and has also lent support to the speculations advanced by Vygotsky about the way in which cultural tools such as language can amplify our thinking. Consider the everyday experience of doing mental arithmetic. Those who are monolingual may not notice any particular tendency to make use of inner speech in their mother tongue, but bilinguals are often aware of the need to switch. They may ask for their cappuccino in English but silently calculate their modest change from a five-dollar bill in their mother tongue. These commonplace observations suggest that when we engage in counting and mental arithmetic we make use of the language that we are most comfortable in, or rather the language in which we are most practiced so far as counting and arithmetic are concerned. Pushing this idea a step further, it is plausible that the particular language in which we are disposed to count might be a more or less effective tool for numerical thinking depending on how rich or poor that language is in number words.

Just as some languages have only a handful of color words, some have only a handful of number words. For example, the Pirahã language has a "one", "two", and "many" number lexicon. When they engage in simple arithmetic, does this restricted lexicon hamper speakers of Pirahã, a small hunter-gatherer tribe living mainly on the banks of the Maici River in Brazil? To answer this question, the psychologist Peter Gordon conducted an experiment, helped and informed by Daniel Everett, a Christian missionary turned linguist with a prolonged and extensive knowledge of the Pirahã language and culture.

Gordon (2004) presented adult members of the community with an array of objects. For example, he might place six batteries in a line from left to right in front of them. Their task was simply to create a similar array, composed of the same number of batteries. This task is virtually identical to the so-called one-to-one correspondence task devised by Piaget to test children's conception of number. Piaget found that, unlike younger children, elementary-school children could construct a correct numerical match by placing items in one-to-one correspondence with a set of items laid out by the experimenter. In principle, then, this should have been an easy task for Gordon's participants who were all adults. Across a set of tasks in which the number, orientation, and spacing of the line to be reproduced was varied, the Pirahã displayed a similar pattern of performance. If the line was composed of only one or two objects, they generally performed flawlessly, setting down one or two items as appropriate. However, if the line to be reproduced contained more objects, their performance was incorrect. Indeed, their accuracy decreased as the number of items in the line increased. Gordon concluded that his results could be readily explained by the limited number lexicon of the Pirahã. Lacking exact words for "three", "four", "five", and so forth, Pirahã speakers produced an approximate rather than an exact match for the array to be copied. Still, it could be objected that members of the Pirahã community also had little previous experience in dealing with larger numbers. Their limited arithmetic experience might explain their difficulties, rather than any restriction imposed by the Pirahã language.

However, support for Gordon's emphasis on the availability of count words has come from a different quarter. Spaepen et al. (2011) tested four deaf adults living in Nicaragua who had each independently developed their own "homesign" system of manual gestures—a system that worked well for communication with family and friends but did not correspond to any conventional sign language. For comparison purposes, the investigators also tested two other groups—hearing adults who had not been to school but could count in Spanish and deaf adults who had learned to sign and could count in sign language. All three groups were living in an environment where—unlike the Pirahã community—exact counting would be appropriate in a variety of contexts, such as buying goods and services or receiving payment. However, the homesigners, unlike the other two groups, lacked a conventional counting system. All participants were given various numerical tasks. For example, they were asked to communicate the number of items shown on a card or to use disks to create an array equivalent in number to an array that they had been shown. In such tasks, the homesigners made no errors when the tasks involved the numbers 1, 2 and 3, but for higher numbers they tended to produce an approximate rather than an absolute match. By contrast, the other two groups made very few errors even on numbers from 4 to 20. Overall, these results underline the importance of having a conventional number system for counting—at least for numbers higher than 3.

Does a limited counting system restrict a person's conception of the number system as a whole? Consider the following thought experiment. You are presented with a line running from left to right. The left-hand end of the line is marked as 0 and the right-hand end is marked as 100. You are asked to think about various numbers in between—25, 50, 75—and asked to say where each number would fall along the line. You conceive of the line as a kind of ruler and place the numbers at appropriate intervals. For example, you place the number 75 three-quarters of the way along the line, starting from the left. If you do that, you are thinking of each number as occupying a fixed and equal amount of space on the line and you might well wonder how anybody could conceive of matters differently. In fact, young children do. When they first go to school and are presented with such a number line, they grasp the overall principle that low numbers should be placed to the left and that higher numbers should be placed increasingly rightward. What they fail to do is to divide the line into equal intervals. Suppose we have shown them that the left-hand end of the line is marked as 0 and the right-hand end is marked as 10, children do not place 5 in the middle of the line—they tend to displace it to the right of the mid-point. More generally, they allocate more space to low numbers and increasingly less space to higher numbers, effectively distributing the numbers along a logarithmic scale. By the time children have reached the end of elementary school, they conceptualize the number line in the same way as adults. They conceive of it as a linear scale, along which numbers are distributed at equal intervals.

One plausible interpretation of this developmental change is that as children's mastery and use of the counting system extends to higher and higher numbers, they find the same patterns recurring again and again. Just as 11 is one more than 10, so 51 is one more than 50 and 100,001 is one more than 100,000. This might encourage them to think of numbers as equally spaced whether they focus on low numbers or high numbers.

In that case, what do adults do if they have a restricted number lexicon? The French psychologist Stanislas Dehaene and his colleagues tested adult members of the Mundurucu, an Amazonian group of approximately 7000 people living in an autonomous territory in the state of Para, Brazil (Dehaene et al., 2008). Like the Pirahã, their counting system is quite limited: they have words for the numbers from 1 to 5 only. Given the restriction on their number lexicon, adult members of the Mundurucu might display the same logarithmic relationship between numbers and space as young elementary-school children in the USA. On the other hand, if the adoption of the linear, equal-interval scale conception of number emerges with maturity, then Mundurucu adults should adopt it too.

The answer obtained by Dehaene and his colleagues was clear. In general, Mundurucu adults adopted the logarithmic scale—they spaced out lower numbers and compressed higher numbers so that the middle number of the various numbers that they responded to was displaced toward the right of center. They could map numbers onto space and they could arrange them from left to right in increasing order of magnitude, but, unlike older American children and indeed most Western adults, they did not conceive of the difference between 2 and 3 as equivalent to the difference between 52 and 53.

There was one intriguing exception to this straightforward pattern. Some of the older adults had received some education and spoke Portuguese. They differed from their fellow tribesmen in adopting the linear rather than the logarithmic solution. Still, even these adults did not adopt that solution across the board. When presented with numbers in Portuguese they adopted the linear solution but not when they were presented with numbers in Mundurucu or even with a series of beeps. So, even among these educated Mundurucu adults, the inclination to think about numbers in terms of a logarithmic scale rather than a linear scale still seemed to be the default.

Two different interpretations of these findings seem feasible: one narrowly focused on the impact of language and the other on the broader impact of education. In line with the Whorfian hypothesis, we might conclude that a language that offers an indefinitely large number of count words—such as English or Portuguese—allows speakers to realize that numbers are arranged on an equal interval scale: the difference between 1 and 2 is equivalent in magnitude to the difference between 10 and 11 or 100 and 101. In each case, it is simply a difference of 1. On this hypothesis, adult Mundurucu who speak Portuguese have been given a chance to grasp this notion, whereas monolingual Mundurucu have not. This line of interpretation would obviously comfort Whorf. But another interpretation is plausible. Exposure to Portuguese is correlated among the Mundurucu with exposure to education. Basic education provides experience in measurement. Perhaps it is these experiences, not language per se, that evoke the concept of an equal-interval scale. Consider a simple measuring device such as a ruler, a tape measure, or a thermometer. All of these devices depict numbers along an equal interval scale. Arguably, it is this exposure to measurement and measuring instruments—rather than the lexicon—that is critical for conceiving of numbers along a linear scale.

Still, no matter which of these two interpretations is correct, we are left with the Vygotskyan conclusion that the tools and practices of a culture, be it the number lexicon or exposure to measurement practices via education, induce a conceptual change in the way that numbers are conceived.

Language and time

Recall the earlier comment on the way in which we talk about time in English—with the future ahead of us and the past behind us, as if events were lined up in a queue in the horizontal plane with future events up in front and past events at the rear. This horizontal schema is also available in Mandarin, but, in addition, the succession of months can be talked about in a different way, notably with reference to the vertical plane, with past months above and future months below. So, last month is effectively referred to as the "ascending" month, whereas next month is the "descending" month.

Lera Boroditsky (2001) asked if this was just a figure of speech or if the orientation implied by the language enters into speakers' thinking about time. To test for this latter possibility, native speakers of English and Mandarin were given temporal sentences to judge for their truth or falsity. For example, they were presented with the sentence "September comes earlier than October" (and expected to judge it true) or the sentence "June comes later than August" (and expected to judge it false). But just before receiving these sentences, speakers were primed to think either about horizontal spatial arrangements (for example, they saw a picture of blocks arranged from left to right) or about vertical, spatial arrangements (for example, they saw a picture of two circles, one above the other). English speakers made quicker judgments about the temporal sentences if they had just been primed with a horizontal rather than a vertical arrangement. By contrast, Mandarin speakers showed the opposite pattern. They made quicker judgments if they had just been primed with a vertical arrangement. Moreover, this effect emerged even though the Mandarin speakers—who were all bilingual—were tested in English. By implication, the habit of thinking about temporal relationships in terms of a vertical axis carried over to their processing of English sentences. Their judgments about those sentences were speeded up if they had just been primed to think of items arranged on a vertical axis. Further support for this conclusion emerged in a follow-up study of these bilingual Mandarin-English speakers. Those who had started to learn English late, and had therefore spent most of their childhood speaking Mandarin, showed a stronger benefit from vertical priming than those who had started to learn English earlier. The number of years spent in childhood speaking only Mandarin predicted how readily native speakers of Mandarin thought of time in terms of a vertical axis.

On the basis of this last finding, it is tempting to think that the effects of language on thought build up slowly over several years: the longer one speaks Mandarin, the more firmly entrenched the vertical conception of time becomes. It turns out, however, that such effects can be established quite quickly. Boroditsky invited English speakers to start thinking about time along the vertical axis. They practiced with sentences such as "Nixon was president above Clinton" and "World War I happened lower than World War II", learning to judge the former sentence as true and the latter as false. After this training period, they were tested in the same way as in the first experiment. They were primed with vertical or horizontal arrangements and then given sentences to judge as true or false. Now, their judgments were faster if they were given vertical primes. So, after a brief training, these native speakers of English displayed a pattern of results akin to those shown by Mandarin speakers. By implication, the conceptualization of time that we arrive at on the basis of a given language, such as English, is not so very deeply entrenched. We can gain another, hitherto alien, type of spatial thinking after a relatively brief period of language training.

Conclusions

Is language simply a tool for the expression of our thoughts or is it a mental device whose deployment can change the way we think? Developmental evidence indicates that overt speech is gradually internalized and used in thinking and planning: children can increasingly engage in a silent monologue, telling themselves what to do next. Developmental evidence also underlines the fact that language is an excellent tool for gathering material to think about. Young children ply their caregivers with questions, thousands of them. Many of their questions are factual: they ask *what*, *when*, and *where*. But—especially when they are talking to a familiar caregiver at home—they also ask more probing *why* and *how* questions. Sadly, opportunities to engage in such information-gathering dialogues are much rarer in the classroom. In that context, it is the teacher who asks most of the questions.

Whorf argued that the particular language that we speak influences the particular conceptions that we use in our private reflections. This hypothesis has a tantalizing experimental history. Initially promising findings have disintegrated in the wake of further analysis. Still, recent findings on number and time are suggestive. Even if we all initially depend on a preverbal Mentalese, rather than any given language, to conduct our inner monologues, it looks as if the format of Mentalese is not fixed and universal. The use of a given language can cue us to deploy a particular format within Mentalese—for example, to deploy either a vertical or a horizontal axis when mentally arranging events in time. Further research should help us to figure out how far such rebound effects—from spoken language to Mentalese—are infrequent and modest or common and deep.

4

Do children live in a fantasy world?

Pretending and the origins of the imagination

In thinking about children's attachments, it was natural to adopt a wide-ranging, cross-species perspective, following in the footsteps of Lorenz, Harlow, and Bowlby. After all, we can see signs of attachment in many different species: geese and monkeys as well as human babies. It is more difficult to approach pretend play in a comparative fashion. There is scant evidence for pretend play in any species except human beings. True, there are anecdotal reports of chimpanzees reared in captivity playing with dolls or toys, but such reports are rare. By contrast, in a wide range of cultures, most young children readily engage in pretend play (Harris & Jalloul, 2013). Indeed, by around the age of 4 or 5 years, some children can sustain a particular piece of pretense—the invention of an imaginary companion or the adoption of another's identity—over weeks or months. So, unlike attachment, we have no comparative framework in which to think about pretend play. It is distinctively and remarkably human.

Pretend play is disconcerting if we view it from an evolutionary perspective. It is not hard to think of ways in which staying close to an attachment figure would increase young children's chances of survival, but how does the ability to pretend do so? What adaptive value could there be to "drinking" from empty cups, feeling scared of a pretend monster, or becoming attached to an imaginary companion? At a stretch, we might argue that pretend play allows toddlers to rehearse the roles they may adopt in later life, to practice ministering to a baby or fleeing a wild animal. But is practice with lifeless props or make-believe creatures very instructive? Might we not expect Mother Nature to ensure that young children pay careful attention to real events and activities rather than allowing them to become absorbed in a fantasy world?

Granted these points, we could retreat and conclude that children's imaginative flights are just a fleeting indulgence, harmless in the cocooned world of early childhood, but suppressed or abandoned as children get older. In fact, this is a classic psychological stance toward pretend play. For example, Freud and Piaget had very different theories of childhood—Freud stressed the drives and emotions of early childhood, whereas Piaget focused on the gradual emergence of logical thinking. Yet they were united in their negative stance toward pretense and fantasy (Harris, 2000). Both of them thought of it as a hallmark of immaturity, a mode of thought that would gradually give way, in the course of development, to a more objective, reality-oriented way of thinking.

The intriguing similarity between the two theorists is no coincidence (Harris, 1997). In 1919, after the end of World War I, Piaget left his native city of Neuchâtel for Zurich, where he learned about psychoanalytic ideas from Carl Jung and from Eugen Bleuler, director of the renowned Burghölzli psychiatric clinic. At the time, both Jung and Bleuler were loyal supporters of Freudian theory. Bleuler was particularly impressed by Freud's provocative contrast between primary process thinking—the kind of free association and wishful thinking that characterizes our dreams and fantasies—and secondary process thinking—the more objective cognitive mode by which we cope with reality.

Subsequently moving to Paris, Piaget began to study children's intellectual development. Thanks to Théodore Simon who, together with Alfred Binet, had devised the first tests of intelligence, Piaget was able to interview children each afternoon in Binet's former laboratory, housed in a Parisian school at La Grange-aux-Belles. In thinking about the results of these interviews, Piaget concluded that the increasingly logical stance that he observed as children got older must be inhibiting or suppressing the kind of primary process thinking that he had learned about from Freud—via Bleuler—in Zürich.

In 1922, Piaget attended the 7th International Congress of Psychoanalysis in Berlin, and, with Freud in his audience, he presented a developmental and theoretical synthesis (Piaget, 1923b). He argued that pretend play, which to him displayed the hallmarks of primary process thinking, such as free association and wish fulfillment, was destined to disappear in the course of development as more rational and logical thinking increasingly prevailed. Indeed, to the extent that older children and adults do not, on the face of it, engage in much pretend play, it is tempting to agree with Piaget's negative conclusion: pretend play is a mental cul-de-sac from which older children eventually retreat.

But there are two good reasons for disagreeing with Piaget, and indeed with Freud. First, as I noted earlier, pretend play emerges spontaneously in almost all normal children, even if the exact timetable varies from culture to culture. Granted that ubiquity, it is unlikely that pretend play serves no adaptive function. Second, when pretend play does not emerge in a given child, or is very restricted, it is often associated with social and cognitive difficulties. Ever since the psychiatrist Leo Kanner first identified the syndrome of autism, limitations in pretend play have been one of the defining features of the syndrome and children with autism have cognitive difficulties on several fronts (Kanner, 1943). As discussed in Chapter 5, they have persistent problems in making sense of other people, as well as a narrow range of preoccupations, and difficulties in planning for the future. By implication, whatever Piaget and Freud argued, it is the absence of pretend play, not its presence, that is likely to augur major psychological difficulties.

With these points in mind, it is worth considering a radically different and more positive conception of pretend play. My proposal rests on three interrelated claims. First, pretend play is not so fantastical or wish-based as Piaget and Freud imply. It is deeply regulated by children's understanding of everyday, causal constraints. In much the same way, our own adult fantasies and fictions generally honor the everyday constraints of physics, biology, and psychology, even if they sometimes embrace the heroic, transgressive, or implausible.

Second, and somewhat paradoxically, the ability to mentally set reality aside turns out to be critical for understanding reality. Setting reality aside is not necessarily an escapist retreat but a way to better gauge what actually happened in light of what might have happened instead. Finally, as we will see, there is little indication that children are fundamentally confused about the difference between the world of make-believe and the world of reality.

Pretend worlds

Suppose we play a game of pretend with a 2-year-old toddler. We introduce the child to Teddy, a hand puppet, and explain that, "Teddy's being naughty again." The child watches intently as Teddy is made to lift an empty teapot, carry it over to a pair of identical toy pigs, and, with a tipping gesture, pour (make-believe) tea over one of them. We hand the toddler a tissue, saying, "Oh dear! Can you dry the pig who's all wet?" The 2-year-old will generally play along with this fantasy. He or she will pick up the "wet" pig and wipe it down with the tissue. At first glance, this smooth meshing with the adult's playful invitation is unsurprising. After all, 2-year-olds surely know that a tissue can be used to dry something. But on closer examination, it becomes clear that the 2-year-old's response is complicated. First, note that both pigs, objectively, at any rate, remain dry. So, how the does the child pick out the one that is wet? The most plausible interpretation is that the child sees the teapot being tipped in a pouring motion and imagines tea coming out of the spout. Further, the child does not imagine this liquid spurting in all directions but falling vertically onto only one of the pigs—the one directly beneath the teapot. Finally, the child realizes that make-believe tea, just like real tea, makes you wet, or at any rate makes you "pretend" wet. So, the "wet" pig that the adult is talking about must be the one that was the target of Teddy's mischief and it is this "wet" pig that needs to be "dried" with the tissue. Plausible though this interpretation is, it actually credits 2-year-olds with a good deal of sophisticated thinking. It implies that they realize that the make-believe world behaves in pretty much the same way as the real world: a liquid will emerge when you tip a container such as a teapot; that liquid falls vertically not horizontally; and it wets a dry surface that happens to be in its path. In other words, we should not think of the fantasy world of young children as one in which undisciplined, free association holds sway. Rather, it is a world in which they readily imagine objects behaving in line with everyday causal constraints just as they do in the real world.

Various other pieces of evidence show that this interpretation of 2-year-olds' understanding of pretend worlds is correct. By the end of the third year, when children have more language at their disposal, they can produce an appropriate description of an imaginary transformation. For example, if they are asked, "What happened— what did Teddy do?" they say that Teddy "poured tea over" his victim (Harris & Kavanaugh, 1993). Objectively speaking, of course, Teddy did no such thing. He lifted the empty teapot, tilted it, and put it back down again. But 2-year-olds never describe his actions in that literal fashion. Presumably, in their mind's eye, they see him doing something more mischievous and that is what they describe. Also, if 2-year-olds watch a pretend pouring and are then asked to choose a picture showing what has happened, they point to a picture of a pig with an appropriate, tea-colored stain on its back, not to a picture of a pink and pristine pig or a picture of a pig with some irrelevant change such as a red mark on its snout (Kavanaugh & Harris, 1994). Again, children do this even though the pretend tipping actually leaves the victim unmarked. Finally, 2-year-olds can keep track of a succession of imaginary, causal changes. Suppose that some children watch pretend milk poured from an (empty) milk carton into a cup, whereas others watch pretend powder shaken from a (closed) can of talcum powder into a cup. All the children then see the adult lift the cup, hold it above a toy horse, and turn it upside down. What has happened to the horse? In the former case, he will have been doused with pretend milk and in the latter case, sprinkled with pretend talcum powder. But for children to realize this, they would first have to imagine the relevant substance entering the cup and then imagine the consequences for the horse when the cup, together with its contents, is turned upside down. Two-year-olds are well able to do this. Asked what happened to the horse, they say that he's "covered in milk" or "got powder on him" depending on which pretend sequence they have watched (Harris & Kavanaugh, 1993).

These various studies demonstrate that the toddler's imagination is disciplined and well structured. Children can observe a pretend change and, based on their knowledge of everyday causality, imagine what will happen next, and indeed what will happen after that. In their mind, the world of make-believe is not fundamentally different from the real world. Its successive events are held together by the same type of causal cement.

Much the same picture emerges if we watch children generating their own pretend play episodes. We will see them reproducing the familiar scripts of everyday life—pretending to cook, eat, or clean. If they often spend time with adults who are busy going about their work, children will seek to re-enact those adult activities—of grinding, hoeing, fishing, or gathering. Admittedly, stories and films for young children often depict an unreal world of talking animals, superheroes, witches, and magical transformations, but those fantastical scenarios are created by adults for children. By contrast, when children generate a pretend world for themselves, it is mostly grounded in reality. Children rarely invent a fantastical identity or conjure up impossibilities even if witches, monsters, and superheroes make an occasional appearance (Harris, 2021a).

A retreat from reality?

Freud and Piaget thought of the imagination as a place where the constraints of reality are cast aside. This conception of the imagination has some validity. In real life, we may not be especially adventurous, but we fantasize about the bold choices that we are actually too afraid to make. As we leave our host's apartment or exit a tough job interview, we may fantasize about the penetrating reply that we actually failed to deliver—"*l'esprit de l'escalier*" ("the wit of the staircase"), as the French call it. Still, the notion of the imagination as a place where the shackles of reality are broken by triumphant and exceptional powers can be misleading. We often use our imagination to think about a parallel track that reality could have taken, a track that is realistic, not grandiose, a track that calls for no special powers. Indeed, in trying to figure out why and how the present is as it is, we frequently compare the choices that we have made with others that we could, just as plausibly, have made. And we feel regret or relief, as the case may be. When we ruminate about what might have been, we do not leave reality behind completely. Rather, we use our imagination to get another take on reality. In thinking about what other people have done, we do much the same thing. We compare what they have actually done with what they might plausibly have done instead. In conjuring up these alternative scenarios, we don't invest other people with extraordinary or superhuman powers. We simply imagine how they might, realistically, have acted differently, and we express approval or disapproval depending on the way in which their actual choices met or fell short of some desirable alternative.

Two social psychologists, Wells and Gavanski (1989), devised a neat experiment to probe our tendency to think about such alternative courses of action when we evaluate what someone has actually done. They gave adults one of two slightly different versions of a story about Karen who dines one evening with her boss, Mr. Carlson—who chooses from the menu for both of them. In one version, Carlson hesitates between ordering either mussels with wine or scallops without wine. He eventually chooses mussels with wine. In the alternative version, Carlson hesitates between mussels with wine and a beef dish that also contains wine. Again, in this story version, he eventually chooses mussels with wine. So, in each version of the story, Carlson chooses the same dish.

At this point, in both versions, the story takes an unexpectedly tragic and somewhat lurid turn. It turns out that Karen has a serious hereditary allergy to wine and dies shortly after eating her mussels. After reading the story, participants were asked to evaluate Mr. Carlson's responsibility for Karen's sad demise. Those who had read the first story version, when he vacillated between mussels with wine and scallops without, placed more of the blame on his shoulders than those who read the second. Why the difference? If we look only at what Mr. Carlson actually did, it's not so obvious that he really deserves more blame in the first version. After all, as noted, he chose mussels with wine in both versions—so shouldn't he shoulder the blame to the same extent in both? However, it is evident, at least to our imagination, that in the first version he would have avoided the tragedy had he chosen the scallops with no wine. By contrast, in the second version, poor Karen is doomed no matter what he chooses. Had Carlson chosen the alternative beef dish, Karen would have died anyway. Apparently, when participants made judgments about Mr. Carlson's blameworthiness, they thought not just about what he actually did but also about what he could have done instead. If the alternative was equally deadly, their intuition told them that Carlson was not so blameworthy. No matter what he chose, the outcome would have been fatal. On the other hand, if Carlson could easily have made a different choice that would have saved Karen, participants were tempted to hold him more responsible. Making the same point more broadly, our causal thinking does not focus narrowly on what someone actually did. Our imagination supplies alternatives to reality. We also ask ourselves what someone might, and indeed should, have done instead.

Is this tendency to imagine plausible alternatives confined to adults or do young children display a similar tendency, especially when they hear about negative outcomes? To answer this question, 3- and 4-year-olds were given various (child-friendly) versions of the Karen story (Harris et al., 1996). Instead of hearing about Karen's deadly dinner, children heard, for example, about Sally's inky exploits. They were told that Sally wanted to do a drawing. In one version, her mother gave Sally the choice of using either a black pen or a pencil. She chose the black pen and, guess what, she ended up with inky fingers! In the other version, Sally's mother gave her the choice of using either a black pen or a blue pen. Again, Sally chose the black pen and again she ended up with inky fingers! Children were then asked to say what had caused the mishap and how it could have been prevented. Both 3- and 4-year-olds were likely to consider what Sally had *not* done. In the black pen vs. pencil version, they often mentioned Sally's failure to choose the other instrument: "She didn't use a pencil" or "She should have used the pencil." Indeed, this tendency to imagine what Sally might have done instead sometimes emerged even in the black pen vs. blue pen version of the story, but in that case children conjured up more exotic and unmentioned alternatives: for example, "She should have worn gloves." So, children responded in much the same way as adults. As they thought about the sequence of events and about what had led to Sally's mishap, they focused on choice points, moments when Sally could have acted differently and forestalled the mishap. Their explanations effectively contrasted what she had done with what she should have done instead.

This early readiness to think about alternative courses of action emerged in another set of studies. Preschoolers listened to stories in which child protagonists were given parental permission to do something provided they met some precondition. For example, John's mother told him that he could paint, provided he wore an apron. Children were then shown four different pictures: John was depicted either painting or busy with some other activity, and in each case he was shown either wearing his apron or not. Asked to point to the picture showing John being naughty, children zoomed in on the picture where John was painting but not wearing his apron. Asked to explain what he was doing wrong, they mostly talked about what he was *not* doing: "He hasn't got his apron on" (Harris & Núñez, 1996).

These studies show that when children use their imagination, they do not abandon all thoughts of what actually did happen. Rather, they compare what actually happened to an alternative possibility, identifying causes or misdemeanors as the case may be. Sally did not use a pencil and John did not wear an apron, but in each case they should have. This shuttling between reality and its close, but unrealized, neighbors does not disappear in the course of development. Recall that Freud and Piaget thought of the child's involvement in a fantasy world as a sign of immaturity. But the contemplation of alternatives to reality is a lifelong disposition, not a transient stage. In the wake of a mishap or a tragedy, adults also ruminate intensely about what might have been done to forestall it and mete out blame to those who failed to do what they could or should have done (Roese, 1997).

Confusing fantasy with reality?

So far, I have argued that young children are quite disciplined in their imaginings. They bring their understanding of everyday causality to their pretend play. They think about realistic alternatives to what has actually happened. But one aspect of their pretend play is not easy to reconcile with this portrait. Not only do children sometimes become absorbed in their fantasies, but also they respond to those fantasies with emotion. They pretend that there is a monster behind the door, only to start displaying signs of apprehension toward that same monster. Alternatively, they imagine that they have a companion who accompanies them everywhere, only to get upset when the companion fails to "meet" them or is "accidentally" left behind on the bus (Taylor, 1999). Why, in these instances, do children become fearful or distressed at what is only an imaginary event—indeed, an event that they themselves have conjured up? Alternatively, since they have invented these creatures in the first place, why not imagine creatures that are less fearsome or more reliable?

A possible explanation for these emotional reactions is that children get "carried away" by their imagination. For example, they might invent a monster or a companion and then mentally elaborate on their invention: "The monster might be waiting to pounce on me in the dark" or "My companion is lost or lonely." They might then start to believe that these self-generated fantasies are actually true. So, they become fearful or concerned. According to this account, children's fantasy life is not reliably tagged as mere fantasy. Possibilities that they have elaborated in their imagination come to be treated as emotionally charged actualities.

But there is a plausible alternative explanation for children's emotional reactions. Consider the impact of the cinema. Even as adults, we may experience a quickening of our heart rate when the heroine is about to do battle with aliens aboard the spacecraft. We know full well that the dangers she faces are mere fictions, but still they drive our emotional system, including its physiological aspects. Our emotional reaction is genuine even if its target is purely imaginary. Perhaps children are no different from adults in this respect. They may also be prone to lucid absorption in a fictional world. They realize that the monster waiting to pounce or their companion who is lost are both products of their imagination. Still, like adults, they react with fear or distress to those products. This line of explanation fits one otherwise puzzling aspect of children's fantasy-driven emotions. Reassurances from adults—that monsters do not exist—do not seem to help much. This makes good sense if children are afraid of what they imagine, even when they are reassured by an adult that it is imaginary.

So, we have two opposing explanations for children's emotional reactions to what is purely imaginary. Their emotional reactions might reflect confusion about what is real versus what is imaginary. Alternatively, they might index the kind of emotional absorption in an imaginary world that adults can also exhibit. To assess these two alternatives, we asked 4- and 6-year-olds to close their eyes and imagine various kinds of entities: some prosaic—for example, a pair of scissors—and some extraordinary—for example, a witch (Harris et al., 1991). Children were then asked whether they thought of these imagined entities as real in any way. For comparison purposes, children were also asked about visible and obviously real entities, for example an actual pair of scissors placed on the table in front of them. Children were quite clear that the scissors on the table were real, whereas the scissors they imagined while closing their eyes were not. But they were equally clear that the extraordinary entities we asked them to imagine—for example, a witch—were not real. Children continued to make this clear-eyed assessment even when we invited them to make the imagined entities still more anxiety provoking. For example, we asked them to close their eyes and imagine a monster chasing after them. This emotional boost had no impact. Children often acknowledged that thinking about a monster chasing after them was scary, but they still showed no signs of getting into a muddle about whether the monster was real.

The children in these studies were prompted to conjure up imaginary entities for only a short time. Maybe when they generate and sustain a fantasy for a longer period, they are more prone to losing track of its status. In fact, however, children who have an imaginary companion for weeks or months at a stretch also remain lucid about the status of the companion. They realize that nobody could actually see or play with their imaginary companion even if they themselves regard the relationship as meaningful (Goy & Harris, 1990).

Overall, these findings show that young children are not confused about the status of the various imaginary beings that they conjure up. Their interaction with them may be emotionally charged, but children know that the witch, or friend, or monster that they imagine is not real. By implication, children are not so different from adults who also become emotionally involved in mere fictions.

How does this involvement work exactly, be it in children or adults? A plausible explanation, one that fits our familiar, everyday experience, is that our absorption in a fictional world shuts off our connection to the real world. Temporarily, our real-life concerns are sidelined and instead it is the fictional events that take center stage in our consciousness. Subjectively, and physiologically, these fictional events can have as strong an impact, at least in the immediate or short term, as real events. For example, sitting in the cinema or reading a good book, we sometimes undergo physiological changes toward fictional events: our heart beats faster or a lump comes to our throat, equivalent to those we might experience in real life.

Experimental evidence backs up these familiar impressions. When adults read descriptive texts, they respond with a gradient of visceral arousal. The more the text includes anxiety-provoking content, the more their heart rate accelerates (Lang et al., 1970). The strength of these text-induced reactions varies from one adult to another, but that variation mirrors the variation that would occur during exposure to the real thing. For example, if adults are asked to read a passage about a frightening experience with a snake, an increase in heart rate is especially pronounced among snake phobics—individuals who would display marked cardiac acceleration if shown a live snake (Lang et al., 1983). This correlation backs up the general point that, so far as our emotional reactions are concerned, our emotional system does not make a sharp distinction between fiction and real life. It resonates with both mental and real-life encounters in much the same way.

Of course, as adults, we can step back from fictional material and remind ourselves that what is disturbing us is "just" a book or "just" a film. And such reminders do serve to dampen down our physiological reactions. A classic experiment by Berkeley psychologist Richard Lazarus and his colleagues underlined this point (Koriat et al., 1972). They presented adults with an industrial safety film that included gory depictions of accidents in the workplace. Participants were asked to watch the film in one of two ways—to let themselves become emotionally involved or alternatively to remain detached but attentive. As they watched the film, participants assigned to these two groups were monitored for changes in their heart rate. When it came to the disturbing sections of the film—during and immediately following the accident—the involved group showed a much greater increase in heart rate than the detached group. When asked afterwards about what strategies they had used, participants instructed to become involved emphasized "identification". They said that they deliberately imagined that the events in the film were happening to them. Of course, such a strategy would help to minimize reality checking. It would tempt participants to temporarily respond to the accident as if it were really taking place. By contrast, participants who had been asked to remain detached talked about "reality-checking" strategies. They reminded themselves that it was a film rather than a real occurrence. They strove to reduce their absorption in the film by mentally stepping outside of it, by telling themselves that it was "just" a film.

Adults' flexible self-regulation of their emotional reactions raises an interesting developmental question. Can young children do the same thing? For example, can they remind themselves that the film they are watching, the story they are listening to, or the make-believe situation they have created are mere fictions, and will those self-reminders dampen their emotional reactions? In fact, elementary-school children can manage this. Six-year-olds were given a sad story to listen to; some children were asked to adopt an involved stance, some a detached stance, and some were left to their own devices (Meerum Terwogt et al., 1986). The results were strikingly similar to those obtained by Lazarus and his colleagues with adults. The reactions of the involved children were more intense than those of the detached children, as shown by their self-reports and by their addition of emotionally charged details on retelling the story. Also, when asked about their strategies for involvement or detachment, children echoed what the adults had said. Children in the involved group said, "I pretended it was happening to me", whereas children in the detached group said, "I told myself it was just a story."

These children were 6-year-olds in elementary school. It is possible but unlikely that preschoolers have the same self-regulatory strategies at their disposal. Everyday experience shows that when preschoolers watch a scary movie, its emotional impact is not something that they can easily hold in check. They show distress as they watch or complain later that the film goes round and round in their head when they try to go to sleep. Even if, as argued above, preschoolers ultimately know that fictions are just that—fictions— we should not assume that they can strategically remind themselves of that fact. More generally, young children are probably less able than adults to moderate their emotional reactions to fictions, not because they are muddled about the distinction between fantasy and reality but because they have more trouble in effectively using that distinction to counter their emotional absorption in a fiction.

The child's imagination—fantastical or reality-oriented?

Given that young children often leave the real world behind and become absorbed in a make-believe world, it is tempting to think of them as blessed with a powerful imagination. But the evidence reviewed in this chapter invites a less exuberant conclusion. With some exceptions, the make-believe worlds that young children create are similar to the real world. When they engage with a play partner, they assume that everyday causal regularities also apply to the pretend world. As we saw, they assume that make-believe tea pours downward—just like real tea. Indeed, when young children generate pretend scenarios, they typically re-enact familiar scripts such as cooking, eating, or cleaning (Gaskins, 2013). When they think about how things could have turned out differently, they invoke realistic alternatives to what actually happened, not fanciful or magical alternatives. Indeed, when asked to judge what could and could not happen in reality, young children are actually more conservative than older children or adults. They doubt that improbable departures from everyday reality would ever actually materialize (Shtulman & Carey, 2007). They insist, for example, that it is impossible for someone to wake up and find an alligator under their bed. Summing up, we can say that children's imagination is often constrained by their past experience of reality. It tends to plod rather than soar. This is worth keeping in mind when thinking about the evolutionary function of the imagination and its close links to our emotional lives.

An evolutionary puzzle

Even if adults are better than children at switching off, or dampening, their emotional reactions to imaginary characters and imaginary events, there is still an evolutionary puzzle. Why is it that, for children and adults alike, the default reaction to an imaginary scenario is emotional involvement? It is not immediately obvious how such hyper-emotionality could be adaptive. Surely, we human beings would be better off limiting our emotional reactions to real events, not shedding tears over soap operas or taking fright at make-believe creatures. On reflection, however, there are a couple of plausible, albeit speculative explanations for this intimate link between imagination and emotion. One explanation emphasizes the importance of the link in planning for the future; the other explanation emphasizes how it might help us engage with and learn from other people's experiences.

The evolutionary history of our species shows that over time, thinking about the future weighed more and more upon our mind and brain. The archeological record reveals both a dramatic expansion in the size of the frontal cortex, the area of the brain closely associated with future-oriented planning, and a dramatic expansion in the temporal and geographic scope of our plans, as indexed by the fact that we transported materials for tools and shelter across greater and greater distances.

Planning ahead calls for choices. We conjure up in our mind's eye different courses of action and choose what might yield the greatest benefit. But choosing among those different prospects calls for a metric, a way to assess the potential risks and benefits. This is where emotion might play a key role. If, as we contemplate an imagined course of action that we might take, our emotional system kicks in, flashing emotional red or green lights, then it can help us to make wiser choices.

Persuasive evidence for exactly this link between the imagination, emotion, and good planning has emerged from the work of the neuropsychologist Antonio Damasio (1994). He reports that adults with damage to the frontal cortex appear to lack the usual connection between imagination and emotion. When contemplating pictures of emotionally charged scenes or contemplating a potential future course of action, they fail to show the physiological changes that are typical of ordinary adults. This disconnection appears to hamper their ability to choose. In their everyday lives, such adults are inclined to become involved in ambitious but risky or harebrained schemes. In experimental studies, involving a choice between risky versus less risky investments, they tend to persist in making risky choices even though they can talk lucidly about the dangers involved (Bechara et al., 1994). It is as if the red emotional light that inhibits normal adults when they contemplate a risky course of action has been switched off and they plough ahead, regardless (Bechara et al., 1997).

The second possible interpretation of the imagination–emotion link is closely connected to our language abilities. Much of the information that we gather about the world, we gather not from direct observation but from what other people tell us, a theme I explore in Chapter 9. Other people tell us about events that we have not experienced ourselves. In listening to what other people tell us, we are likely to conjure up a mental picture of what they describe. Suppose that we were to react in a cold-blooded fashion to the events and experiences being described even when they are dramatic or charged with emotion. Not only would that place us out of sympathy with our conversation partner, but also it would mean that our stock of knowledge would be oddly partitioned. If we had no emotional reaction to events that we learn about vicariously, events that took place but are not part of our own personal experience, we would be creating a strange chasm between events that we experience first-hand, to which we typically have appropriate emotional reactions, and events that we conjure up in our imagination on the basis of what we are told. In other words, it looks as if our emotional reactions to events that we only imagine can benefit us. They enable us to use our imagination to appraise the implications not just of a made-up narrative that a storyteller recounts but also the true narrative that our friend recounts. The distressing encounter or the risky venture that our friend describes will provoke appropriate emotional reactions as we contemplate them, via our imagination, in the course of his or her narration. On this view, our emotional engagement will be similar—whether we contemplate reality first-hand or learn about it from other people in the course of conversation, or gossip, or listening to the news.

Conclusions

The classic stance toward children's early pretend play and fantasy has been either negative or overly romantic. On the one hand, children have been seen as immature fantasists who will eventually buckle down and face reality. Alternatively, they are held up as inventive creators, whose imaginative talents warrant protection from a gray and dulling world. I believe that both the negative and the romantic stance are fundamentally mistaken. When children use their imagination, they typically entertain possibilities that unfold according to the same causal logic as actual events. In addition, they can compare such possibilities to what actually took place, so as to pinpoint important causal factors or allocate praise and blame. Furthermore, on careful inspection, young children appear to be no more confused about the distinction between fantasy and reality than are adults. Admittedly, children respond in an emotional fashion to mere fictions, but so do adults. But the ability to respond emotionally to events that are imagined, and not just to events that are experienced first-hand, plays a key role in making choices about what to do in the future. It enables us to enlarge our stock of experience via our imagination. We can engage emotionally with all sorts of events that we are told about but have not yet experienced.

5

Are children natural psychologists?

One or two early theories of mind

In the early twentieth century, psychologists fell under the spell of behaviorism. In an effort to be rigorous, they banished talk of mental states and concentrated on producing accurate descriptions of overt behavior, whether it was pecking by pigeons or running by rats. But such lean accounts of behavior are difficult for ordinary human beings to sustain. We rarely focus exclusively on behavior. We readily attribute desires and beliefs to the simplest acts: we interpret an extended index finger as a desire to point out something of interest or an extended arm as a desire to grasp something. Are these mentalistic interpretations confined to human beings? In a landmark paper, two primatologists, David Premack and Guy Woodruff, asked if non-human primates have a natural intellectual affinity with behaviorism. When chimpanzees watch a piece of behavior maybe they just see finger and limb movements or perhaps, like us, they more or less automatically attribute desires and beliefs (Premack & Woodruff, 1978).

Does the chimpanzee have a theory of mind?

To start to answer this question, they showed Sarah—a domesticated chimpanzee—films of a human actor engaged in various practical activities, for example, reaching up and jumping in an apparent effort to get some bananas hanging overhead. Sarah then watched film clips depicting what the actor might do next. One clip showed the actor doing something that would help him reach his goal—for example, dragging some crates into position under the bananas, presumably with the idea of climbing onto them to reach the bananas. Other clips showed the actor doing something irrelevant or counter-productive.

When invited to choose among the film clips, Sarah proved to be good at figuring out the actor's likely next move. Her choice of the appropriate clip—pushing crates into position, for example—implied that she had not simply registered his motor movements. When she had seen the actor reaching up to the bananas, she realized what he wanted—to get hold of them—so that his positioning of the crates was seen as a means to fulfil that desire. Apparently, Sarah—like human beings—was operating with what Premack and Woodruff called "a theory of mind"—an inclination to interpret ongoing behavior in terms of mental states, notably desires and beliefs.

Commenting on these results, three philosophers—Jonathan Bennett, Daniel Dennett, and Gilbert Harmon—wondered if Sarah was really that good at attributing mental states. We know that chimpanzees can be adroit problem-solvers themselves. They too are capable of fetching a crate in order to climb on it to reach for something too high to reach otherwise. So, maybe Sarah was not working out what was going on in the mind of the actor in the film clip. Maybe, she was effectively saying: "Well, if I were in that situation, this is what I would do . . . ." Genuine psychological attributions, insisted the philosophers, call for a less egocentric type of thinking. At least some of the time, we human beings can recognize that if someone wants—or believes—something different from us, they may well act differently from the way we would. Even if we are invariably late, we can anticipate that a friend who values punctuality will be waiting for us at exactly the agreed time.

Wimmer and Perner (1983) devised an experiment testing for the ability to engage in this type of self-abnegating prediction. The experiment involved preschool children rather than chimpanzees, but the theoretical issue at stake was essentially the same: do young children make psychological predictions by expecting other people to behave as they themselves would in that particular situation? Alternatively, do they grasp that people can sometimes act on their own independent desires and beliefs? The preschoolers watched a simple puppet play acted out in front of them. First, Maxi, the main character, put some chocolate in a cupboard and then left the stage. Next, his mother took the chocolate out of the cupboard, used some of it to make a chocolate cake, put the rest in a different cupboard, and left. Maxi came back and—as the experimenter explained—wanted his chocolate. Children were asked to "Think carefully!" and to say where Maxi would go to get it: in the first cupboard, where he had left it, or in the second cupboard, where his mother had put the remainder? Older children, 5-year-olds, easily solved this prediction problem. They realized that Maxi, not having seen his mother move the chocolate, would head for the first cupboard on the mistaken belief that the chocolate was still where he had left it. Three-year-olds, on the other hand, answered wrongly. They said that Maxi would go to the new cupboard where his mother had put the remaining chocolate. Of course, having watched the mother's activity, the children knew where the chocolate was and presumably knew exactly where they themselves would search, i.e., in the new cupboard— but they had been asked to say what Maxi would do, not what they would do.

These results suggested that the philosophical trio of Bennett, Dennett, and Harmon had unwittingly put their finger on a developmental divide. Younger children, 3-year-olds, did seem to fall back on the type of egocentric strategy that the philosophers had tentatively attributed to Sarah. By contrast, older children, 5-year-olds, were able to grasp that Maxi would search in the wrong place, even if they themselves knew the right place to search.

Knowing your own mind

Subsequent results forced an important revision—or rather a deepening—of the interpretation of the mistake made by younger children. Alison Gopnik and Janet Astington presented Canadian preschoolers with an instantly recognizable tubular box of candy (Gopnik & Astington, 1988). Asked what was inside, the children more or less invariably came up with the right answer: "Smarties!"—similar to M&Ms in the USA. The lid was then taken off so that children could look inside. To their surprise—and disappointment—the box contained pencils rather than Smarties. Once the lid had been replaced, children were asked to say what they had first thought was inside—before the lid had been taken off. The observed age change echoed that found by Wimmer and Perner (1983) with the Maxi task. Three-year-olds wrongly claimed that they had thought there were pencils even before the lid had been taken off, but 4- and 5-year-olds acknowledged that they had initially thought there were Smarties.

Clearly, the difficulties of the 3-year-olds in this Smarties-box experiment are not easily explained in terms of egocentricity, which generally implies an inability to grasp *another* person's perspective. Here, children were invited to acknowledge their *own* initially mistaken perspective. The 3-year-olds failed to realize that when they first saw the container, they had mistakenly thought that Smarties were inside rather than pencils. So, the problem displayed by 3-year-olds is surprisingly wide-ranging: not only do they fail to grasp that other people might not share their beliefs, they also fail to grasp that a few moments earlier they may have held a belief that they no longer hold.

By implication, 3-year-olds live in a benign world where nobody is ever misled or mistaken in their beliefs. They assume that whatever they themselves believe at present is what everyone else believes and indeed what they themselves believed all along. If this interpretation is correct, the insight gained by older preschoolers is radical. They appreciate that everyone, their past and future selves included, can be mistaken about reality, even about such a straightforward and uncontroversial matter as where an object is located or what is inside a box. This insight opens up various possibilities for the child. In particular, it enables them to understand lies, which are typically aimed at getting someone to believe something false.

Such a profound change in children's understanding of the mind is a good candidate for universality. After all, if children change their basic conception of how the mind works, and more specifically of whether or not the mind faithfully mirrors reality or sometimes misrepresents it, it is not very likely that the change occurs as a result of explicit formal teaching. Adults and older brothers and sisters are unlikely to offer 3-year-olds a tutorial about the ways in which beliefs can be false as well as true. Children presumably arrive at this insight without any explicit instruction even if various everyday informal experiences, such as talking to adults or playing with friends, might help them on their way. So, we might expect the same insight to emerge among children growing up in very different cultures.

A summer vacation with the Baka

To test that possibility, Jeremy Avis, then a student at Oxford University, spent his summer vacation among the Baka, an ethnic group living in the rainforests of the Cameroons. With the help of two young men from the Baka village, he arranged a simple test for the children. First, some pfeke nuts—a local specialty—were cooked in a covered pot on the fire inside one of the huts. When the nuts were ready, the senior of the two men, Mopfana, explained to the child participant that he was just going for a pre-prandial smoke in a hut nearby but would return shortly to enjoy his share of the nuts. Once he had left, the younger man, Mobissa, suggested in a conspiratorial fashion that they play a trick on Mopfana—he invited the child to remove the nuts from the covered pot on the fire and to hide them elsewhere in a different container. Then, just before his return, the child was asked to say where Mopfana would go to get his nuts—to the covered pot on the fire where he had left them or to the place where they had just been hidden. The familiar age change reappeared: older children were more likely than younger children to realize that Mopfana would go expectantly to the pot on the fire (Avis & Harris, 1991).

A robust age change

The early studies just described led to a cascade of research. A decade later, Henry Wellman and his colleagues were able to pool the findings from well over a hundred different studies of false belief understanding (Wellman et al., 2001). These studies varied in terms of the background of the children, the exact nature of the testing procedure, and the way that children had been questioned. By grouping similar studies together, it was possible to see what factors, if any, affect the overall pattern of developmental change.

Several clear findings emerged. First, there is indeed a robust improvement with age. Across the various studies, most 3-year-olds are wrong in their predictions, whereas most 5-year-olds are right. This is consistent, of course, with the three studies I have described so far. However, that does not mean that exactly the same proportion pass or fail in each and every study. Some investigators introduced procedural variations that helped boost performance. For example, compare Wimmer and Perner's classic experiment (1983) with the study carried out with Baka children by Avis and Harris (1991). In the former case, children were spectators who watched puppets not real people. In the latter case, children were not just spectators, they were actively involved in hiding the pfeke nuts and they interacted with real people not puppets. It turns out that children perform better if they are actively involved. On the other hand, children respond in much the same way whether they are asked to think about the beliefs of puppets or people. However—and this is the more important point—factors that boost performance—such as being actively involved—turn out to help younger and older children alike. They do not eliminate the performance gap between the two age groups.

So, despite the discovery of procedures that can improve the overall performance of a range of children, younger children still display a less accurate understanding than older children across a wide variety of tasks, implying that the underlying age difference is hard to eliminate. Stated differently, we have strong evidence of a robust developmental change, one that holds across all sorts of conditions. But figuring out exactly what it is that older children have come to understand that younger children do not has proven to be a challenge—as we will see.

Many developmental psychologists concluded that 3-year-olds have a conceptual problem in understanding the way that beliefs guide our behavior. According to this analysis, 3-year-olds realize that people pursue their desires—they seek bananas and chocolate, fame and fortune—but 3-year-olds don't realize that people pursue their desires in the light of their beliefs, no matter whether those beliefs are true or false. By implication, 3-year-olds grasp—at best— only half of our everyday psychology. We ordinarily think of other people as motivated by their desires and guided by their beliefs. Their desires specify the destination that they aim for and their beliefs serve as a kind of map indicating how to get there. Three-year-olds appear to understand only one part of the picture. They understand that people are aiming at a particular destination, but they fail to appreciate that it is people's beliefs, whether true of false, that guide them along a given path toward that destination.

Changes in children's language lend support to this developmental claim. Two- and three-year-olds often use the word "want" to talk about both their own desires and those of other people. On the other hand, they use the words "know" and "think" less often. Only at around 4 years of age does talk about knowledge and belief become as frequent as talk about desires. Moreover, just as we might expect from the findings with Baka children, this age change is stable across different languages. For example, it is found among Chinese- and German-speaking children as well as English-speaking children— even though the grammar of mental verbs like "want", "think", and "know" varies considerably across Mandarin, German, and English (Bartsch & Wellman, 1995; Perner et al., 2003; Tardif & Wellman, 2000).

A spanner/wrench in the works

Despite the solid evidence for a major shift in preschoolers' understanding of the mind, we may have radically underestimated 3-year-olds—and even preverbal toddlers. Think back, once more, to Sarah as she watched the actor in the video reaching upwards. To the extent that she interpreted his movements as an attempt to reach for the bananas overhead, she was making a simple psychological attribution—she saw the reaching movement as desire-based, aimed at the bananas. We know that human infants can also make these attributions. Suppose an object is placed in one of two boxes. Infants will stare less at someone reaching into that box than at someone reaching into the empty box. Their staring is an index of surprise: "Why would someone reach into an empty box!?" they seem to be thinking. This interpretation of infants' prolonged looking is backed up by many investigations. Infants typically look longer at an action that is novel and unexpected as compared to an action that is familiar and predictable (Woodward, 1998).

Kristine Onishi and Renée Baillargeon (2005) made use of this behavioral index of early thinking to assess toddlers' understanding of belief. They showed 15-month-olds a film in which a woman placed a toy in one of two empty boxes and then reached for it a couple of times. Once the toddlers were familiar with this set-up, the researchers moved on to probe the toddlers' sensitivity to the woman's beliefs about the toy's location. For example, toddlers saw the toy moved from one box into the other, hitherto empty box. In one condition, the woman also saw this movement, but in another condition, a screen blocked her view. Adults watching this set-up would readily conclude that the woman knew where the toy ended up if she saw it move but mistakenly believe it to be in the original box if she did not. Indeed, 5-year-olds would conclude the same thing because, as should be clear, this set-up is a variant on the classic task involving Maxi and his chocolate, devised by Wimmer and Perner (1983).

What did the 15-month-old toddlers conclude? When the woman had seen the toy moved to the new box, they stared more if she reached into the now empty original box rather than the new one. This is not so surprising—after all, infants presumably realize that someone will adjust their reach if they have just seen the toy that they want moved to a new box. However, if the woman had not seen the toy moved (because of the screen), toddlers stared more if she reached into the new box rather than the empty old one. By implication, the toddlers had worked out what she (mistakenly) believed—that the object was still in the initial box—and expected her to act on that belief by reaching to that empty box. When she reached to the new box instead, the toddlers stared in surprise, as if thinking: "How could she possibly know it had moved there?" By implication, toddlers had expected the woman to hold a false belief and to reach toward the now empty box.

Other researchers have built on these striking findings. For example, Senju and his colleagues (2011) gave 18-month-olds experience with distinctive blindfolds made of black cloth with pink trimming around the edge. Half the toddlers discovered that they could not see when they wore such a blindfold. However, the other half were given "trick", translucent blindfolds—the center had only a thin layer, so that these children discovered that they could still see, despite the blindfold. All the toddlers then watched as a woman reached toward one of two boxes to find a toy. On the critical test trial, a puppet put the toy in one box, waited for the woman to don the blindfold, then took the toy out of the box, and left. Toddlers watching this might reasonably reach different conclusions about whether or not the woman—who was ostensibly wearing the same type of blindfold as they had—would be able to see the puppet's removal of the toy. Indeed, toddlers who had experienced the fully opaque blindfolds looked at the box as if expecting the woman to fruitlessly reach there. Apparently, they expected the woman to mistakenly think that the toy was still there. By contrast, toddlers who had worn the thinner translucent blindfolds showed no such expectation.

These various findings effectively tossed a hefty spanner in the works. Some psychologists applauded them as long overdue support for their assumption that human beings, babies included, have a natural disposition to attribute not just desires but also beliefs to human agents, even if hundreds of false belief experiments had failed to uncover much evidence for any such disposition. Other psychologists, bolstered by the many studies that Henry Wellman and his colleagues reviewed, thought it safe to conclude that an understanding of belief was something gradually constructed during the preschool years. From that perspective, it seemed quite implausible that toddlers who were not even close to their second birthday could understand false beliefs. Compounding these divergent reactions, the findings with infants and toddlers have not proven so easy to reproduce. Some investigators have reported successful replications or extensions (Southgate et al., 2007; Surian et al., 2007), but others have not (Kulke et al., (2018).

Two planes of understanding

Stepping back from either of the above reactions—the first of unalloyed satisfaction and the other of surprise and skepticism—it would be a mistake to conclude that research with toddlers somehow trumps research with older children. Even if toddlers reveal—through their non-verbal reactions—some nascent grasp of belief, we should not immediately conclude that the large body of findings with preschoolers is somehow invalidated. Equally plausible is the idea that there might be two successive planes to the development of psychological understanding—a tacit, preverbal plane and a more reflective, postverbal plane. Insights understood at a tacit level may or may not get elevated to the reflective plane. The toddler who shows a tacit understanding of the false belief that prompts her mother's mistaken reach into an empty box may eventually turn into a 3-year-old who fails to predict—when asked—that her mother will search there. Knowledge that is expressed behaviorally via expectant glances may be too fragile to underpin the kind of slower, contemplative predictions that are called for when we ask a 3-year-old, "What did you think was in this candy box before I took the lid off?" or "When he comes back, where will Mopfana look for the nuts?"

One key difference between these two levels of knowledge is that the first level may not be open to any kind of explicit formulation or verbal questioning. It operates chiefly at the level of more or less automatic behavior such as visual fixation time. The second level, by contrast, is clearly amenable to explicit formulation and verbal questioning. Most assessments of children's understanding of false beliefs call for children to provide a verbal answer to a question about what someone—a puppet, a story character, a real person—might think, say, or do. Indeed, there is strong evidence that language is closely implicated in the changes that are observed in children's understanding of belief during the preschool years. The evidence comes, somewhat surprisingly, from deaf children, but it is helpful to first set the stage for those findings by reflecting on the ways that we ordinarily figure out what someone believes.

When she watched films of the human actor struggling with various practical problems, the chimpanzee Sarah could base her interpretation of his activities on what she could see him doing. Her interpretation did not call for any understanding of human language. Indeed, because the test was designed to be suitable for a chimpanzee, the films were deliberately created so as to be interpretable simply from watching the visible behavior of the actor. However, we ordinarily interpret other people not just in light of what we see them doing but also in light of what they say. Particularly when we are assessing what another person thinks and believes, we talk to them. To take a familiar example, when a teacher tries to gauge a student's thinking about a newly introduced topic, a roundabout way to do it would be to watch the student attentively, to note how much time he or she spends in the library and what books the student reads. But teachers rarely engage in this type of surveillance. They get the student to talk or write about the topic. Similarly, meeting someone for the first time, we might be curious about the books they have on their bookshelf, but if we really want to know their opinions, we talk to them. Stated more broadly, many of our insights into what other people think and believe are grounded in conversations with them—even if we sometimes have an opportunity to track their behavior. Consider another example: if we know that a friend went to see a recent film, we will expect them to have certain beliefs and thoughts about it. That said, unless they are tiresomely predictable in their film reviews, we need to talk to them to find out in more detail just what they think about this one. The mere knowledge that they saw it tells us very little about what they think of it.

This preamble implies that although we sometimes infer people's beliefs simply from their behavior, we human beings often use another route—we have a conversation with them and ask them what they think. In fact, having conversations might be especially important for realizing how much people vary in what they know and think. When young children acquire language and start to talk to other people, they can begin to discover that mental diversity. Depending on the topic, some people will know nothing, some people will know a lot, and still others may know less than they think. These variations will become evident as two people voice what they think or ask what each knows. So, we can ask what would happen if children have difficulty in engaging in such conversations? If the above line of thinking is valid, it is likely that such children will have a problem in realizing that people vary in what they know and believe—at least when tested in the classic fashion with variants of the Maxi task or the Smarties task (Harris, 1996).

Lessons from deaf children

Candi Peterson and Michael Siegal tested two groups of deaf children. One group was composed of "native" signers—deaf children growing up in families with a fluent signer. So, despite their auditory disability, these children could acquire sign language from that fluent signer and they learned to communicate in much the same way and at much the same pace as hearing children do. The other group was composed of deaf children born into ordinary, hearing families where no one was a fluent signer. Lacking early access to a communication partner, these children were typically delayed in their acquisition of language, be it signing or spoken language.

Peterson and Siegal found that the two groups differed markedly on standard tests of false belief understanding, such as the Maxi task described earlier. Deaf children who were "native" signers showed a good understanding of belief, equivalent to that shown by hearing children of the same age. By contrast, deaf children born into non-signing families showed a marked delay. These findings confirm that language and communication are important, possibly vital, for the developmental change in understanding beliefs that routinely occurs between 3 and 5 years of age among typically developing hearing children (Peterson & Siegal, 2000).

Various other pieces of evidence also point to a key role for language. First, preschoolers' language ability is a very good predictor of their performance on standard false belief tasks (Happé, 1995; Milligan et al., 2007). Second, the elaborateness and quality of the conversations that children have at home are also linked to their theory-of-mind performance. Mothers who make frequent references to mental states have children who display a better grasp of beliefs and of belief-based emotions (Harris et al., 2005). Finally, training studies that employ mental state language have a positive impact on children's understanding of beliefs (Harris, 2005). All these results support the idea that conversation, especially conversation about mental states, serves as a kind of insistent and repeated tutorial for young children, underlining the fact that people vary in what they think and know. Does this tutorial build on the tacit understanding of belief that seems to be present in typically developing infants and toddlers or does the preschooler simply make a fresh start on the concept of belief, using help from everyday conversation? For the moment, we do not have a very firm answer to that important question, but it is starting to frame various lines of investigation.

Meantime, the decades of research on children's understanding of belief are a salutary reminder of the complex nature of that understanding. Especially when studies accumulate in a consistent fashion, it is tempting to conclude that we are gaining a solid, unshakeable insight into the hidden workings of children's minds. However, the conclusions that we reach about children's thinking and its development often depend on the measures that we use as external indicators of their thinking. Focusing on one particular index, such as visual looking time, would be fine if children's understanding were all of a piece. In that case, the conclusions that we draw from one indicator should fit the conclusions we draw from another indicator. But maybe children's understanding is not a single integrated piece of machinery but a conglomeration of different components and functions. These different components and functions do not have the same developmental timetable—some functions may start working early in life and last more or less an entire lifetime—the mental equivalent of breathing. But other functions may need considerable environmental support to get started and remain operational. More generally, the readings that we obtain from one measure of children's thinking may be quite different from the readings that we obtain with another. In this respect, contemporary developmental psychology offers an unexpected echo of the teachings of Freud and the psychoanalytic tradition. The various ways that adults think are not necessarily coherent and the same applies to children and toddlers.

Children with autism

Children with autism display four key symptoms: they have difficulty in making relationships with other people; they are slow to acquire language and can rarely manage to have a conversation with other people in a completely normal fashion; they may be easily distressed by departures from routine; and their pretend play is limited or nonexistent.

What accounts for this cluster of problems? Simon Baron-Cohen, Alan Leslie, and Uta Frith were inspired by the findings of Wimmer and Perner (1983) with the Maxi task. They speculated that children with autism might fail to acquire a normal theory of mind. A pioneering experiment promptly offered strong support (Baron-Cohen et al., 1985). When they gave a version of the Maxi task to children with autism, the majority made the same mistake as normal 3-year-olds. The children with autism were, on average, 11 years of age, with an average mental age (as measured by their verbal ability) of 5 years and yet they failed to take account of the story character's false belief. This failure could not be explained in terms of any general impairment in intellectual functioning because another group of Down's syndrome children with no signs of autism but similar, if not greater impairments in terms of verbal ability mostly answered correctly.

Subsequent work consolidated this basic finding. Children with autism proved to have difficulty in various situations calling for the recognition of someone's belief. For example, when we deliberately lie, we intend to cause someone to believe something that is not true. Children with autism have difficulty in producing lies—even when encouraged to do so—in order to trick a mean puppet, for example (Sodian & Frith, 1992). Their problem in understanding beliefs also restricts their understanding of emotions. Many of our emotions spring from our beliefs about reality rather than from any direct or accurate reading of reality. For example, we can feel genuinely afraid if we hear sounds of an intruder in the house even if the "intruder" turns out to be a harmless sparrow. We can feel proud of a piece of writing that turns out to contain humiliating mistakes. Children with autism have difficulty in understanding such belief-based emotions (Baron-Cohen, 1991). Their difficulty in understanding beliefs also impairs their grasp of non-literal language. Some of our remarks do not directly convey what we believe. For example, "Great job!" can be said with irony rather than genuine approbation and children with autism have trouble understanding such ironic remarks (Happé, 1993). Finally, naturalistic studies show that children with autism are slow to start using the words "know" and "think"—just as we would expect if they have difficulty in grasping the concept of belief (Tager-Flusberg, 1993).

The hypothesis that children with autism have difficult in acquiring a theory of mind neatly explains these various aspects of autism—their difficulty in understanding beliefs, as well as lies, belief-based emotions, jokes, and irony. Because such difficulties would, in turn, make it hard for them to interact with other people, the hypothesis also begins to make sense of their difficulties with human relationships. At a pinch, we might even speculate that a difficulty in understanding mental states can explain some of the other problems displayed by children with autism. Arguably, a problem in understanding and relating to other people might hamper their acquisition of language. It might also undermine children's involvement in pretend play, which is often a social activity, not just a solitary endeavor.

There is, however, a problem facing the hypothesis. Ultimately, the connection between performance on theory-of-mind problems and the defining features of autism is not that tight. On the one hand, there are children who fail standard false belief tasks but never show the classic signs of autism. On the other hand, some children with autism do eventually acquire an understanding of beliefs, yet their interpersonal difficulties persist. Let us consider each of these two cases in turn.

The onset of autism

It is not easy to pick out babies who are at risk for autism. Clinicians often hesitate to make a firm diagnosis until the child is 2 years old or more. As noted earlier, one of the diagnostic signs of autism is a marked delay in the onset of language. Yet language can be quite limited between 12 and 24 months even among typically develop-ing children, so that a firm diagnosis of autism might be premature. However, by the time a child is 3 years of age a diagnosis can be made with more confidence.

Consider, however, a typically developing 3-year-old. We can be confident, following the comprehensive analysis reported by Well-man et al. (2001), that at this age the child will routinely fail classic false belief tasks such as the puppet play involving Maxi or the Smar-ties box with its unexpected contents. We can also be confident that this apparent limitation in their theory of mind is no barrier to their normal, healthy interaction on various fronts. Three-year-olds can interact comfortably with other people even if some trickier aspects of social interaction such as lies and irony elude them. Although children with autism and typically developing 3-year-olds each fail the classic false belief task, they are clearly on a different develop-mental trajectory. By implication, children with autism must have other, deeper problems that eventually lead to a diagnosis of autism. Moreover, these other problems antedate the emergence of false be-lief understanding in the classic verbal set-up because it is possible to diagnose autism with some certainty by 3 years of age.

Investigators have identified two early indicators. At the age of 18 months, typically developing children are usually able to engage in what is commonly called joint attention—to follow another person's direction of gaze or to direct another person's attention to an interesting object by pointing at it. Typically developing children can also produce simple acts of pretense. In a large survey study, Baron-Cohen and his colleagues identified some children who failed to show either joint attention or pretense. Follow-up assessments of these children confirmed that all of them received a diagnosis of autism (Baron-Cohen et al., 1992). By implication, children with autism have interpersonal difficulties well before the age of 3 or 4 years. Investigators are uncertain of the full scope of those difficulties, but whatever they are they antedate their problems with classic verbal false belief tasks. Next, we may ask if children with autism continue to display problems on theory-of-mind tasks as they get older.

Persistent difficulties among high-functioning children

The pioneering study by Baron-Cohen and his colleagues in 1985 showed that most children with autism failed the standard false belief test—but not all of them did so. Of the 20 children that they tested, 4 children answered correctly despite having a clear diagnosis of autism. Follow-up studies have confirmed that the correct replies produced by this minority are not an artifact. Among so-called high-functioning children with autism—those with reasonable language skills—it is common for them to pass the classic verbal false belief task. Admittedly, they find it harder to deal with more complex problems involving belief—for example, they have difficulty when they have to keep track not just of one character's beliefs but the beliefs of one character about another character's beliefs. Still, there are adults with autism who can solve even these more complex tasks (Ozonoff et al., 1991). These results clearly undermine the idea that a persistent or pervasive problem in understanding belief is a core aspect of autism.

Does this mean that the interpersonal difficulties of people on the autistic spectrum are resolved as they move into adolescence and adulthood? Three pieces of evidence show that they are not. First, when they are presented with subtle facial cues—for example, a photograph showing a person's eyes—and asked to say what mental state the person is experiencing, adults on the autistic spectrum make more mistakes than normal controls (Baron-Cohen et al., 1997b).

Second, when they watch people, their pattern of fixation is markedly different from that of ordinary adults. They spend less time looking at people's eyes and more time looking at physical objects (Klin et al., 2002). Moreover, this tendency is a good predictor of how they behave in everyday life. Those who spend a disproportionate amount of time looking at objects rather than people score lowest on a measure of social adaptation but highest on a measure of autistic-like behavior.

The third piece of evidence is especially striking. Senju and colleagues tested a group of adults with Asperger syndrome, commonly regarded as a mild form of autism in which there is less delay in the acquisition of language (Senju et al., 2009). Many adults with Asperger syndrome have no difficulties with the classic, verbal false belief task, and this was true for the sample that Senju and colleagues tested. In addition, they were presented with a looking task devised by Southgate and her colleagues (2007) for toddlers.

Adults with Asperger syndrome and normal adults watched as an actor first reached for an object in a box. Then, on test trials, the object was moved from the box without the actor knowing. Normal adults behaved just like toddlers—their gaze pattern suggested that they expected the actor to search at the box where she mistakenly thought the object was located. But the adults with Asperger syndrome failed to display this expectation. Apparently, their success on the classic verbal false belief task had been attained despite persistent poor performance on the toddler-friendly looking version. Once again, we are forced to the conclusion that different indices can point in different directions. Toddlers display an understanding of false beliefs via their gaze pattern but not when answering questions. By contrast, adults with Asperger syndrome display an understanding of false beliefs if we question them but not if we study their gaze pattern. By implication, there are two planes of understanding, and indeed one can function without the other.

Conclusions

Research on the child's theory of mind has had a major impact on developmental psychology. It has drawn attention to the fact that children's social encounters call for an understanding of mental states. In the 1960s and 1970s, a great deal of work in cognitive development focused on children's understanding of the physical world—for example, on their concepts of number, space, time, and volume. Children's understanding of the social and mental world was much less studied. Now, however, the field of social cognition, as it is often called, is one of the most dynamic areas of developmental psychology. It is interesting to note that children with autism display many fewer difficulties in dealing with the physical or inanimate world than they do with the social and mental world. Their difficulties highlight the striking social competence of typically developing children.

Still, the exact nature of that competence is puzzling. In particular, it remains hard to reconcile the finding that normal toddlers appear to pass an eye-gaze version of the false belief task but fail the classic verbal task. Conversely, it is hard to reconcile the fact that many adults on the autistic spectrum eventually solve false belief tasks but continue to have social impairments in their everyday interactions. It looks as if we do need to make a distinction between tacit and explicit mentalizing. Perhaps children with autism come into the world with a deep and persistent impairment in tacit mentalizing, as reflected in the persistence of their awkward behavior in social situations, their deviant gaze patterns when they watch everyday social interactions, and their early emerging problems with joint attention. To the extent that they acquire advanced language, however, and begin to engage in conversation, they do eventually arrive at something like an explicit understanding of belief, even if they arrive at that understanding much later than normal children. Still, children with autism continue to lack the more tacit and automatic understanding that normal children display even before they have mastered language and conversation.

6

Can we trust children's memory?

The vulnerable eyewitness

Babies can remember things. A few days after birth, they start to recognize their mother, turning preferentially toward her face or the smell of her breast rather than a stranger's. By the age of 3 months, they recognize a distinctive mobile that they saw some days earlier, as shown by their production of an action that they had learned to do with it—for example, kicking to make it move (Boller et al., 1990). By the age of 9 months, they can watch an adult act in an odd and unexpected way with an object—for example lean over to touch it with the forehead—and copy that same action a day later (Meltzoff, 1988). However, we know from our own childhood that such early memories do not stay with us. Almost no-one has any clear memories from their first or second year of life. How can we explain this amnesia if, as babies, we were able to take in information and remember it from one day to the next? Are our early memories completely lost or can we, in exceptional circumstances—perhaps via therapeutic intervention—recover some of them? And beyond the period of earliest infancy, how reliable is the memory of young children? Can we trust them to give us an accurate report of something they saw days or weeks ago? In the context of accusations of sexual or physical abuse sometimes leveled at parents or caregivers, the answers to these questions have obvious practical significance.

The phenomenon of infantile amnesia is now well documented. When adults are asked to recall their first memories, there is an early period that is almost entirely void. With occasional exceptions, nobody reports incidents that took place in the first 2 years of life. Only when the event took place from around 2–3 years of age and upward is there subsequent recollection. For example, Usher and

Neisser (1993) asked college students about different events likely to be salient to them as a toddler. Many students recalled the birth of a younger sibling or a hospitalization that had occurred when they were 2 years of age. Follow-up studies in Britain by Eacott and Crawley (1998) reached similar conclusions. Students who had a younger sibling were asked what they remembered about the birth of that sibling. Those who were only 2 years old at the time of the birth had reasonably accurate memories of the event. Nevertheless, even among these students, there was evidence of an increase in re-membering if they were somewhat older when the sibling was born. Those who had just turned 2 (24–27 months) recalled less about their sibling's birth than those who were slightly older (28–31 months). Moreover, when students were questioned again 1 year later, their memories for the birth proved to quite stable, but this stability was less in evidence for those who had only just turned 2 at the time of the birth.

Both the fragility and the durability of early memories were appar-ent in a study of preschoolers. At the Wellesley College preschool in 1985, a small drama played out. The fire alarm went off and chil-dren were quickly evacuated from the building. As they sat beside the sandboxes in the outside playground, the firefighters arrived, went inside, and turned off the alarm. When the children went back to their classrooms, they were told what had happened: burning popcorn in the basement had triggered the alarm.

Two weeks later, David Pillemer, a psychology professor at Welles-ley College, took advantage of this incident to probe children's memory for the unexpected event. Both 3-year-olds and 4-year-olds could provide some information about what had happened, but the two age groups differed in the quality of their recall. The 4-year-olds included more information about where they were when the alarm went off, the urgency with which they had to leave the building, as well as the actual cause of the alarm (Pillemer, 1992). Happily, most of the children were available for a second interview 7 years later. Some could still produce a fairly coherent account of what had hap-pened: for example, "Well, it was popcorn, and it caught on fire, I guess. And I was stapling something. And I think I was the last one out, because I wouldn't leave until I had stapled it . . . And I remember they were pulling me out, because, uh, that's pretty much it. And they figured out that it was, uh, umm, just the popcorn. And then we went back in." Others could only offer a fragmentary account. They failed to mention the cause of the alarm and gave only a brief description of going outside to the playground and the sandbox. Overall, slightly more than half of the children who were 4-year-olds at the time of the incident managed to remember something, whereas less than 20% of 3-year-olds could do so (Pillemer et al., 1994). So, we have further confirmation that memories laid down in a more mature brain have a better chance of later retrieval.

The amnesia that characterizes very early childhood and the increasingly coherent memories of somewhat older children invite two related questions. First, what causes the amnesia for early memories and second, what leads to the gradual improvement in memory as children get older? Freud, who first called attention to the phenomenon of infantile amnesia, suggested that early memories are difficult to retrieve because they are imbued with anxiety-provoking sexual and aggressive impulses (Freud, 1973, p. 326). But it's hard to imagine that this can account for the wholesale forgetting of the first 2 years—especially the forgetting of benign as well as negative episodes. Katherine Nelson proposed a more credible and intriguing explanation (Nelson, 1993). She argued that although we may sometimes engage in independent rumination about what has happened when we are alone, reminiscence is often a shared activity—we talk about the past with our family and friends. Indeed, young children's first efforts to review and talk about a past episode—a visit to the zoo, a quarrel with a sibling—will ordinarily need the support that can be provided by a familiar adult, someone whose comments and questions can help the child turn memory fragments into something more coherent. Gradually, children can do this for themselves. They can interrogate their memory and draw out a well-structured narrative. According to this theoretical account, recollection of the past is something that children first do with the help of other people. The type of private rumination that we engage in as adults is something that children are only gradually able to do. The scaffolding provided by the adult can eventually be removed because children become capable of recollecting a past episode on their own.

This Vygotskyan theory has two notable strengths. First, it offers a plausible explanation for the phenomenon of early amnesia. In the infancy period—before children learn to talk—adults can scarcely provide the conversational scaffold that children need. Of course, adults can organize the child's activities, be it washing, dressing, or going to a crèche, and sure enough, children begin to master and remember such scripts, anticipating what comes next. But such ritualized and recurrent activities are not ordinarily the stuff of autobiographical memory. To recollect specific incidents, children appear to need the support that is provided by having an adult talk over the particularities of an incident, and, clearly, that type of conversation is not something children can participate in before they acquire language.

A second virtue of Nelson's theory is that it predicts and explains variation among children in their biographical memory. Listening to mothers reminisce about the past with their children, Susan Engel had noticed that mothers differ in the way that they conduct the conversation (Engel, 1986). So-called elaborative mothers listen to the fragments offered by their child and help to elaborate them into a coherent narrative by offering reminders and connections. Other mothers play 20 questions—they quiz the child about where the episode took place, who was there, and so forth. If the child doesn't supply the answer, these mothers are inclined to repeat the question rather than help their child out with prompts and reminders. Elaborative mothers seem to view the conversation as a joint effort to recreate a past experience, whereas mothers who repeatedly pose questions view it as a context in which their child ought to remember independently. It turns out that mothers who elaborate rather than quiz have children who produce richer narratives about the past, consistent with the proposal that children need adults to help them organize their memory fragments into a coherent whole.

In one especially persuasive analysis of variation among mothers, Elaine Reese and her colleagues asked mothers to reminisce with their children about one-off episodes they had recently experienced together. These conversations were recorded when children were 40, 46, 58, and 70 months (Reese et al., 1993). On the basis of recordings of these conversations, mothers were scored for the relative frequency with which they elaborated on their child's contribution or alternatively repeated the same question ("Do you remember who was there?") or request ("Tell me about it"). All the mothers became more elaborative as their children got older—presumably because children were more actively contributing to the conversation so that there was more for mothers to elaborate upon. Nevertheless, variation among the mothers persisted. The mothers who were particularly prone to elaborate did so both when their children were 3½ years old and also some 2½ years later when their children were nearly 6 years old. In that sense, the variation among the mothers remained quite stable.

The frequency with which children made a memory response—by either supplying a new piece of information or asking for one— proved to be correlated with the style that their mother had adopted. Mothers who were highly elaborative at the beginning of the study had children who offered more memory responses both at the start of the study and toward the end—when children were 58 and 70 months. By implication, having an elaborative mother helps a child to get involved in the activity of recollecting.

A closer look at particular conversations will illustrate in more detail how the mothers differed. Here is an exchange between a highly elaborative mother and her child:

MOTHER: Right. Where were our seats?
CHILD: Um, I forget.
MOTHER: Way up high. How high?
CHILD: In the balcony.
MOTHER: So high we could see all the way over the . . .? Do you
   remember? The stage?

Notice that when the child cannot remember, this mother does not repeat her question. Instead, she supplies a helpful elaborative cue:

"Way up high." She then moves on to a different question; the child successfully provides an answer; and the mother elaborates further.

Here is an exchange between a less elaborative mother and her child:

MOTHER: You saw giraffes? Ah. And what else?
CHILD: RRROAR
MOTHER: What's roar?
CHILD: Lion.
MOTHER: What else did you see?
CHILD: ROAR!
MOTHER: What else did you see?
CHILD: No, I want to go watch my T.V.
MOTHER: Well, you can go back and watch that in a second. What other animals did you see?

In this exchange, the mother repeats the same question—what animals did the child see? She does not take her child's contribution to the conversation and build upon it. Perhaps it's not surprising that the child would like to do something else.

However, a word of caution is appropriate. Although these data suggest an impact of the mother on the child, they are purely correlational. It is conceivable that the apparent link between mother and child is not really due to the fact that the child learns from the mother how to engage in recollection. Maybe for genetic reasons, mother and child are both quite fluent and articulate—or taciturn—or maybe they both have a similar long-term memory, whether good or bad. A stronger way to check on the mother's influence is a training or intervention study. More specifically, if some mothers are encouraged to produce more elaborations, we can ask if this increment has an impact on their children's memory. With this possibility in mind, Reese and Newcombe (2007) studied a large group of mothers and children. Half were randomly assigned to the training group and half to the no-training group. When the children were 21, 25, and 29 months, the mothers in the training group were asked to talk with their child—at some point during the ensuing week—about some novel or one-off experience that the child had been interested in. Mothers were also given an instruction sheet with suggestions for elaborative talk about the past. Tips included the selection of one-off events, drawing the child into the conversation with *wh* questions (*what*, *where*, *who*, and *when*), praising the child's responses, following up the child's responses with related questions, or, if the child failed to respond, offering an elaboration by rephrasing the question together with some new information. (Remember the elaborative mother quoted earlier: "Way up high. How high?") At the initial reminiscence session, before the training started, the investigators checked to see whether there were any differences between the mothers and children in the training group as compared to the no-training group and, as expected, found none.

The picture was different at two later follow-up sessions—one took place when children were just over 2½ and a second 1 year later when children were just over 3½. In both sessions, trained mothers did as they had been instructed. They produced more open-ended, elaborative questions ("What did we feed the baby sheep?") than untrained mothers. Moreover, in both sessions, children of trained mothers replied with more memory responses than did children of untrained mothers. Finally, in both sessions, trained mothers offered more confirmations (e.g., "Yes, that's right . . .") than did untrained mothers. These results provide strong evidence that children remember more or less depending on how their mothers approach the conversation and, equally important, they provide evidence that a mother's style of reminiscence—although generally stable as indicated by the earlier findings—can be altered by a modest intervention.

Cultural variation

Katherine Nelson's proposals are also consistent with evidence showing that the age at which infantile amnesia ends varies from one cultural group to another. For example, European-American adults tend to have earlier memories from their childhood than do East-Asian adults (Wang, 2001; 2006). A likely explanation for this difference is that adult–child reminiscing serves different purposes for East-Asian as compared to European-American families. Wang and Fivush (2005) asked mothers living in Ithaca, New York and in Beijing to discuss two, one-off events with their 3-year-old children—one extremely positive and one extremely negative. Even though the mothers were all middle-class and the majority in both locations had a college education, differences still emerged in the way that they talked about the past events. Most of the positive events in each location were about family activities, parties, and vacations, but there was much less overlap with respect to the type of negative event. In the USA, mothers often focused on child injuries or illnesses as well as scary events such as thunderstorms and monsters. In China, by contrast, mothers often talked about a conflict between parent and child (or between a caregiver and the child). Mothers also framed these negative events differently. European-American mothers offered more causal explanation for their children's emotions, whereas Chinese mothers produced more didactic comments. The following extracts highlight these differences:

European-American mother–child pair

MOTHER: What were you crying about?

CHILD: 'Cause I didn't wanted to leave yet; it was because I wanted to eat.

MOTHER: Oh you wanted to eat some more (laughs); is that why?

CHILD: Yeah.

MOTHER: Hmm. I remember Mommy tried to pick you up and you put up a little bit of a fight. You were crying real hard. Maybe it was 'cause the balloon and maybe it was 'cause you were hungry. But we knew that you could get another balloon, right?

CHILD: Yep.

Chinese mother–child pair

MOTHER: How were you not being obedient?

CHILD: (I) threw the pieces on the floor.

MOTHER: All over the floor, right? And did you do it on purpose?

CHILD: Umm. I'll be careful next time!

MOTHER: Right! That's why Dad spanked your bottom, right . . .? Did you cry then?

CHILD: (I) cried.

MOTHER: Did it hurt?

CHILD: It hurt.

MOTHER: It hurt? It doesn't hurt anymore, right?

CHILD: Right. I'll be careful next time.

MOTHER: Umm, be careful.

This cultural signature in the pattern of recall shows up not just among mothers but also among their children. Wang and Song (2018) invited European-American mothers and Chinese immigrant mothers living in the USA to nominate two salient recent events, one positive and one negative—for example, a family outing or activity. Mothers and their 6-year-old children were asked (separately) to recall what had happened during each nominated event. They described what had happened in roughly the same way. So, whether the event was positive or negative, the accounts of mother and children often included information about when and where the event happened, who was involved, and what people had done—for example, "We were riding on the beach."

Despite the stability of this basic recall schema, cultural differences were found. For example, European-American mothers mentioned thoughts and feelings more often than Chinese immigrant mothers—and the same was true of their children. Wang and Song (2018) conclude that European-American adults are more prone to mention the subjective or mentalistic features of a past event—and this pattern gets established relatively early in life (Wang, 2021).

Bilingualism and memory

Because Nelson's theory implies that language is intimately connected to the process of recollecting the past, we can also ask what happens when someone is bilingual. At one extreme, we can imagine that memories are laid down in some Universal Mentalese, as described in Chapter 3. Presumably, any given memory would then be equally available for retrieval no matter which language the person uses for later reminiscence. Whether the person uses one language or the other, the memory would be translated from Universal Mentalese into a given spoken language. But suppose—in line with Nelson's proposals—that the act of remembering is intimately connected with the act of joint reminiscing in the context of dialogue. In that case, we can anticipate that the particular language in which an event is discussed and retrieved will influence the way in which it is remembered.

Findings with bilingual children lend intriguing support to this latter idea. Wang and her colleagues (2010) interviewed bilingual children in Hong Kong—some in English and some in either Mandarin or Cantonese. Children were asked to recount four past events. In addition, they were questioned to assess how far they emphasized autonomy versus interdependence, and how far they thought of themselves as a separate individual or as part of a social group. The language in which children were interviewed had a pervasive, even a cascading effect. First, those children who were interviewed in English were more inclined to stress the value of autonomy (e.g., "When I have a big decision to make, I make my own plans") and describe themselves as a separate individual (e.g., "I enjoy books"), but also to recount incidents in which the focus was on their own thoughts and feelings (e.g., "I wanted to drink Coca Cola"). By contrast, those interviewed in Mandarin or Cantonese were more inclined to stress interdependence (e.g., "When I have a big decision to make, I ask my parents for advice"), to describe themselves in an interconnected fashion (e.g., "I have many friends"), and also to recount incidents in which such interconnections were highlighted (e.g., "My father bought a Game Cake for me").

Wang and her colleagues propose that the speaking of a given language activates the core values associated with that language. In turn, those values bring to mind a particular representation of the self—for example, as being more or less autonomous—which in turn favors the retrieval and narration of episodes, or particular aspects of episodes, that are consistent with that representation of the self. In future research, it will be important to figure out whether the very same event might be recalled and recounted differently depending on the language of recall. For the moment, this intriguing study suggests that bilingual children and adults are prone to construct two partially distinct autobiographies, each attuned to the values and preoccupations of a given language and culture.

Recovered memories

If conversation is helpful, and possibly essential, in making memories fit for long-term recall, what about episodes that are never talked about? Some of these episodes might be banal and not worth discussing. Others might be disturbing or subject to a family taboo. Do these episodes fall into oblivion if they are never discussed? Alternatively, if reminders are eventually provided—for example, in the context of a clinical interview about the past or looking at a long-lost photo album—can these memories be dredged up and organized into a coherent narrative?

One striking example of such a recovered memory is connected to the case of George Franklin, who, at the age of 51, was accused of having murdered an 8-year-old girl some 20 years earlier. The main evidence against him was supplied by his adult daughter, who was also aged 8 at the time of the murder and a friend of the murdered girl. Her memory of the murder "returned" to her gradually. She eventually provided a detailed description of events that fitted newspaper reports at the time, including the crushing of a silver ring. On the basis of her recovered memory, Franklin was eventually tried for murder and found guilty (Loftus, 1993).

Despite the well-documented nature of this particular case, it is important to place it alongside a great deal of other evidence showing that childhood memories, including so-called recovered memories, may sometimes be false rather than genuine. More generally, there is considerable evidence that conversations about the past can not only strengthen genuine memories—just as Nelson's theory implies—but also "manufacture" memories. Engaging in conversation can convince someone that they witnessed or participated in a particular episode when, in fact, they did not.

Piaget (1962) describes a telling example of one of his own childhood memories that turned out to be manufactured and illusory. For many years, he was able to "recall" being with his nurse in the park when she foiled a threatened kidnapping. Years later, however, the nurse admitted to his family that she had made up the whole story. Presumably, Piaget, who had heard her "report" the incident to his family, had constructed in his mind an incident corresponding to what she had reported, but without realizing that his mental construction did not actually take place but was the result of listening to her misleading narrative. In due course, this conversation-based mental construction became indistinguishable from a genuine memory. Piaget "remembered" the threatened kidnapping even though he had experienced no such thing.

A striking demonstration of such memory manufacture—and its risks—was devised by Ofshe, a clinical psychologist. In 1988, Paul Ingram was arrested for child abuse. Although Ingram initially denied everything, after 5 months of questioning by lawyers and psychologists he confessed to rapes, assaults, child sexual abuse, and participation in a Satanic cult. Ofshe doubted that all these supposedly recovered memories were genuine. To illustrate the potential risks of repeated questioning, he invented a sexual scenario, telling Ingram that it had been reported to him by Ingram's children. After an initial "failure" to recall this episode, Ingram eventually wrote a three-page graphic "confession" detailing what Ofshe had fabricated (Loftus, 1993).

How exactly does such a "false memory" get manufactured in the mind? Arguably, the process is set in motion by a conversation. This might be a conversation led by a clinician or a police officer in the wake of an accusation—as in the case of Paul Ingram. Alternatively, it could be a conversation conducted between parent and child— or overheard by a child, as in the case of Piaget. In the course of such a conversation, events, sometimes of a dramatic nature, are described or are the target of repeated questioning. Even if there is no explicit implication that these events have actually taken place, it is likely that those involved in the conversation will create some kind of mental image or schema to represent the event under discussion. For example, when asked about a potential threat or assault, a child might easily—in their imagination—construct a mental image of what such an event would have been like, had it happened. When the same event is revisited again in conversation, it is likely that the same mental image will be retrieved. Now, however, the image might be experienced as a slightly familiar image. If this process is repeated, what started off as a hypothetical scene in the imagination may eventually come to feel just as familiar and authentic as a genuine biographical memory. By implication, if children are prone to such confusions about the source of their "memories", inviting them to think about an event repeatedly may have the paradoxical effect of leading them to wrongly conclude that an imagined event actually took place. They will have difficulty in deciding whether the source of the "memory" is an actual experienced event or an event that they have imagined in the context of a conversation.

Stephen Ceci and his colleagues tested this provocative idea by asking children to think about, and make a judgment about, a variety of events—some that had really happened to them as well as some that had never happened to them. For example, in the latter category, children might be asked: "Think real hard. Did you ever get your hand caught in a mousetrap and go to the hospital to get it off?" (Ceci et al., 1994). Children aged 3–4 years and 4–5 years were asked these questions each week over a period of 10 weeks. At the first interview, children were almost completely accurate. Almost invariably, they denied that the made-up events had ever happened to them. Five weeks later, however, children were showing confusion. They said that around a third of the made-up events had befallen them. In week 10, at the end of the experiment, the younger group assented to more than half of the made-up events and the older group to more than 40%. Such suggestibility in young children is clearly very problematic if their testimony is to be used in a law court. How are we to know if their "recollections" are genuine, especially when they have been repeatedly questioned about a given episode?

It is possible that children talk differently about manufactured as opposed to genuine memories. Perhaps tell-tale expressive signs reveal which type of memory is which. To examine this possibility, Ceci and his colleagues invited clinicians to watch videotapes of 10 children giving their answers. The clinicians were asked to decide which events did versus did not occur. These professionals were at chance in differentiating true from false claims. By implication, even when children claimed that one of the made-up events had actually happened to them—they claimed that they had gone to the hospital to have a mousetrap removed—they did so with sufficient conviction that the clinicians were misled.

How unusual is this transformation from imagined episode to "remembered" episode? It could be argued that the conditions for the transformation do not often happen. Ordinarily, children will not be repeatedly questioned about the same event and, certainly, they will almost never be asked to "think about" a fictitious event 10 weeks in a row. On this skeptical argument, even if false memories can occasionally be manufactured, their manufacture rarely happens in the course of everyday life.

Principe and her colleagues explored this issue with an experiment that was much more akin to children's everyday experience (Principe et al., 2006). Children aged 3–5 years watched a magic show at their preschool in which the magician—Magic Mumfry—ran into trouble in performing one of his tricks. Despite several attempts, he failed to pull a rabbit out of his hat. Later, children were divided into four groups who differed in the explanation they received for the rabbit's disappointing no-show.

One group of children overheard a conversation between two adults in which one adult said that the missing rabbit had been spotted eating carrots in a classroom. A second group did not hear the conversation between the adults but had access to classmates who had heard it and who might well pass on its content to them. Children in a third condition actually got to see a rabbit eating carrots in their classroom. Finally, a fourth group of children were given no access to a ready explanation for the rabbit's non-appearance.

A week later, children were interviewed about the magic show and then 2 weeks later, questioned again by a new interviewer. In each case, analysis focused on the number of children who reported having seen the missing rabbit. As might be expected, virtually all the children who had actually seen the rabbit in the classroom reported having done so. However, a considerable number of children claimed to be eye-witnesses merely on the strength of what they had heard: they reported seeing the rabbit in the classroom even though they had only overheard adults discussing its being seen or heard about its being seen from their classmates.

These findings clearly show that repeated interviewing over a 10-week period is not necessary for the fabrication of false memories. Children who eavesdropped informally on an adult conversation or who heard about that conversation from their classmates ended up creating a false memory. They claimed not just that the alleged event had happened but that they had personally witnessed it. By implication, conversation can have a powerful impact on what young children think they have observed.

Still, it is worth emphasizing that children do sometimes resist the misinformation that can arise in the context of conversation. Galindo and Harris (2017) invited mothers and their children (ranging from 3 to 5 years) to watch a short film about a visit to the park. They watched the film separately and, unbeknownst to them, were shown slightly discrepant versions. For example, the mother might see a child protagonist in the film playing on the swings at the park, whereas her child might see the same protagonist playing on the slide at the park. Afterwards, mother and child were reunited and asked various questions about what they had seen—with some of the questions focusing on discrepant portions of the film. Not surprisingly, mother and child offered different answers to these latter questions. For example, given the discrepant versions they had been shown, the child might claim that the park visit included playing on the slide, whereas the mother might claim that it included playing on the swings. Later, children were interviewed separately and once again they were asked about the film. At this point, we might expect children's recall of the discrepant items to suffer—after all, in the preceding joint interview, their mothers had unwittingly provided answers that amounted to misinformation, at least with respect to the film version that their child had actually watched. In fact, children proved quite resistant to such misinformation. Why were they unaffected by their mothers' misleading input? We cannot be certain, but one reasonable conjecture is that children are good at hanging on to clear-cut, observable facts—seeing a slide rather than swings. They may be more prone to misinformation in the context of more ambiguous events such as the reason for a rabbit's mysterious non-appearance. It is also worth noting that mothers were often quite accepting when their child ventured a different memory from them. Here, for example, is one exchange that took place:

MOTHER: I sort of remember her running to the swings first because I remember she jumped onto the swing and she started pumping her legs.
CHILD: Mmm (nods).
MOTHER: But do you think, you think it was the slide? You don't have to say what Mommy says. You can say something different if you want.
CHILD: I think, no, first she runs to the structure and then she goes down the slide.

   In future research, it will be important to figure out in more detail when children are susceptible to misleading input from other people and when they stick to their guns about what they saw.

Conclusions

After a long, relatively dormant period throughout much of the twentieth century, the study of young children's memory is one of the most exciting and active areas of developmental psychology. Recent memory research connects to theorizing about the nature of the self, as well as to potential variation in basic psychological functions from one cultural group to another. The research is also relevant to practical and consequential questions about the veracity of human memory.

One general conclusion seems firmly established. Even if it is possible to lay down an authentic memory trace, the way in which that trace is retrieved and reworked in the context of later discussion can have a major impact on its fate. At its most benign, such conversation can ensure that a given experience is elaborated into a coherent narrative with no significant departure from "the facts". At the other extreme, however, the power of narrative is such that the overhearing of a credible account—a threatened kidnapping in the case of the young Piaget or the reappearance of the missing rabbit in the case of Magic Mumfry's puzzled preschoolers—can lead its recipients to say that they remember witnessing the non-existent event. In other words, the human mind makes it difficult for us to maintain a firm distinction between what other people have (allegedly) witnessed and then reported to us as compared to what we have seen for ourselves. Our capacity to listen to a narrative and render it into a vivid mental picture can sometimes be enough for us to insist: "I was there. I saw it with my own eyes." We will return to this fecund ability to "learn" from the testimony of other people in Chapter 9.

7

Do children understand emotion?

Children's insight into their inner lives

Early expressions of emotion

"Use your words!"—preschool children who are upset or angry are often given this advice. It may or may not help them to express their feelings and calm down. Still, it is remarkable that children do gradually learn how to put their feelings into words. That is a unique human capacity. Like our primate cousins, we express our emotions non-verbally via an array of facial, bodily, and vocal signals, but language brings about a revolution in our emotional experience and our emotional relationships. In the course of this chapter, I try to describe that revolution, but before doing so, it will be helpful to take a backwards look at earlier research.

Charles Darwin was not only an evolutionary theorist; he was also a pioneering developmental psychologist. In 1877, he published *A Biographical Sketch of an Infant* in the somewhat austere London journal *Mind*, whose authors rarely ventured into the nursery (Darwin, 1877). Granted that Darwin thought of human beings as yet another animal taking their place alongside so many others in the animal kingdom, he brought the eye of a naturalist to human growth and development. So, when his first child William was born, Darwin kept careful notes, with special attention to emotion and its expression. Some of those observations were also included in Darwin's book published in 1872, *The Expression of the Emotions in Man and Animals* (Darwin, 1998), and they helped to consolidate his general thesis that our primate heritage is evident in the way that we humans express and understand emotion.

In discussing Darwin's research, I have regularly asked students to try to visualize how babies look when they scream and then to answer two questions: "Do babies have their eyes open or closed?" and "Is their mouth open or shut?" The students are rarely unanimous in their replies, but Darwin's description provides an unequivocal—and detailed—answer: "Infants, when suffering even slight pain, or discomfort, utter violent and prolonged screams. While thus screaming their eyes are firmly closed, so that the skin round them is wrinkled, and the forehead contracted into a frown. The mouth is widely opened with the lips retracted in a peculiar manner, which causes it to assume a squarish form: the gums or teeth being more or less exposed". A glance at the photographs that Darwin included in his book confirms his point: the eyes are shut tight, but the mouth is wide open.

This expression of distress helps to illustrate two key claims made by Darwin. First, he argued that babies have an innate repertoire for the expression of particular emotions. The way they express pain and distress is different from the way they express disgust or fear or pleasure. Because such expressions appear to be innate, they might form a universal language that recurs across cultures. Subsequent work in different cultures has lent support to Darwin's claim not just for pain and distress but for other emotions as well. For example, when members of the Fore, a remote New Guinea tribe having little contact with Westerners, were asked to say how someone would look when he or she came across a rotting carcass, they tended to pick out a photograph of someone looking disgusted, just as American adults had done. Moreover, when asked to mimic that facial expression of disgust, they did so in ways that were recognizable to American participants (Ekman, 1973). More recent studies have emphasized that the interpretation of a given facial expression of emotion can be markedly affected by contextual factors: the same expression can convey agony or ecstasy depending on the context (Barrett et al., 2011). Moreover, there is evidence of an in-group advantage—we are better at recognizing the emotions expressed by members of our own cultural group (Elfenbein & Ambady, 2002). Nevertheless, even for a diverse sample, it is feasible to create facial stimuli that are recognized as expressing sadness vs. disgust vs. happiness, etc. (Tottenham et al., 2009).

In addition to his claims about the expression of emotions, Darwin made a further claim that has remained controversial and difficult to assess. Consider once again the facial expression of a screaming baby. Clearly, we do not look at the various components of that expression—the closed eyes, the open mouth—and reason our way to the conclusion that the baby is in distress. Our impression of the baby's distress is visceral and rapid—we barely have time to consciously register its specific facial components, as is highlighted by the disagreement among the students that I have polled. That is consistent with the possibility that the recognition of distress might be automatic and even "instinctive". Darwin raises that possibility in the following way: "Do our children acquire their knowledge of expression solely by experience through the power of association and reason? As most of the movements of expression must have been gradually acquired, afterwards becoming instinctive, there seems to be some degree of *a priori* probability that their recognition would likewise have become instinctive." In other words, to the extent that we evolved a repertoire for expressing emotion, we might also have evolved an inbuilt mental dictionary that tells us, even before we even start to think about it, what a given facial expression means about the emotional state of the person we are facing.

Darwin used the records that he had kept about his infant son's development as suggestive evidence for such "instinctive" or innate recognition: "When a few days over six months old, his nurse pretended to cry, and I saw his face instantly assume a melancholy expression with the corners of the mouth strongly depressed; now this child could rarely have seen any other child crying, and never a grown-up person crying, and I doubt whether at so early an age he could have reasoned on the subject. Therefore it seems to me that an innate feeling must have told him that the pretended crying of his nurse expressed grief: and this, through the instinct of sympathy, excited grief in him."

Research with babies has lent some support to Darwin's speculation. In the course of the first year, babies begin to respond selectively and appropriately to the emotional expressions of adults. Indeed, when uncertain about how to respond to a novel object or situation, they can be swayed by a caregiver's emotional expression. If the caregiver smiles encouragement, they will be emboldened and proceed. If, on the other hand, the caregiver expresses fear or anger, they are likely to stop or retreat (Adolph et al., 2010). Still, it remains unclear exactly how discriminating they are—do babies simply make a broad distinction between positive as compared to negative expressions? Alternatively, do they make more fine-grained distinction between, for example, a fearful and an angry expression? Furthermore, although it is true that a competence that emerges in the course of the first year is not likely to be acquired on the basis of explicit instruction or "reasoning"—to borrow Darwin's choice of word—it is conceivable that more informal learning of some kind plays a role.

Darwin's discussion and much of the subsequent research on babies has focused on interpersonal recognition—asking, for example, when and how babies come to recognize that someone else, for example a caregiver, is upset, afraid, or happy. A different but equally important question focuses on the origins of self-knowledge. Babies express basic emotions such as anger, fear, disgust, and joy during the first year of life, but at what point are they aware of the various emotions that they feel? A 12-month-old who is wary of a stranger and edges back to his mother for reassurance may or may not have some conscious awareness of what emotion he feels. After all, there is not ordinarily any possibility of seeing his own fearful face and using that as a sign or index. Presumably, at some point in development there is likely to be a different route to self-knowledge. Toddlers not only express emotion, but also arrive at some conscious awareness of the emotion that they are expressing—yet they have no need to look at themselves in the mirror to achieve that awareness.

Some of the most persuasive evidence for the early emergence of such self-knowledge comes from children's early talk about emotion. Henry Wellman and his colleagues took advantage of a large database (briefly introduced in Chapter 3) that included the spontaneous remarks of five children studied in the first instance by psycholinguists interested in children's gradual mastery of syntax (Wellman et al., 1995). Two of the children—Adam and Sarah—both children living in Cambridge, Massachusetts, but from different backgrounds—were closely followed as they talked in their own homes with members of their family by the psycholinguist Roger Brown and a team of graduate students who recorded what was said. Three additional children, Abe, Naomi, and Ross, who had been systematically observed by their academic parents, were eventually added. All five of these children were audio-recorded for somewhere between 30 minutes and 2 hours every 1 or 2 weeks between the ages of 2 and 5 years. This vast set or recordings totaled more than 120,000 utterances. Happily, the utterances had been transcribed and entered onto a computerized database that could be easily searched for key emotion terms and phrases—*feel good*, *glad*, *happy*, *afraid*, *cry*, *mad*, *sad*, *yuck*, etc.—as well as a parallel set of feeling words referring to pain rather than emotion—*hurt*, *itch*, *ouch*, *sting*, etc. The five children differed from one another in several ways. There were two girls and three boys; one was African-American and the others were white; one child came from a working-class family, another from a middle-class family, and three were children of academics interested in language acquisition. So, although it is important to keep in mind that this sample is far from representative of the US population as a whole, there was some diversity.

The analyses revealed that even at 2 years of age—a few short months after they had started to produce language—children were able to talk systematically about positive emotions (*feeling good*, *feeling better*, *feeling love* or *loving*) as well as negative emotions (*feeling afraid*, *angry*, *frightened*, *mad*, *sad*, or *scared*). One possible interpretation of such early emotion talk is that it is just a verbal supplement to children's non-verbal expressions of emotion. For example, as well as expressing disgust via a facial expression, children might learn to say "Yuck". As well as crying or screaming in pain, children might also learn to say "Ouch" or "Hurt". Wittgenstein (1953) implies that early talk about feelings is expressive in precisely this way. Prompted by adults, children learn to convey what they are feeling by means of language rather than through non-verbal signs. Effectively, children learn to "use their words" to express their feelings.

However, even at 2 years of age, the children used emotion talk in a more comprehensive fashion. This was evident in two important ways. First, although they talked mostly about their own emotions, they also referred to the emotions of other people (including the emotions of dolls, stuffed animals, and made-up characters). So, when children used words like *hurt*, *mad*, or *scared*, these were not just verbal exclamations that were substitutes for non-verbal expressions of their own feelings; children also used the words to describe other people's feelings. Second, although about half of children's remarks about emotion focused on current feelings, the remaining half focused on non-current feelings. Children did not use emotion talk simply to express their ongoing emotions. They also used it in a more contemplative fashion to describe emotions felt in the past and those that might be felt in the future—their own as well as those of other people. One final point is worth noting—the children varied considerably in the frequency with which they talked about feelings. For example, Ross made more than twice as many references to emotion as Naomi—despite the fact that her language was as complex as his and they came from similar backgrounds. We will take a closer look at this individual variation in due course.

Children not only talked about emotions—feeling happy or afraid—they also often identified the target or object of those emotions. For example, they might simply say, "I'm happy" or "He was scared", with no explanation of what the emotion was about—but other utterances did include such an explanation. For example, Adam opined, "You happy I hafta poop" and Sarah explained, "I'm afraid he will bite me."

Because these utterances were audio-recorded and not on video there was no way to go back to check whether the children's remarks accurately captured the emotions that were felt at the time. However, follow-up work with slightly older children is encouraging. In one study, preschoolers aged 3–5 years were observed in daycare centers. As soon as an emotionally charged incident occurred, one of the researchers would approach a nearby child and ask what had happened. Even the 3-year-olds were able to provide an account that agreed with an adult observer's about two-thirds of the time and this proportion rose to about four-fifths for 5-year-olds (Fabes et al., 1991).

A nasty surprise

Granted that preschoolers can report on various types of emotion, both their own and other people's, with a fair degree of accuracy, how do they manage that? One possibility is that in the course of their everyday encounters, they gradually notice and remember recurrent "scripts" for various basic emotions. The happiness script, for example, might go as follows: "A person approaches a situation or outcome that is desirable; the person feels happy; they express their happiness with a smile and/or go toward the situation." The fear script might go as follows: "A person encounters a situation that is dangerous or threatening; the person feels afraid; they express fear in various ways—for example, via a fear expression and/or by trying to avoid the threatening situation." The surprise script might be: "A person encounters an unforeseen situation; the person feels surprised; they express surprise facially or vocally and/or seek more information."

Having memorized these various scripts, children ought to be in a position to "fill in the blanks". For example, seeing someone about to have an inoculation, they might recognize this as a potentially painful situation, retrieve the fear script, and anticipate that the person will feel and look afraid. Conversely, seeing someone with an emotional expression on their face, for example a look of surprise, they could work backwards and infer that the person must have come across something unexpected. Indeed, there is good evidence that preschoolers can make such forward- and backward-looking inferences (Borke, 1971; Trabasso et al., 1981). Such scripts would also help children to identify their own likely emotions. On their way to a goal or outcome they know to be desirable or threatening, children would be able to infer what they are feeling—to categorize their state of mind as a feeling of happiness or fear.

Still, there is an important limitation to such script-based analyses of emotion when they are used to figure out what someone else feels.

Consider what happens when someone is in for a nasty surprise. The story of Little Red Riding Hood offers a good example. When she knocks at the door of her grandmother's cottage, Little Red Riding Hood is about to confront a dangerous situation. The wolf does not have the best of intentions toward her. But as she knocks at the door of the cottage, Little Red Riding Hood is blithely unaware of this danger. In fact, even when she goes inside the cottage, she does not immediately grasp the situation. She is puzzled rather than terrified by the appearance of her "grandmother". To appreciate how she feels, we need to analyze the situation from her point of view. Even if the wolf has devoured her grandmother and dressed up in her grandmother's clothes, Little Red Riding Hood is oblivious at first. So, at this point the "fear script" is not applicable. Actually, because Little Red Riding Hood expects to see her grandmother, the happiness script is much more applicable. From her point of view, she is approaching a desirable situation.

Granted that Little Red Riding Hood is a children's classic, we might suppose that young children readily grasp this paradoxical feature of the story—the discrepancy between what Little Red Riding Hood actually feels and what she ought to feel given the mortal danger she is in. In fact, young children miss this dramatic irony. What captivates them is the danger that they already know about— even if Little Red Riding Hood does not. So, if 4- to 5-year-olds are asked, "How does Little Red Riding Hood feel when she knocks on the door of the cottage?" they typically say that she feels afraid. Only at around 5–6 years of age do most children realize that, actually, Little Red Riding Hood is not afraid. At the moment she knocks on the cottage door she feels fine, even if she is eventually terrified (Harris et al., 2014).

Thinking back to the discussion of false beliefs in Chapter 5, it might be argued that the problem for the younger children is that they don't realize that Little Red Riding Hood has a false belief about who is inside the cottage—younger children might wrongly assume that Little Red Riding Hood knows there is a wolf waiting to pounce and so they invoke the fear script when they think about how she feels. On this diagnosis, the difficulty encountered by younger children is not really a problem in understanding what Little Red Riding Hood feels but a problem in understanding what she believes. However, this argument is only partly right. When younger children are asked who Little Red Riding Hood thinks is inside the cottage, many are actually quite lucid about the fact that she doesn't know about the wolf. Yet, surprisingly, they still claim that she is afraid. So, even though they understand that Little Red Riding Hood doesn't realize she is in danger, they still claim that she feels afraid (Bradmetz & Schneider, 1999).

Various other studies have highlighted this developmental puzzle. For example, children watched a film in which a toddler, who had been briefly separated from his mother, turned hopefully toward the door when someone knocked. Unexpectedly, a stranger came in rather than the mother. When children were asked how the toddler felt on hearing the knock, many children realized that the toddler had mistakenly expected his mother's return. Yet despite that insight, they claimed that the toddler felt sad rather than happy at hearing the knock on the door (de Rosnay et al., 2004).

Overall, there is a marked shift in the preschool period. In trying to figure out how someone feels, younger preschoolers—3- and 4-year-olds—typically focus on the actual situation that a person faces and they attribute the emotion that would normally be triggered by that situation. They ignore the question of whether the person in that situation is fully aware of what the situation implies. Older preschoolers—5- and 6-year-olds—are much more likely to take the person's awareness—or lack of it—into account. They understand that the emotions that we feel depend on how we appraise the situation we find ourselves in. Even if we are wrong in our appraisal, it is still our appraisal that drives our emotion, not the objective situation. So, older preschoolers appreciate the dramatic irony of Little Red Riding Hood feeling happy about seeing her grandmother when her grandmother has actually been devoured and replaced by a wolf. That irony eludes younger preschoolers—they focus on the threat from the wolf and assume that Little Red Riding Hood feels afraid.

Returning to the question of whether children attribute emotions to other people in terms of scripts, this turns out to be a reasonable description for younger children. They focus on the situation that a person is in and assume that some scripted emotion will be triggered by that situation. So, for example, knowing that Little Red Riding Hood is in danger, they attribute fear to her. Older children are more subtle. They realize that it is the situation we *think* we are in that is critical—not the actual situation. More generally, these developmental findings show that young children's developing understanding of emotion is part of a broader story—it has to be linked to their developing understanding of the role of other mental states, especially desires and beliefs, in the appraisal of an emotionally charged situation.

The happy victimizer

So far, I have talked only about simple emotions—happiness, fear, anger, surprise, and so forth. When do children begin to grasp that people also feel more complicated emotions, such as guilt after a wrongdoing? On the one hand, children certainly realize that people have desires and feel happy or sad depending on whether those desires are fulfilled or not. In addition, as discussed in Chapter 8 on morality, they judge that certain actions—for example, hitting another child or stealing from another child—are bad. But can children work out the emotional consequences of allowing desire to triumph over obligation? For example, what do they think about someone who yields to the desire to grab something belonging to another child or to hit another child? Do they think that a person who acts on these malevolent desires will feel good—having acted on their desires—or bad—having broken a moral rule?

Two German psychologists, Gertrud Nunner-Winkler and Beate Sodian, devised a simple and elegant experiment to study this question. Children ranging from 4 to 8 years old listened to stories in which the main character pursued some base desire: for example, pushing another child off the swing or stealing another child's toy. The children were then asked to say how the main character would feel. Younger children—4- and 5-year-olds—were surprisingly oblivious to the transgression. They said that the character would be happy about his or her misdeed—after all, the character had wanted to get on the swing or play with the other child's toy and had succeeded in doing so. By contrast, older children, around 8 years of age, acknowledged that the character would feel sad or bad (Nunner-Winkler & Sodian, 1988). By implication, younger children are insensitive to the conflict between desire and obligation. They expect someone to feel good about getting what they want even if has involved a wrongdoing. Young children's indifference to the possibility of feeling guilty about doing wrong has come to be known as the "happy victimizer phenomenon".

The following dialogue, reported by Chen (2009), illustrates the flavor of younger children's thinking:

INTERVIEWER : John took Anne's toy without telling her. Is that right or wrong?
CHILD : Wrong.
INTERVIEWER : Why?
CHILD : Because he took Ann's toy.
INTERVIEWER : After he got home, John took out the toy and put it on his table. Now, how did John feel—good or bad?
CHILD : Good . . . Happy.
INTERVIEWER : Why?
CHILD : Because he has it.
INTERVIEWER : Is it possible that John felt bad?
CHILD : Um . . ..
INTERVIEWER : Actually, John felt bad. Why?
CHILD : . . . I don't know.

The mother of the child being interviewed was listening to this exchange and—disconcerted by her daughter's replies—suggested that she might answer differently if the story were framed in terms of her stealing from her own friend. Here is the ensuing dialogue between the mother and her daughter:

MOTHER : If you take your friend Amy's toy home without telling her,
    is that right or wrong?
CHILD : Wrong.
MOTHER : How would you feel if you do that?
CHILD : Happy.
MOTHER : Why?
CHILD : I have the toy.
MOTHER : Would you tell me that you took Amy's toy?
CHILD : No.

Apparently, young children's "happy victimizer" stance is quite
firm—surprisingly firm—even in the presence of a parent. How can
we explain this puzzling indifference to wrongdoing—and how can
we explain the emergence of more guilt-ridden attributions among
older children? One possibility is that younger children simply don't
know that hitting or taking another child's possessions is wrong, and
so they assume that a perpetrator of such acts will feel just fine. However, this explanation does not fit the evidence on young children's
moral judgments, as discussed in more detail in Chapter 8. Three-
and four-year-olds judge that it is bad to hit and steal. In fact, they
even judge that it is bad to do such things in a school with no rules—
where you would not get punished. Also, the idea that preschoolers
are simply amoral does not fit the dialogues just quoted. Note that
the girl being interviewed readily acknowledges that you should not
take another child's belongings without permission. Finally, a study
by Keller et al. (2003) confirmed that both younger and older children judge transgressions like hitting and stealing to be wrong, but
it is only the younger children who expect the victimizer to be happy
about having committed such transgressions.

A second possible explanation of the happy victimizer pattern
is that both age groups realize that hitting and stealing are wrong,
but older children are more anxious about the possibility of getting
reprimanded. And, of course, they might have good reason to be
more anxious. After all, because they are older—and ought "to know
better"—their punishment for such transgressions might be more
serious than the punishment meted out to younger children. In fact,

however, older children rarely mention punishment in explaining why a transgressor might feel bad. Instead, they think in terms of the distress brought on by self-criticism—that is to say, they focus on a bad or guilty conscience (Keller et al., 2003; Nunner-Winkler & Sodian, 1988), as opposed to any fear of external sanctions.

A third line of explanation for the developmental change is that older children might be more empathic—more sensitive to the suffering of the victim—and therefore more likely to expect the transgressor to feel badly about the distress that he or she has caused. However, when Arsenio and Kramer (1992) explicitly asked about the emotional reactions of the victim, younger children proved to be just as aware as older children of the victim's likely distress. Yet the happy victimizer pattern still emerged among the younger children. Further evidence against an empathy-based explanation of the age change emerged when Lagattuta (2005) told children stories about victimless transgressions. For example, the story character did something very risky—such as dashing out into a busy street to rescue a ball—but that did not cause distress to any victim. Again, younger children were likely to claim that the transgressor felt fine afterwards, whereas older children attributed remorse to him or her. Clearly, this age change cannot be ascribed to greater empathy on the part of the older child, because no victim was involved in these risky behaviors.

The most plausible explanation of the age change is that it is actually part of a revolution in the way that children see the relationship between desires on the one hand and obligations on the other. In certain respects, younger children are libertarians about emotion. They assume that people's emotional well-being is mostly determined by whether or not their desires are met. They reckon that people feel good if they get what they want and feel bad if they do not. So, in their eyes, when desire triumphs over duty—for example, you set about taking something even though you shouldn't—you'll feel fine, provided you succeed in getting what you want. This seems to capture the spirit of the girl's replies quoted above.

Older children are more obligation-oriented. They assume that people's emotional well-being is impacted by how they stand in relation to their obligations. If people fall short, they will feel bad. So, a child who hits or steals from a peer will feel bad. A child who runs across the road without looking properly will feel bad. From this perspective, your feeling bad is independent of whether anyone is hurt or not. The fact that you did not do what you ought to do is what counts.

One way to test this account is to ask children about a protagonist who is a "rightdoer" rather than a wrongdoer—a protagonist who does his or her duty even if that means thwarting a desire. If the account just described is correct, younger children should say that such a person will feel bad—after all, the person did not do what he or she really wanted to do. Older children, by contrast, should say that a rightdoer will feel good because in their eyes emotional well-being is dictated by how someone stands in relation to their duty as opposed to their desires. So, if someone has fulfilled their duty, they should feel good even if it has meant the denial or frustration of a desire.

Lagattuta (2005) presented children with such "rightdoer" stories. For example, the protagonist was tempted to break a rule but showed willpower and resisted. When asked how the protagonist would feel, the predicted age change emerged. It was essentially the mirror image of the happy victimizer pattern. Younger children said that the rightdoer would feel bad, whereas older children said that the rightdoer would feel good, and when asked to explain their attributions, younger children focused on thwarted desires, whereas older children focused on obligations fulfilled.

Saying sorry

How do children come to shift in their perception of the conflict between desire and obligation? This is an important question for future research, but major clues have emerged from looking at children's understanding of apologies. Apologies are found in many different cultures. They reduce the likelihood of angry retaliation by the victim and they help to ameliorate damaged interpersonal relationships. Witnessing a tussle between two young children, parents will often intervene and prompt one or both to say sorry. Yet parents sometimes have misgivings about the effectiveness of such interventions. How do young children regard such parent-induced apologies—do they grasp their emotional implications?

Smith and colleagues (2010) gave 4- to 8-year-olds two happy victimizer stories. In one story, the main protagonist grabbed something belonging to another child—a bag of marbles. In the other story, the protagonist pushed another child off the swing. However, at the end of one story, the protagonist said, "I'm sorry", whereas at the end of the other story, the protagonist was unapologetic. When the protagonist failed to apologize, children showed the classic pattern of happy victimizer attributions, especially in the younger group. They expected the transgressor to feel good despite the misdeed and they explained those feelings in terms of desirable gains—the chance to play with the marbles or go on the swing. However, the presence of an apology dramatically altered children's interpretation. They expected the apologetic transgressor to feel bad and in their explanations they no longer focused on the protagonist's gains. Instead, they called attention to the misdeed and its impact on the victim. They also expected that if the victim received an apology, he or she would not feel so bad.

These findings offer some reassurance to parents. Apparently, preschoolers do not think of an apology as an empty pronouncement that parents oblige you to deliver. They realize that it signals a different emotional stance on the part of the transgressor and will bring about some alleviation of the victim's hurt feelings. More generally, a transgressor's apology is surprisingly effective in getting young children to realize that someone who gets what they want may not feel good about it. It prompts younger children to make a more obligation-based interpretation of the transgressor's feelings—one they would not ordinarily make until around 8 years of age.

Understanding mixed feelings

We sometimes experience mixed feelings—a combination of positive and negative emotion toward an opportunity or a person.

Judging by the findings of attachment theory, some infants express such ambivalence from an early age. Recall that they express ambivalence even toward their mother—they oscillate between approach and avoidance. When do children acknowledge that such mixed feelings are possible? Susan Harter and her colleagues (Harter, 1983; Harter & Buddin, 1987) asked children to describe situations that might evoke positive and negative feelings at the same time. Children found the task surprisingly challenging—it was only at around 9–11 years of age that they could produce appropriate examples: for example, "I was happy that I got a present but mad that it wasn't what I wanted." Younger children either flatly denied that such mixed feelings were possible or described situations that would evoke mixed feelings successively rather than simultaneously: for example, "If you were in a haunted house, you'd be scared, but then you'd be happy after you got out of it."

Still, remembering or proposing situations that would provoke mixed feelings is a challenging task. Perhaps young children can recognize that certain situations would provoke ambivalent feelings even if they are not good at proposing them. To explore this possibility, 6- and 10-year-olds were presented with stories like the following (Harris, 1983): "Late one night there is a bark outside the door. It's Lassie, your dog. She has been lost all day and she has come home, but she has cut her ear in a fight." Children were asked how they would feel in such a situation. More specifically, they were asked whether they would feel each of four emotions—happiness, anger, fear, and sadness. Six-year-olds typically focused on either a positive emotion or a negative emotion but not both—so, for the Lassie story, they said they would feel happy (because Lassie has come home) or sad (because she has cut her ear in a fight). Ten-year-olds were better at acknowledging that they might feel both emotions. The age difference could not be attributed to the fact that younger children remembered the story less accurately than older children— when they were asked to repeat it, most children, irrespective of age, mentioned both Lassie's return and her cut ear. Rather, the results tended to support Harter's contention that young children have trouble with the very idea of ambivalent feelings. Indeed, when asked directly if such feelings were possible, they mostly said no, whereas older children acknowledged that they were indeed possible.

Individual differences

Much of the work described so far has focused on changes with age. The results have repeatedly shown that with age, children get better at understanding emotion. This improvement is, of course, part of the broader story that we can tell about their understanding of various mental states—not just emotions, but also beliefs and desires, as discussed in Chapter 5. Beyond the regularity of such age changes, however, it is important to note that children vary a lot in the speed with which they come to understand mental states in general and emotions in particular. To measure these individual differences, Pons and colleagues (2004) devised a test to probe children's understanding of various aspects of emotion—some quite easy to grasp—for example, the link between particular situations and particular emotions—and some more difficult—for example, the fact that emotions depend not on actual situations but on the beliefs brought to those situation—and some mastered by only a minority of older children—for example, the fact that certain situations evoke a mix of positive and negative emotion.

When this Test of Emotion Comprehension was given to children ranging from 3 to 11 years, there was the expected improvement with age in performance, with older children passing more of the tasks than younger children. In addition, however, at any given age, there were marked individual differences. Effectively, some children responded like children 2 or 3 years younger or like children 2 or 3 years older. These individual differences among the children were not simply due to chance fluctuations in attention or understanding—when the same group of children was tested twice with a year-long interval between the first and second test, the pattern of individual differences remained quite stable (Pons & Harris, 2005).

Why do children of the same age vary so much in their understanding of emotion? One clue is that children's verbal ability emerged as a strong predictor of their performance on the Test of Emotion Comprehension (Pons et al., 2003). This fits in with what we know about other aspects of children's mental state understanding, as discussed in Chapter 5. Recall the notable differences in false belief understanding between deaf children born into families with or without a proficient signer. Other evidence also points to an important role for family conversation. Some children are likely to grow up in a family where family members often talk about emotion, whereas others grow up in a family where such talk is rare. Judy Dunn and her colleagues obtained striking evidence of such variation. In an observational study, they found that some children never made any mention of emotion during an hour-long home visit, whereas others made more than 25 such references, and variation among the mothers was equally great. Such variation was correlated with children's later ability to identify how someone feels (Brown & Dunn, 1996; Dunn et al., 1991).

Certain kinds of family discussion seem especially helpful in promoting children's understanding of emotion. For example, Laible (2004) showed that amongst 2- to 3-year-olds, emotion understanding was related to mother–child conversations that were high in clarity and stayed on topic, rather than to the sheer number of references to emotion per se. Garner and colleagues (1997) found that the emotional perspective-taking of 3- to 5-year-olds was correlated with family discussions of emotion that focused not just on what someone felt but also on why they felt that way. More recent findings also indicate that it is important for discussion to go beyond the simple labeling and identification of emotions in order to help children to understand the thought processes that can lead to one emotion rather than another (Taumoepeau & Ruffman, 2006; 2008). Parent–child reminiscence about the past appears to be an especially good vehicle for promoting the understanding of emotion. When mothers were trained to engage in "elaborative" reminiscing—as discussed in Chapter 6—their 3- and 4-year-old children subsequently displayed better understanding of the causes of emotion than did children of mothers in a control group (Van Bergen et al., 2009). By implication, "emotion recollected in tranquility"—to borrow a phrase from Wordsworth—helps children reflect on and remember what situations lead to particular emotions.

Finally, recent research points to the broader longer-term benefits of emotion understanding. Young children with better understanding tend to be more popular and socially adroit in their interactions with other children (Harris et al., 2016; Trentacosta & Fine, 2010). They also tend to perform better on measures of educational achievement. For example, 4-year-olds' knowledge about emotion helps to predict how well they will perform on tests of math and reading 1 year later in kindergarten and even 3 years later in elementary school (Ursache et al., 2020).

Conclusions

Darwin argued that our emotional expressions are a universal language. Because we all "speak" the same language of emotion no matter what culture we grow up in, our facial expressions readily convey our feelings to people from a different culture. Subsequent psychological research provides some support for this claim about the universality of facial expression. Darwin's further claim that babies have a kind of inborn mental dictionary that enables them to grasp the emotional meaning of various facial expressions has been harder to prove. We can say, however, that in the course of the first year, babies begin to respond appropriately to the facial expressions of adults, and indeed they use those expressions of emotion as a guide if they are unsure how to respond to an uncertain or ambiguous situation.

Although Darwin stressed the continuities between human beings and other species so far as the expression of emotion is concerned, there is also a major discontinuity. We human beings can put our feelings into words. Children start to do that at an early age. Even 2-year-olds talk systematically about emotion, including past, future, and recurrent emotions—their remarks are not confined to here-and-now expostulations, such as "Yuck!" or "Yummy!"

Some investigators have argued that as children build up their knowledge of emotions such as happiness, anger, or fear, they arrive at a kind of script for each emotion. When they have such a script they can use it to make predictions. For example, knowing what situation a person is in they can anticipate whether the person feels happy, sad, angry, or afraid. However, children's grasp of emotion eventually moves beyond this script-based understanding. They realize that how someone feels is not determined by the actual situation but by the situation as he or she perceives it. They appreciate that a person who is unaware of the mortal danger that he or she is in—Little Red Riding Hood, for example—may feel just fine. Older preschoolers grasp the fundamental impact of a person's subjective appraisal, even if younger preschoolers have more trouble with that insight.

How do children come to understand more complicated emotions? Guilt offers an interesting case study. A large set of findings has suggested, somewhat surprisingly, that young children have little insight into this emotion. Asked to predict how a wrongdoer will feel, they are likely to say that he or she will feel good, especially if the transgression produced some tangible gain—stolen candies or a chance to get onto the swing. By implication, young children are not very concerned about conflicts between desire and duty: so long as you get what you want, they assume you will feel fine, even if you did something bad en route. However, young children are not totally oblivious to guilty feelings. In particular, when they are asked to think about an apologetic wrongdoer—someone who says sorry to his or her victim—they acknowledge that the wrongdoer feels bad. We may speculate that parents who prompt children to apologize will thereby nurture children's susceptibility to guilty feelings—for better or for worse. It is also worth noting that apologies offer a quintessential illustration of the human capacity for putting feelings into words.

There are marked individual differences among children in the speed with which they develop insight into emotions—both their own emotions and those of others. Various lines of evidence suggest that family conversations about emotion, especially conversations that delve into the thought processes that trigger emotion, help to promote children's understanding.

8
How do children tell right from wrong?

The origins of morality

Psychological research on the development of morality has a long and checkered history, but one question comes up repeatedly. Should we think of children as basically amoral and dependent on adult authority for guidance? Alternatively, can they make their own independent, moral judgments, at least some of the time? In *Lord of the Flies*, a novel about a group of English schoolboys stranded on a desert island, William Golding offered his fictional answer (Golding, 1954). In the absence of adult authority, tyranny and savagery will rapidly sweep away any semblance of a moral order. But what does psychological research show?

An inner moral compass?

In an early, monumental investigation, three American psychologists, Hartshorne, May, and Shuttleworth (1930), examined children's moral behavior. They asked whether something like an inner moral compass could be discerned at least among some children. Their strategy was to test a very large sample in a variety of situations in which it would be possible to observe who did the right thing and who did not. For example, after completing a quiz, children handed in their answer sheets, which were then discreetly copied before being returned to their owners. Children were asked to check their answers and to give themselves an overall grade. By comparing children's self-assigned grades to their true grades, it was possible to detect who had been honest and who was guilty of self-serving grade inflation.

Using a variety of such probes, Hartshorne and colleagues attempted to figure out who displayed moral character—who consistently did the right thing across all sorts of different situations—and who lacked moral character—who consistently transgressed. The results were both disappointing and surprising. Overall, children were quite inconsistent from one situation to the next. The child who graded herself accurately was not necessarily the child who resisted the temptation to do the wrong thing in other situations. By implication, most young children lack a stable moral compass—even the best of them are prone to cheating, selfishness, or lack of consideration, at least in certain circumstances. A guiding adult hand would seem advisable.

In subsequent research, two different directions were taken, one by developmental psychologists and the other by social psychologists. Developmental psychologists asked whether more consistency is found if we look not at moral behavior but at moral judgment. Perhaps the framework that children use when they make moral judgments is fairly consistent across different situations even if their behavior varies from one situation to another. By contrast, social psychologists accepted the idea that people might be less than consistent and began to focus instead on various aspects of the social situation. What circumstantial factors, they asked, push someone—anyone—toward immorality? Are there situations where most of us would fail to do the right thing?

Not taking responsibility

Stanley Milgram created what is undoubtedly one of the most dramatic and disturbing illustrations of the power of the situation (Milgram, 1974). Adults were invited to assist a researcher apparently conducting an experiment on learning. Their task was to play the role of a teacher and, following the experimenter's instructions, give electric shocks of increasing intensity to a learner whenever he gave the wrong answer in a memory test—supposedly to investigate the effects of punishment on learning. Unbeknownst to the teachers, the electric shocks were not actually delivered to the learner, who, in any case, was an actor whose pain and distress were feigned rather than genuine. The teachers were remarkably compliant toward the experimenter's instructions. Even when they had heard the screams of the learner strapped into a chair in an adjoining room, and even when the gauge on the machine delivering the electric shocks eventually indicated "Danger: Severe Shock", a surprising number of adults from all walks of life remained compliant. They did what the experimenter asked and continued to press the switch delivering punishment to the learner. In an initial study, 65% were willing to deliver the maximum shock level, labeled as 450 volts (Milgram, 1963, Experiment 1).

Milgram identified a variety of situational factors that promoted either obedience or disobedience. If the suffering and resistance of the learner were made salient—for example, if teachers were asked to actively hold the learner's hand down on the plate at the same time as they delivered the electric shock—they were more likely to disobey the experimenter. Conversely, if the experimenter was standing beside the teachers, rather than giving his instructions either via the phone or by means of a set of taped messages, they were more likely to obey. It was as if two competing forces acted on the teacher. The more immediate the suffering of the learner, the less they complied; the more immediate the authority of the experimenter, the more they complied. Milgram concluded that human beings have a fundamental disposition toward obedience. That disposition serves them well if the authority issuing the instructions is benign, but, as he noted, history is full of examples where the authority is not benign. It issues instructions to torture, bomb, and exterminate.

Milgram emphasized that most individuals who administered the more powerful shocks displayed signs of stress: "Subjects were observed to sweat, tremble, stutter, bite their lips, groan and dig their fingernails into their flesh" (Milgram, 1963, p. 375). A third of them showed "definite signs of nervous laughter and smiling", insisting afterwards that they did not enjoy shocking the victim. Indeed, watching the film that Milgram made of his experiments, it is evident that some obedient teachers were extremely concerned about what the learner was suffering as a result of their actions. They displayed enormous relief when they learned in the debriefing session at the end of the experiment that, in fact, they had been misled— they had not actually delivered any electric shocks to the learner, even if the machine with its array of switches looked very convincing. Apparently, adults in this situation do not do what they are told because they have some psychopathic insensitivity to the suffering that they inflict. They are concerned about the victim, but follow orders nonetheless.

Recent analyses of the exchange that took place between the experimenter and the teacher have added more nuance to the focus on obedience. It is true that the teachers were prone to do what they were asked, but they often construed their compliance as honorable, as serving a higher purpose, notably the advancement of science— in line with the framing offered by the white-coated experimenter asking them to deliver shocks to the learner. Moreover, as Milgram points out, participants had entered voluntarily into the experiment, effectively making a commitment to help the experimenter complete it. In other words, we should not conclude that the teachers were following orders in an unthinking or blind fashion. They saw themselves as committed to making a contribution to a worthy enterprise. Indeed, analysis of historical atrocities, notably the holocaust, suggests that Hitler's henchmen, such as Eichmann, saw themselves as working voluntarily and proudly for the Nazi cause (Haslam et al., 2016). Likewise, the US pilots who dropped atomic bombs on the defenseless civilians of Hiroshima and Nagasaki saw themselves as saving lives in the long run, not simply following orders.

Nonetheless, other moments in Milgram's film reveal a disturbing tendency to yield ultimate responsibility to a supposedly higher authority. One participant, clearly distressed by the audible suffering of the learner in the room next-door, turns to the experimenter and explicitly asks who is taking responsibility. He insists that someone must take responsibility, but in the end, he does not take it upon himself to decide what should be done and proceeds to follow orders.

The issue of responsibility reappears in another famous experiment in social psychology. Bib Latané and John Darley (1970) asked when a bystander would intervene to help someone in obvious need. They arranged for an actor to mimic having a sudden seizure or heart attack while walking along a city street. The striking result was that bystanders were more likely to help the apparent victim if the street was otherwise empty: the greater the number of people in the immediate vicinity, the smaller the likelihood that any particular bystander would offer help. When plenty of other people were close by, it was as if bystanders said to themselves, "Why me?" On the other hand, when they found themselves alone with the victim, they were prepared to take on the role of Good Samaritan. This inner weighing of who should take responsibility seemed to take place outside of conscious awareness. When bystanders were subsequently interviewed about their behavior and explicitly asked whether or not the number of other people close by had been a consideration in their decision to help or not, they typically denied any such influence.

Pulling the results of these two classic studies together, there is not much reason for optimism about the human inclination to take responsibility for a morally acceptable outcome. It is not that we are deliberately immoral but rather that we are disinclined to take it upon ourselves to act responsibly. We leave it to others to decide or act for us. It is often the dictates of authority or the chance presence of other people that determine whether people do the right thing—not the considered judgment of autonomous individuals (Sanderson, 2020). There is, however, one encouraging result that emerged from Milgram's research. He had little success in identifying any personal or social characteristics that might lead particular individuals to resist authority and bring the punishment of the learner to an end. Neither education nor social class nor personality seemed to make much difference. Still, he did identify one predictor: adults who scored well on a test of moral reasoning were more likely to rebel against authority. That test of moral reasoning, devised by Lawrence Kohlberg, dominated the study of moral development for decades. Before describing it, however, it is useful to look at its main progenitor, Jean Piaget, and his research on children's moral judgment.

The development of moral judgment

Piaget's book *The Moral Judgment of the Child* (Piaget, 1965b) can be read as two sustained dialogues, one with Emile Durkheim and the other with Immanuel Kant. In writing about education, Durkheim, one of the luminaries of French sociology, had argued that social authority, invested in parents and teachers, is needed to cultivate the child's sense of right and wrong. He would not have been surprised by the empirical findings of Hartshorne and his colleagues. They would have confirmed his prior expectations. Durkheim's child has little autonomous capacity to make moral judgments. Adult authority is needed to provide guidance in the absence of such autonomy. Kant, by contrast, proposed that any moral judgment worthy of the name ought to be grounded in independent reflection on what is right and wrong, as opposed to the inclination to follow or obey. Of course, that does not mean that adults do regularly engage in such autonomous reflection. Still, Kant's writings set out an ideal to be aimed at.

Piaget, noting this head-on conflict between the two thinkers, adopted his habitual strategy of looking to developmental research as a way to resolve the debate. Is there, he asked, a developmental narrative to be told that embraces both proposals? Are young children initially disposed to assess what is right and wrong in light of adult authority, and, in the course of development, do children gradually move toward more autonomous reflection, especially after they have considered what does and does not lead to good outcomes in the context of peer interaction? Piaget studied children's judgments about various types of wrongdoing, as well as their broader conception of rule-guided behavior, as shown, for example, by their approach to the game of marbles. He drew two interconnected conclusions. First, he argued that younger children look at a misdemeanor and ask themselves how much damage it has done and how much punishment authority figures will mete out. On this calculus, a child who breaks several plates while helping his mother is judged more severely than a child who breaks one plate when trying to steal a cookie. Older children, by contrast, look at the misdemeanor and ask themselves not about the external consequences—the damage done—but the intention behind the act. If the perpetrator was intent on stealing a cookie, he is more reprehensible than someone trying to help his mother. So, the younger child focuses on the reactions of authority figures to damage done, whereas the older child takes a more obviously Kantian stance by considering the reasons for the protagonist's act, rather than its unintended consequences.

Subsequent research chipped away at Piaget's empirical findings. Maybe younger children could take intentions into account provided they were presented with a narrative that did not distract them by highlighting the damage caused. However, the most sympathetic and enduring reaction to Piaget's findings came from Lawrence Kohlberg. Rather than putting particular findings under the microscope, Kohlberg sought to position the developmental shift that Piaget had described within a much larger framework, extending from childhood through adolescence into adulthood. Starting in 1958 with a cohort of 10-year-old boys, Kohlberg studied the way that their moral thinking developed through adolescence, young adulthood, and into their mid-30s (Kohlberg, 1969). His key instrument was a set of story-based dilemmas in which the protagonist was faced with a moral conflict: for example, between stealing to help a family member in dire need versus the obligation to uphold the law. What, Kohlberg asked, should the protagonist do and why should the protagonist take one particular course of action rather than another?

Kohlberg found that pre-adolescents focused mainly on tangible costs and benefits. For example, 10-year-olds typically justified the course of action that they recommended for the protagonist in terms of whether it would provoke punishment or serve the protagonist's interests. Adolescents and adults focused more on abiding by rules, expectations, and laws. They emphasized the desire to be perceived as a good person or the desire to meet the dictates of conscience, rather than the avoidance of punishment or the pursuit of self-interest. Finally, a small proportion of adults claimed that occasional non-conformity or law-breaking was morally justified if it was in the service of some higher-order moral principle such as equality (Colby et al., 1983). The overall direction of developmental change was largely what Piaget would have expected. Younger children and adolescents think of external authority as a constraint on self-interest or as a source of prescriptions and laws. Only adults, or rather only some adults, focus on what is intrinsically right, rather than on what external authority prescribes.

Steady developmental progress through the early stages of Kohlberg's scheme, similar to the progress that Kohlberg himself observed in his initial cohort of American males, has been found in many cross-cultural replications. Given the number and diversity of these replication studies, it is reasonable to conclude that Kohlberg has identified a widespread, even universal, pattern of developmental change. Children and adolescents everywhere increasingly focus on the conflicting obligations that a moral agent should choose among or on the approbation or disapprobation that different courses of action might warrant, rather than on personal costs and benefits. However, support for non-conformity in defense of some higher-order moral principle is rare among people in traditional rural communities or among adults with no higher education (Snarey, 1985). Apparently, it is uncommon for people to think that non-conformity is morally justifiable.

Overall, Kohlberg's findings imply that the tendency to think about whether an action is intrinsically right or wrong—independent of the dictates of the law or social mores—is not attained until adulthood, and even then, by only a minority. Admittedly, one might object that such a tendency is, in any case, just a rhetorical skill, a verbal acknowledgment that occasional non-conformity is morally warranted. On this skeptical view, progress on Kohlberg's scale does not index a mode of thinking that actually guides moral behavior. Rather, it mostly reflects a way of engaging in moral debate. Yet, that deflationary reaction to Kohlberg's findings is probably misplaced. Recall the earlier indications that Kohlberg's scale does, in fact, predict behavior. Those who fell into the small minority of participants who thought of non-conformity as morally justifiable were more likely to disobey the experimenter's order to administer painful electric shocks in Milgram's experiment. That connection makes good sense. After all, resistance to authority in Milgram's experiment depends precisely on a recognition that no matter what one is ordered to do by some supposed authority, one can—and sometimes one should—make an autonomous moral choice. That recognition was what Kohlberg focused on when looking for advanced moral reasoning. As noted earlier, the film of Milgram's experiment includes charged moments when a participant, disturbed by the pain he is inflicting, turns in distress to the experimenter for guidance, whereupon he is reminded that he must proceed, and does so, apparently unwilling or unable to exercise his own judgment about whether to stop or go on.

Autonomy among preschoolers?

Surveying the findings from both social and developmental psychology, we end up with a dismal picture. Children and adults are prone to various situational pressures. They frequently reject opportunities for morally based action and act instead at the behest of other people. When adults think about how someone should decide what to do, few argue that a particular course of action would be morally appropriate if it flouts the dictates of external authority. By implication, moral autonomy is in short supply.

Paradoxically, a more optimistic picture has emerged from research with young children. Kohlberg used relatively complicated dilemmas and did not interview children below the age of 10 years. Judith Smetana, using a simpler test, found a way to probe the early emergence of moral judgment (Smetana, 1981). She gave preschoolers—3- and 4-year-olds—basic transgressions to think about—for example, hitting another child or stealing from another child—and asked them to answer two questions about the transgressions. First, how bad was it to hit or steal—very bad, a little bit bad, or OK? Second, what if adult authority were suspended—as it was in *Lord of the Flies*? Children were invited to imagine a school with no rules where nobody got punished. Would it be OK under those unusual circumstances to hit other children or steal their belongings?

Both the 3- and 4-year-olds judged transgressions such as hitting and stealing to be serious rather than mild. More importantly, they judged that it would be wrong to do such things even in a school with no rules where you would not get punished. Here, for the first time, we have some data suggesting that there may be an early developing inner compass—not one that emerges in adulthood among a few special individuals. Preschoolers seem to understand that the wrongness of basic transgressions, such as hitting and stealing, is not tied to how adult authority reacts. Note that this understanding is consistent with the interviews reported in Chapter 7. There, too, we saw that young children judged hitting and stealing to be wrong, even if they did not view either action as especially guilt-inducing.

Still, it could be argued that children of this age are martinets about rules. It is not that they think there is anything that is intrinsically wrong about hitting and stealing. Rather, adults issue rules such as "No hitting!" or "It's wrong to steal", and children assume that such rules apply willy-nilly, irrespective of whether or not the rules are enforced in a given setting. On this hypothesis, children are simply unthinking sticklers about rules—rules that are arbitrary and conventional as well as those that are moral. To examine this possibility, Smetana (1981) invited preschoolers to think about various social-conventional transgressions—for example, wearing pajamas to school—and asked the same two questions as before: how bad was the transgression and would it be OK in a school with no rules? Children judged these transgressions of convention to be less serious than transgressions of morality. In addition, they were inclined to think that it would be OK to behave in such an unconventional fashion if there were no rules against doing so. A large body of research has reinforced these basic results. Young children grasp the difference between actions that would be bad no matter what anyone, adults included, might say and actions that are only bad insofar as they are violations of more or less arbitrary social conventions, be they rules of politeness or the code of conduct in a particular institutional setting, such as a school or church.

How do young children arrive at this differentiation between moral obligations and merely conventional obligations? One plausible explanation is that preschoolers are intuitive utilitarians. They ask themselves how much happiness or distress a particular act will cause, and when distress is the obvious and more or less inevitable outcome, they conclude that the act is wrong. For example, they know from first-hand experience that it is painful to be hit and upsetting to have one's belongings snatched away. Likewise, they can see that other children react in a similar fashion if they are the victims of such transgressions. By contrast, they realize that infractions of a conventional nature are less upsetting. Neither they nor their peers get especially upset at someone who wanders around during snack time or wriggles endlessly during show-and-tell—and if someone came to school in his or her pajamas it would be odd or funny but scarcely distressing. So, they conclude that hitting and stealing are wrong, and would remain wrong even in a school with no rules, whereas what you do during snack time or what you wear to school is ultimately up to you, at least so long as there is no teacher telling you what to do.

Implicit in this account is the idea that children can and do figure out what is right and wrong for themselves. They make their own intuitive assessments of what is distressing, independent of what adults tell them. In fact, the messages that adults provide might even be somewhat unhelpful. Teachers and caregivers in a preschool react negatively to social-conventional transgressions as well as moral transgressions. Indeed, they respond to a higher proportion of social-conventional transgressions. By contrast, children themselves react to moral transgressions but are often indifferent to social-conventional transgressions (Smetana, 1984). So, this lends support to the idea that children learn primarily from the clear and differentiated emotional feedback that they receive from their peers as opposed to the more encompassing and undifferentiated feedback provided by adults.

Further support for the idea that preschoolers learn what is right and wrong by interacting with other children comes from research on preschool veterans as compared to preschool novices. Siegal and Storey (1985) found that children who were preschool novices—having just started at preschool—tended to be equally judgmental about various transgressions. The differentiation between moral and social-conventional transgressions was more evident among the preschool veterans, consistent with the idea that children come to calibrate the seriousness of a transgression on the basis of observation and experience with other children. Moreover, children growing up in families in which they had suffered abuse and neglect showed the same differentiation between moral and social-conventional transgressions as children growing up in more nurturant homes—a finding that might seem counter-intuitive at first. But, note that these children were attending preschools, underlining the possibility that social interaction with peers is the critical factor in helping children figure out right from wrong, rather than moral instruction by parents (Smetana et al., 1984).

Summing up this program of research, there is persuasive evidence that young children are good at making up their own mind about moral matters. They know what it is to feel pain and distress and they regard acts that cause those feelings as wrong. Indeed, when children are explicitly asked to explain why it is wrong to hit other children or take their possessions, they mostly refer to the consequences for the victim—the harm and distress the actions will cause (Davidson et al., 1983).

When do young children start to display these moral intuitions? Much of the research on children's ability to distinguish moral from conventional rules has focused on preschoolers, but what about infants? Do they display any sensitivity to good versus bad actions? In a striking set of experiments, Hamlin and colleagues (2007) presented infants with brief cartoons in which a protagonist was visibly pursuing a goal: for example, trying to climb a hill or retrieve a ball. After seeing the protagonist helped by one individual but hindered by another, infants of 6 and 10 months subsequently preferred to look at and reach for the helper rather than the hinderer. Follow-up studies showed that 8-month infants were even able to take intentions into account: they preferred someone with good intentions to someone with bad intentions, no matter what outcome they had achieved (Hamlin, 2013). It is too early to say whether these early preferences amount to genuinely moral intuitions—judgments about how individuals *ought* to behave (Van de Vondervoort & Hamlin, 2016). Still, their reactions do show that infants prefer good actions to bad actions and good intentions to bad intentions. And given that they are infants, it seems very unlikely that they have arrived at these preferences on the basis of any type of moral teaching.

Acting morally

Granted that young children show signs of making autonomous moral judgments, how far do they act on those judgments? Here the research findings again take a depressing turn. Preschool life may not be a jungle, but tussles, disputes, and petty theft are rife. Preschoolers do not systematically practice what they preach. Even if they know that an action is wrong, that knowledge scarcely restrains them from doing it. Conversely, even if they know that an action—for example, sharing with another child—is the right thing to do, that knowledge is no guarantee that they will do it (Smith et al., 2013). More generally, the moral judgments that young children make are a poor guide to whether they will actually behave in a moral or prosocial fashion (Tan et al., 2021). So, at the very least, there would appear to be a key role for adult authority in encouraging children to put their best foot forward—to act in accordance with their own moral judgments. In that sense, it looks as if the case in favor of young children's moral autonomy is thin. At best, we can say that children can arrive at some moral conclusions with little instruction from adults—but they scarcely treat those conclusions as moral imperatives.

However, this conclusion does not always apply. Some children do take a moral stand—a stand that can sometimes be different from that of the adults in their family. They may even act on that stand with surprising consistency. Consider the case of children growing up in ordinary carnivorous families. Some of those children—to the inconvenience and occasional consternation of their parents—opt to become vegetarian. Is this just a transient rebellion or a genuinely moral stance?

To find out, Karen Hussar interviewed a group of these "independent" vegetarian children. She compared them to regular meat-eating children and also to "family" vegetarians—children growing up in vegetarian families (Hussar & Harris, 2010). All three groups of children were invited to think of a particular type of meat that they did not eat—even the meat-eating children could identify a particular kind of meat they did not eat—and then to explain why they did not do so. All the independent vegetarians mentioned harm to animals in their explanation, with only an occasional mention of health or taste considerations. The welfare of animals was less evident in the replies of the family vegetarians—they cited family or religious reasons just as often. Strikingly, none of the meat-eating children ever cited harm to animals—instead they all cited health or taste considerations for not eating a particular kind of meat (Hussar & Harris, 2010). So, this initial study suggested that independent vegetarians had stopped eating meat for good moral reasons. They knew that meat eating entailed harming animals and they did not want to be part of it. Regular meat-eating children, by contrast, did not mention such considerations.

Despite this sharp variation among the three groups of children about the rights and wrongs of eating meat, they were quite similar in their thinking about moral rules in general. For example, in line with the findings just reviewed, all three groups judged that moral transgressions, such as hitting another child, were more serious than an assortment of social-conventional transgressions. Similarly, all three groups judged that such social-conventional transgressions were bad to some degree—worse than purely personal, albeit somewhat idiosyncratic choices, such as reading a book during recess. Finally, all three groups said that it was OK for someone to eat meat. This last finding came as a big surprise. The independent vegetarian children did not eat meat and they refrained from doing so for sound moral reasons—they wanted to avoid the hurt and suffering of animals. So, we had expected them to condemn eating meat.

On reflection, their lack of condemnation bolstered the idea that the vegetarian children were independent-minded. After all, in not eating meat, they were setting a moral standard for themselves, and sticking to it, but they did not condemn others for failing to abide by that standard. Nevertheless, their tolerance toward meat eating by other people remained puzzling. When adults take a strong moral stand—for example, against abortion or animal experiments—some of them can be quite belligerent toward people who do not share their views. A possible explanation for the tolerance displayed by the independent vegetarian children was that they regularly saw people in their own family eating meat and felt pressured to avoid condemning such actions. However, our findings also showed that family vegetarians—who rarely saw people eating meat in their own home—were equally tolerant of meat eating by other people. For that reason, another explanation of the tolerance shown by vegetarian children seemed feasible. Perhaps independent vegetarian children think that meat eating is bad but only if you have made a *commitment* to be a vegetarian.

To assess this line of explanation, Hussar and Harris (2010) again interviewed three groups of children: independent vegetarians, typical meat-eating children, and family vegetarians, all ranging from 7 to 10 years of age. The children were asked to think about someone who had initially made a moral commitment—a promise—not to eat meat but then reneged on that promise. All three groups—even the meat-eating children—condemned this as a bad thing to do. Children were also asked about a person who had made a personal commitment (e.g., for health reasons) not to eat meat and broke that commitment. Again, all three groups said this was bad, although they were less severe in their condemnation. In addition, children were asked about a person who had made no commitment. All three groups unanimously said that in this case it was fine for the person to eat meat—condemnation was inappropriate. Finally, we asked children to say what reaction they would have to eating meat themselves. For this question, there was a sharp divergence among the children. The two vegetarian groups, independent and family vegetarians, said that it would be wrong for them to eat meat, whereas the meat-eaters said that it would be fine.

Clearly, the notion of commitment plays a key role in children's moral thinking. Even if meat-eating children and vegetarian children have different views about eating meat, they agree that a commitment is a commitment: if you have made a commitment, you do wrong to break it. The findings also explain the intriguing combination of autonomy and tolerance shown by the independent vegetarians. Despite having made—and stuck to—a commitment not to eat meat, and despite having done so on very reasonable moral grounds, namely to avoid harm and suffering for animals, they were reluctant to condemn meat eating by other people. They appeared to take into account the fact that most people have not made a commitment to vegetarianism.

Still, it is worth underlining a lingering paradox. Suppose we discover that someone has lied to us, but when we castigate him or her, the person protests: "Hold on a moment—I never made a commitment not to lie to you!" At that point, we would be unlikely to say, "Oh! Right you are—in that case, all is forgiven." By implication, except in games of poker or espionage, we ordinarily expect people to avoid misleading us. Even if they have never expressed any commitment to being honest, we still feel entitled to condemn them if they end up acting dishonestly. Why is the situation different for eating meat? Why do children condemn only those who have made a commitment? Why do they not condemn carnivores, irrespective of whether they have made a commitment to vegetarianism or thought about the morality of meat eating? This question warrants more research, but for the time being a plausible answer is that children are good observers. They know from sociological observation that most of the people in their community accept that it's wrong to lie, whereas very few people think that it's wrong to eat meat. By implication, children avoid judging other people in terms of what they know to be a minority position. Despite their moral independence in not eating meat themselves, they hesitate to swim against the powerful tide of the majority by condemning those who do.

Reasoning and emotion

Children who choose to become vegetarian do so for good reason—they want to avoid harm and suffering to animals. At the same time, these unusual children do not reason differently from other children about various other moral issues. Their exceptional moral commitment is circumscribed rather than all embracing. But why are these children so concerned about the harm and suffering of animals—or asking the same question the other way around, why are meat-eating children so indifferent? Maybe the emotional re-actions of independent vegetarians are more intense or more easily evoked than those of other children—especially in the context of an-imal suffering. Perhaps when faced with the prospect of eating meat, they are so repulsed by the animal suffering that came before that they cannot bear to actually eat it. In that case, the argument that they make, namely that it is bad to hurt animals, offers only a ret-rospective moral framing for their repugnance, but that argument might not be the driving force in their initial decision to become vegetarian. From this skeptical perspective, what ultimately drives that initial decision is the feeling of disgust they have as they con-template how meat arrives on their plate, rather than dispassionate moral reflection.

Jonathan Haidt (2001) has pursued this line of thinking about moral decision-making in research with adults. He presented the following vignette to college students:

Julie and Mark who are brother and sister are traveling together in France on summer vacation from college. One night they are staying alone in a cabin near the beach. They decide that it would be interesting and fun if they tried making love. At very least it would be a new experience for each of them. Julie was already taking birth control pills, but Mark uses a condom too, just to be safe. They both enjoy making love, but they decide not to do it again. They keep that night as a special secret, which makes them feel even closer to each other. So what do you think about that? Was it OK for them to make love?

Having read this vignette, most students concluded that what Julie and Mark had done was wrong. The interesting findings emerged when students were invited to explain their judgment. They were prone to what Haidt called "moral dumbfounding". Although they might at first point out potential risks associated with incest, they continued to feel, even when reminded that those risks had been virtually eliminated by Julie and Mark's precautions, that the act was wrong. They were effectively "dumbfounded"—they could not articulate the reasons why, even in the absence of any risk, they felt that Julie and Mark had done something wrong. A reasonable interpretation—and the one advocated by Haidt—is that the students reacted to the vignette at a visceral or gut level. They found the idea of incest disgusting and this prompted them to condemn it. Any reasons—or lack of reasons—that they produced after that condemnation were post-hoc rather than the true grounds of their condemnation. In other words, they had an immediate negative feeling in thinking about what Julie and Mark had done—and then they cast around for a way to rationalize that feeling in moral terms.

Other work, again with adults, has underlined the same basic point: moral judgments are not likely to be the outcome of pure, unemotional reasoning. For example, Greene et al. (2001) presented adults with two similar but subtly different dilemmas. In the "Trolley Switch" dilemma, a runaway trolley is headed for five people who will be killed if the trolley proceeds on its course. The only way to save the five people is to throw a switch that will redirect the trolley onto an alternate set of tracks where it will kill one person instead of five. Participants were asked if they ought to turn the trolley in order to save five people at the expense of one. Would they hit the switch?

In the "Footbridge" dilemma, a trolley again threatens to kill five people. Participants were asked to imagine standing next to an obese stranger on a footbridge spanning the track at a location somewhere in between the oncoming trolley and the five people. In this scenario, the only way to save the five people is to push this large and unfortunate stranger off the bridge onto the tracks below. He will die if he is pushed, but his body will stop the trolley from reaching the others. Participants were asked if they ought to save the five people. Would they push the stranger off the bridge?

A utilitarian reckoning indicates that the two dilemmas are equivalent. In each case, if you do not act, five people will die, whereas if you do act, only one person will die. So, shouldn't you act in the same way in each scenario? People often rejected this logic. They claimed to be more willing to throw the switch in the Trolley Switch dilemma than to push the obese stranger off the bridge in the Footbridge dilemma. Greene et al. (2001) found via functional magnetic resonance imaging (fMRI) scans that areas of the brain associated with emotion were more active in dilemmas like the Footbridge as compared to the Trolley Switch. Presumably, the thought of actually pushing someone to their death is more repugnant and disturbing than the less-personalized act of throwing a switch. This interpretation is consistent with the argument proposed by Haidt (2001): moral decisions, even in adulthood, may not be the outcome of pure reasoning. They will be often driven by emotional considerations, including feelings of repulsion or disgust, as much as by reflection and rational argument.

Conclusions

A long-standing issue in the study of moral development is the question of whether and when children possess their own independent and autonomous moral compass. Early behavioral research showed that such a compass, if it exists, is far from being a steady and reliable guide to moral behavior. Children, and indeed adults, are readily influenced by incidental situational factors in deciding what to do and what not to do.

More recent research, however, has uncovered a seam of independence in young children's moral judgment. It may not always lead them to do the right thing, but it does enable them to conclude that certain actions are wrong no matter what adult authority says. Even infants prefer benign to mean individuals, and it seems unlikely that such preferences are based on moral instruction from caregivers.

Some children offer an especially vivid illustration of such autonomy. Children growing up in meat-eating households sometimes decide to stop eating meat. Their reasons for doing so appear to be moral reasons. Even if they like the taste of meat, they do not want to be implicated in the suffering and slaughter of animals. Still, it has to be acknowledged that such children are rare.

Research with adults suggests that the vision of moral maturity espoused by Kohlberg and Piaget, a vision in which autonomous moral reflection guides decision-making, is overdrawn. In making moral judgments, people are often swayed by emotional considerations. They condemn actions that arouse visceral feelings of disgust. Post hoc, they may back up their condemnations with moral arguments, but they did not necessarily arrive at their initial condemnation via thoughtful reflection.

Thinking once again about children who decide to become vegetarian, we are left with the question of how they arrived at that decision. Was it triggered by feelings of repugnance at the suffering of animals that meat eating entails? Was it reached via calm reflection about how to minimize their involvement in such suffering? Or is this implied opposition too simplistic? Arguably, mature decision-making in the moral domain involves a balance between feeling and reflection.

9

Do children trust what they are told?

The role of trust in cognitive development

In his analysis of miracles, David Hume defines them not simply as unexpected events but as events that defy all our past experience: "It is no miracle that a man, seemingly in good health, should die on a sudden: because such a kind of death, though more unusual than any other, has yet been frequently observed to happen. But it is a miracle that a dead man should come to life; because that has never been observed in any age or country. There must, therefore, be a uniform experience against every miraculous event, otherwise the event would not merit that appellation" (Hume, 1902).

He goes on to note that we ordinarily learn about miracles not from our own experience but from the testimony of other people. We are therefore faced with a conflict. Should we believe what they say, or should we reject it when—granted Hume's plausible definition of a miracle—it is something that "has never been observed in any age or country?" Hume argues that faced with such a choice between accepting that a miracle has occurred—for example, the resurrection of a dead man—and accepting that the testimony is misleading, we would be wise to choose the latter option—it is much more likely. It is, effectively, the lesser or more plausible miracle. After all, we have plenty of first-hand experience of people being misled or seeking to mislead. Yet we have never observed a dead man come to life.

Hume's pithy advice may be epistemologically sound, but it fails to capture human psychology. Consider the Christian faith. Most believers accept the testimony of the Bible concerning various miracles, including the resurrection of Jesus. By implication, when adults face a conflict between a surprising claim that they hear or read and their own past experience, they often choose to accept the claim even when it flies in the face of all their past experience.

In 1938, an intriguing example of such a conflict took place in the USA on October 30th—the night before Halloween. The Mercury Theatre, under the direction of Orson Welles, broadcast a radio dramatization of H. G. Wells' novel *The War of the Worlds*. There was a clear announcement at the start of the program that this was theater rather than fact, but many people tuned in late and also missed subsequent announcements to the same effect. What they did hear was a series of apparently authentic news bulletins—sudden and unexpected interruptions of a program of dance music by Ramon Raquello and his orchestra. The bulletins began with a relatively matter-of-fact report of "a slight atmospheric disturbance of undetermined origin" over Nova Scotia that was causing a low-pressure area to move down rapidly over the northeastern states. Subsequent bulletins were more and more disturbing, and suggested the arrival of some kind of spacecraft. In New Jersey, a news reporter, Carl Phillips, interviewed a Professor Pierson of Princeton University about a huge object that had fallen on a farm in the neighborhood of Grovers Mill, some 20 miles from Trenton. Listeners heard the professor doubt that it could be a meteorite: "Friction with the earth's surface usually tears holes in a meteorite. This thing is smooth and, as you can see, of cylindrical shape." Phillips interjects: "Just a minute! Something's happening! Ladies and gentlemen, this is terrific! This end of the thing is beginning to flake off! The thing must be hollow!" Some minutes later, Phillips reports on the invaders' first act of aggression: a jet of flame that carbonizes three police officers optimistically bearing a white handkerchief tied to a pole. Phillips' last words—"It's coming this way. About twenty yards to my right . . ."— are followed by dead silence until the station announcer explains that, "there's some difficulty with our field transmission".

This radio broadcast rapidly created alarm and even panic. CBS, the station responsible for the broadcast, commissioned a survey 1 week later of those who had heard the broadcast. Cantril and colleagues (1940) present some of the key findings. About two-thirds of the listeners eventually concluded that the program was only a dramatization after initially thinking that it was a live broadcast. They came to realize their mistake in various ways, typically via input from other people.

The remaining third had received no such clear-cut information and needed to make up their own minds about whether to believe the broadcast. Some made "internal" checks of its content. They concluded, for example, that the shifts of scene were too fast to be plausible. Others set about making "external" checks—they listened in to other radio stations or looked at the program listings in the newspaper. Still others attempted to make an external check but were unsuccessful—they called relatives or the police but got no reply. However, just under half of those who needed to make up their own mind made no checks at all. Fright and disturbance were widely reported by all the respondents but especially among those who had made unsuccessful checks or none at all. One respondent explained: "We didn't try to do anything to see if it were really true. I guess we were too frightened." Another said: "I couldn't stand it so I turned it off. I don't remember when, but everything was coming closer. My husband wanted to put it back on but I told him we'd better do something instead of just listen, so we started to pack."

In summary, when respondents had heard what they took to be a report of an event that could be regarded as a "miracle" (an event that "has never been observed in any age or country", as Hume defines it) and needed to assess its veracity, almost 50% failed to carry out any checks. Only a very small percentage (3%) felt calm—the rest reported either unequivocal fear or emotional disturbance. The obvious implication is that many of these adults were—contrary to Hume's dictum—inclined to trust the testimony they heard on the radio even when it involved an extraordinary event and despite having made no checks. In their defense, it should be noted that the testimony appeared to come directly from eyewitnesses to the scene. Recall the comments made by the supposed reporter Carl Phillips and the interviewee Professor Pierson. Arguably, eyewitness testimony should be accorded greater credence than second-hand news. Still, it is interesting to note that Cantril does not describe any respondents who queried the expertise of the two eyewitnesses even when they described something totally alien to everyday experience. By implication, adults are willing to trust the testimony of other people even when it involves something unexpected and indeed unique in the history of the world.

In fact, we display an inclination to trust the testimony of other people in countless ways, most of them more prosaic than an alien invasion. The philosopher Tony Coady offers the following parable to underline the ubiquity of that dependence: "My first morning in Amsterdam I wake uncertain of the time and ring the hotel clerk to discover the hour, accepting the testimony of his voice . . . I read a paperback history book which contains all manner of factual claims that neither I nor the writer can support by personal observation or memory or by deduction from either: the deeds of a man called Napoleon Bonaparte . . . I reflect that on arriving at a strange city a day or so earlier, I had only the aircrew's word that this was Amsterdam . . .." (Coady, 1992).

Granted this pervasive dependence among adults on the testimony of others, it would not be surprising if children showed the same pattern of trust. Two examples provide illustrative evidence. It takes young children some time to realize that the earth is not flat but a sphere. When Michael Siegal and his colleagues interviewed British children, they found that preschoolers—aged 4–5 years— were fairly evenly divided in their views (Siegal et al., 2004). Nearly half gave predominantly "flat earth" answers when probed with various indirect questions: for example, "If you walked for many days in a straight line would you fall off the edge of the world?" By 8–9 years of age, however, all of the children answered predominantly in terms of a spherical earth. They denied that there was an edge to fall off and insisted that the sky encircled the planet—it was not just something "up there". Some developmental psychologists, looking at data like these, have been impressed at the way that young children's own observations of the earth initially mislead them into thinking that it is flat. When children look at the terrain in front of them and its extension to the horizon, it suggests that the earth is a flat surface, with the people moving around on top. However, the developmental change charted by Siegal and his colleagues is also noteworthy. It shows that, notwithstanding these early misconceptions, likely based on their own first-hand perceptual experience, children eventually set them aside. They come to trust the testimony they hear about a spherical earth and gradually integrate it into a coherent conception of the earth's shape.

The role of testimony is neatly underlined by a second set of data collected by Siegal and his colleagues. They gave a parallel interview to children in Australia. The developmental trend was similar but notably accelerated. Even among the 4- to 5-year-olds, only about one-third were flat-earthers, and already by 6–7 years of age, all of them gave predominantly spherical earth judgments. Note that perceptual experience is unlikely to explain the precocity of Australian children relative to British children. Presumably, the earth looks just as flat in Sydney or Perth as it does in London or Glasgow. So, why are Australian children precocious? The most plausible answer is that Australian children are exposed to more informal testimony about the earth and its sphericity than their British cousins. Australian children will learn that they live "down under". They may hear about relatives back in Britain who live in a different time zone and experience different seasons. They may fly—or hear about other people who have flown—"half-way across the globe".

A fascinating study by Margaret Evans further highlights the impact of the testimony that is available to children (Evans, 2000). She talked to children in two different mid-western US communities about dinosaurs. More specifically, she asked them: "How did the first dinosaur get here on earth?" Most of the replies that children gave could be assigned to one of three categories. Some children conceived of dinosaur origins as akin to a spring awakening. A dinosaur was somehow spontaneously generated—it "just appeared" or "grew on earth from eggs, like birds". Second, some children invoked a creator: "God made the dinosaurs." Finally, some children referred to the course of evolution and the transition from one species to another: "Dinosaurs did evolve from water creatures" or "Slowly followed the path of evolution."

In one of the two communities, a developmental pattern emerged that is probably typical of many communities in North America. References to spontaneous generation declined during the early school years. References to a creator were common even among elementary-school children and remained so into adulthood. References to evolution were rare in the early school years, became more frequent in later childhood, but never became the dominant view. So, in this community, adults invoked evolution about as often as they invoked a creator. However, in the second community, a fundamentalist community, the pattern of responding was quite different. References to a creator were frequent at all ages, whereas references to either spontaneous generation or evolution were consistently rare. The clear implication of these findings is that children's ideas about the origin of species are not something that they sort out for themselves. Although they might be expected to rely on their own intuitions, their pattern of responding, and especially the frequency with which they invoke a creator as compared to naturalistic alternatives, varies sharply by community.

These two examples, drawn from cosmology and biology, illustrate a much wider pattern. Children trust adults to help them understand aspects of the world that they cannot easily observe for themselves. Neither the shape of the earth nor the origin of species can be directly observed, so that what children end up believing depends markedly on the beliefs that surrounding adults convey to them. In fact, children look to the testimony of adults not just to resolve scientific questions such as the shape of the earth or the origin of species but also in making decisions about what does and does not exist.

Giraffes, germs, and God

Consider the giraffe. How might children decide whether giraffes really exist? On the face of it, this seems like an easy question to answer. Presumably children have various opportunities to actually see a giraffe. They might see a giraffe at the zoo. Failing that, they might see one in a photograph or on television. So long as they have some grasp of what counts as persuasive visual evidence, they should be able to gather a good deal of it in the case of giraffes.

But now consider the existence of germs. Ordinarily, children have no opportunities to observe germs and they will rarely see photographs of them. Personally, I doubt that I would recognize a germ if I were shown one under a microscope. Still, I acknowledge that germs exist. What about children? Do they adopt a conservative strategy of only believing in those entities and creatures that they have seen first-hand, or for which they have seen some realistic-looking representation? Alternatively, are they swayed by adults' more or less routine remarks implying that invisibles entities, such as germs, also exist?

To investigate children's beliefs, we asked 4- to 5-year-olds and 7- to 8-year-olds to tell us whether they believed in the existence of three different types of entity: impossible entities (e.g., flying pigs and barking cats), visible entities (e.g., giraffes and rabbits), and invisible entities (e.g., germs and oxygen) (Harris et al., 2006). As expected, children confidently denied the existence of the impossible entities and confidently asserted the existence of the visible entities. Our main focus was on the invisible entities. Would children accept their existence? They did—in fact, they were just about as confident of the existence of germs as they were of giraffes. By implication, young children's ideas about what exists are guided by other people's testimony, at least in those cases where they cannot make pertinent observations for themselves.

In a follow-up study, we probed children's belief in the unseen still further. Could it be that young children believe in the existence of more or less anything that they hear adults talk about—not just germs and giraffes but also giants and mermaids? Do they realize that some creatures are mentioned in story books but are purely fictional? And what about the existence of the various special beings that children will hear about—both those that are tied to child-directed rituals such as the Tooth Fairy and those that are part of the adult belief system such as God? We found that 5- to 6-year-olds were selective. They believed in various special beings, including

Santa Claus, the Tooth Fairy, and God, but they were skeptical about the existence of fictional creatures—giants and mermaids. By implication, children are attuned to the way that invisible beings get talked about. They notice, for example, that giants and mermaids are typically mentioned only in fictional contexts, whereas special beings such as the Tooth Fairy and God are linked to actions in the everyday world.

At this point, we may speculate about how exactly children conceive of invisible reality and the various creatures and phenomena that inhabit it. One possibility is that children regard the invisible world as a vast, undifferentiated space with a heterogeneous population—there are tiny organisms that you cannot see (viruses, for example), as well as special beings, such as God. Another possibility is that young children do not think of these various unseen entities as all being on an equal ontological par with each other (Harris & Corriveau, 2020). Indeed, when asked, children typically express more confidence in the existence of scientific as compared to religious entities, arguably because they hear adults talk in a matter-of-fact fashion about scientific entities, generally taking their existence for granted (e.g., "Don't pick that up—it has germs"), whereas adults' talk about religious entities may include references to faith, trust, and particular communities of believers (e.g., "Well, some people think that . . .") (McLoughlin et al., 2021).

Pending more research on how exactly children navigate and chart the varied status of invisible phenomena, we can already conclude that children build up their conception of those phenomena on the basis of testimony from other people. Their conception of the earth's shape as well as their ideas about how various species came to inhabit the earth depend on other people's testimony—as does their belief in the existence of various invisible entities, scientific as well as religious. Children, like adults, trust a great deal of what they are told.

Whom do children trust?

A long tradition of educational thinking worries that children might easily lose their intellectual independence. The basic idea, promulgated by writers such as Rousseau and Piaget, is that when children take over other people's ideas, including those of a teacher, they simply kowtow to an intellectual authority rather than working things out for themselves. They are prone to what Piaget called "verbalism"—the tendency to parrot back received wisdom, without any independent grip on the extent to which what they have been told is well founded or not. Rousseau sets out a clear description in his Enlightenment classic about the education of a hypothetical pupil, *Emile*: "To nourish his curiosity, never hasten to satisfy it . . . Ask questions that he can handle and leave them to him to resolve. Let him not know anything because you have told him but rather because he has understood it for himself: Let him not learn science, let him invent it. If you ever substitute authority for reason in his mind, he will no longer reason; he will only be the plaything of other people's opinions" (Rousseau, 1999).

If the argument in the preceding section is correct, Rousseau's stance is, to say the least, idealistic. In many domains, children cannot gather the relevant evidence to answer the questions that they might ask—what they believe about the shape of the earth, about evolution, germs, and God is almost certainly guided by other people. But does this mean that children invariably accept what they are told? To what extent do they bring their critical faculties to bear? Interestingly, much the same question can be asked about the observations that children gather for themselves. Not just when children are told about a phenomenon but also when they observe it for themselves, there is always a question about how actively or passively they try to understand it. Indeed, there is no particular reason to suppose that first-hand experience is a better vehicle and stimulus for cautious reflection than conversation with a well-informed teacher. Admittedly, one might argue that a teacher is likely to be endowed with authority and may therefore provoke an inappropriately deferential stance—this is the danger that Rousseau underlines. But first-hand observation can exercise its own tyranny. It may be tempting to assume that what we observe, for example, the horizontal plain stretching out in front of us, or the sun rising on the eastern horizon, can tell us about the shape of the earth and the movement of the sun relative to the earth. But we eventually realize, typically via others' testimony or more expert observation, that our own observations are misleading.

Granted these educational considerations, and more generally granted the plausible biological hypothesis that our species has evolved to display the type of trust in other people's testimony that Rousseau and his compatriot Piaget are inclined to denigrate or downplay, we can turn to a pertinent psychological question. Are children prepared to accept information from all-comers or are they selective about the people that they trust? If we look at the most influential account of children's early social development—attachment theory—it would be surprising if children were completely indiscriminate. As described in Chapter 1, when they need emotional reassurance, infants and toddlers seek out and accept comfort from some people but not from others. Children who are indiscriminate in their approach to other people are far from typical. They can sometimes be found among children raised for prolonged periods without predictable and stable caregiving—as is the case for children raised in Romanian orphanages—but that is not the normal course of development. We might reasonably expect, therefore, that just as children seek out particular adults for emotional reassurance, so they will seek out particular adults for cognitive guidance. For example, faced with an uncertain situation, it seems likely that they would be more likely to turn to a familiar caregiver for guidance than to a stranger.

To test this simple prediction, 3-, 4-, and 5-year-olds were shown unfamiliar objects, which were named for them by a familiar as well as an unfamiliar preschool teacher. However, the two teachers proposed conflicting names, so that children could not be sure which name was correct. When asked to endorse one or the other, they showed a marked preference for the name supplied by the teacher who was familiar to them (Corriveau & Harris, 2009a). In a follow-up study, the impact of the attachment relationship was probed more directly (Corriveau et al., 2009a). Five-year-olds were shown pictures of hybrid or ambiguous animals: for example, an animal that was a cross between a cow and a horse. These various entities were named by their mother in one way and by an unfamiliar experimenter in a different way. As in the study with the preschool teachers, children showed an overall preference for the information proposed by the familiar informant—their mother. But in line with what one might expect from attachment theory, the exact way that children responded depended on the type of attachment they had—which had been measured in the standard fashion via the Strange Situation some 4 years earlier when the children were 15 months old.

Securely attached children showed a clear preference for the guidance supplied by their mother rather than the stranger. The same was true of children with a resistant attachment. Indeed, if anything, they were even more likely to be guided by their mother's input than the secure children. The most disconcerting finding was a negative result. The avoidant children showed no preference for the information offered by their mother as compared to the stranger. Recall that the preference for a familiar preschool teacher was very widespread in the initial study—it was striking to see, in this follow-up, that deep, long-term familiarity is not, in itself, a guarantee of trust. Despite knowing their mother much better than the stranger, the avoidant children showed no preference for the information that their mother offered.

Stepping back from these results, it is tempting to conclude that the acceptance of information by toddlers and young children can be fully understood in light of attachment theory. According to this account, children's primary consideration in accepting information is what kind of emotional relationship they have with a potential informant. They accept information from those who have generally provided comfort and reassurance in the past. However, there are reasons for doubting that such an arranged marriage between attachment theory and research on cognitive trust can succeed, especially if we think about how children accept information beyond the period of infancy.

As adults, we make a distinction between those people we trust at some emotional level and those we trust as purveyors of sound information. I do not need to have a deep emotional attachment to my car mechanic to trust their diagnosis of the problems in my car's manifold. There are admittedly some advisors whom we hope can straddle the divide between the emotional and the epistemic: the canonical "family doctor" is—ideally—someone whom we trust in both domains. Still, such a happy conjunction is not always to be found, and children might well realize that. We examined this possibility in two steps.

First, we asked if 3- and 4-year-olds can use cognitive accuracy as a cue. They watched as two strangers named familiar everyday objects. One did so correctly—saying, for example, that a ball was a ball— whereas the other did so incorrectly—saying that a ball was a shoe. Next, the two adults named objects that were unfamiliar. They each proposed a different name for the same unfamiliar object and children were invited to say which name they thought was right. Both 3- and 4-year-olds tended to accept the names provided by the accurate rather than the inaccurate adult (Clément et al., 2004; Koenig et al., 2004).

A variety of experiments have reinforced this basic finding (Tong et al., 2020). Preschoolers keep track of potential informants, noticing who is accurate and who is not, and preferring to seek and accept new information from someone who has been accurate in the past. They show this preference for accuracy even when the informants do not differ consistently: for example, if one informant is mostly right but not always and the other informant is mostly wrong but not always (Pasquini et al., 2007). They show this preference when one informant indicates her lesser competence by repeatedly saying that she does not know the names of familiar objects (Koenig & Harris, 2005) or makes morphological errors rather than semantic errors (Corriveau et al., 2011). The preference is also quite durable: introduced to two informants and given evidence of their differential accuracy, preschoolers prefer to learn from the more accurate of the two informants 1 week later (Corriveau & Harris, 2009b).

Granted this ample evidence for preschoolers' sensitivity to cognitive accuracy, we can now ask the following question: What happens when we pit emotional and cognitive considerations against one another? For example, if a familiar attachment figure starts to prove inaccurate, what will young children do? Accept the information she offers or prefer input from someone less familiar but hitherto accurate? To find out, we asked the two preschool teachers mentioned earlier to assist in a further assessment of their pupils' trust. Some of the children witnessed their familiar teacher start to name objects accurately, whereas an unfamiliar teacher named them inaccurately; some children witnessed the reverse arrangement—the familiar teacher started to prove less accurate than the unfamiliar teacher. Next, the two teachers offered conflicting names for a set of novel objects to assess whether children's exposure to their informants' recent accuracy—or inaccuracy—had an impact.

Three-year-olds were mostly unaffected. They still preferred to learn from the teacher who was familiar to them even if she had just proven inaccurate. By contrast, the 4-year-olds, and especially the 5-year-olds, preferred to learn from whichever teacher had proven to be the more accurate even if she was someone they did not know (Corriveau & Harris, 2009b). By implication, at the end of the preschool period—by the age of 5, if not earlier—children are ready to learn outside of their immediate circle of caregivers. In particular, they are willing to learn outside of the safe haven provided by an attachment figure, especially if they expect to obtain more reliable information by doing so. In the context of human evolution, this shift makes sense. If children were only willing to learn from their nearest and dearest, they would have no ability to profit from a neighbor's expertise or from a well-informed stranger.

To the extent that learning from others often involves learning about the preferred practices and beliefs in a given community, it would be useful if children had some way to identify which practices and beliefs are prevalent and acceptable. One strategy they might adopt is to trust and learn from those people who represent or exemplify the surrounding culture: for example, people that others are inclined to agree with rather than dissent from. Several studies show that children do adopt such a strategy. In one study, 4-year-olds watched as two bystanders frowned and looked dubious at the claims made by one person but smiled with approval at the claims made by another. Asked to say whose claims they agreed with, children systematically sided with the person who had received bystander approval. In fact, children continued to do this even when the bystanders left. It was if bystander endorsement had stamped one of the two informants with a permanent, or at least a durable, seal of approval (Fusaro & Harris, 2008). Similar results emerged in a follow-up study in which bystanders expressed their views not via smiles and frowns but by pointing in concert with one informant rather than another. As before, when the bystanders left, children continued to prefer information supplied by the informant who had received such bystander endorsement (Corriveau et al., 2009b).

Summing up this line of research, it looks as if children are far from indiscriminate in their willingness to trust other people. They employ various strategies to select among potential informants. They prefer to learn from familiar informants but also from competent and accurate informants. Indeed, when those two criteria compete, older children favor competence and accuracy over familiarity. Finally, children appear to be astute at figuring out what is acceptable in a given culture. They tend to agree with the claims of a consensus and to shun a dissenter. They even remember who belonged to a consensus once it has dispersed and treat such a person as a worthy model and informant.

Testing what you're told

As discussed, young children are often unable to check what they are told. They cannot investigate for themselves whether dinosaurs emerged in the course of evolution, how they went extinct, whether a particular virus truly exists, or how it is transmitted. Sometimes, however, children can check what they are told, and they might be especially prone to do so if what they are told flies in the face of their past experience. Do they seize opportunities for empirical investigation when they are readily available or do they simply trust what they are told? Are they budding scientists or budding believers?

Samuel Ronfard designed a simple experiment to explore this issue (Ronfard et al., 2018). The children—ranging from 3 to 8 years—were shown a set of five Russian dolls arranged in ascending order of size on the table and asked to say which doll they thought was the heaviest. Not surprisingly, almost all the children promptly—and plausibly—pointed to the biggest doll. At this point, the experimenter agreed with half of them by saying that the biggest doll was indeed the heaviest but misled the other half by saying that, in fact, the smallest doll was the heaviest. When children were asked once again which doll they thought was the heaviest, the majority now went along with what the experimenter had just told them, even if, for half of them, she had contradicted their initial intuition— evidence, yet again, that young children are prone to trust what they are told even when it goes against their own intuitions.

However, at this point, the experimenter left the room, allegedly to make a phone call, but actually to give the children a chance to quietly investigate what they had been told, especially if they had doubts about it—doubts that would be very reasonable for half the children. In fact, very few of the younger children—preschoolers aged 3–6 years—lifted the dolls in any systematic way; at best, they sometimes touched or poked them. By contrast, a considerable proportion of the older children—elementary-school children aged 6–8 years— picked up the smallest and biggest dolls, lifting them up and down, sometimes simultaneously, as if to gauge their weight. Importantly, this behavior was especially frequent among children who had been told that the smallest doll was the heaviest. By implication, these older children were checking the experimenter's surprising claim. After a suitable interval, the experimenter came back and paused for a few seconds in case any of the children wanted to talk about what they had discovered. Very few did so. Nevertheless, when the experimenter again asked which doll was the heaviest, children who had checked the dolls for themselves answered in light of what they had discovered—setting aside the experimenter's claim if she had misled them. Studies in several different countries—China, the USA, Turkey, and Belarus—show that these findings are very robust. Few preschoolers seize an opportunity to test a surprising claim, whereas older children often do (Ronfard et al., 2018; 2020; 2021).

In sum, young children trust what they are told, even when it goes against their intuitions; older children are equally trusting, but unlike younger children they sometimes engage in their own empirical investigation of a surprising claim. Yet even when they have done so, they are likely to keep the results to themselves—unless explicitly asked what they think. These findings temper a popular trope in developmental psychology, namely that young children busily explore the world like little scientists. It is certainly true that young children are curious and like to explore, but the idea that they are experimental scientists who seek to verify disconcerting claims is overstated. In fact, young children mostly accept what they are told and often leave it untested.

Conclusions

Enlightenment philosophers, like Hume, warned against relying on the testimony of other people, but we adults place considerable trust in the information provided by others. Young children are no different. They come to understand that the world is round, even if it does not look round. Despite Rousseau's strictures about relying on the authority of others, they have not worked out the shape of the earth for themselves. In this particular case, children's trust in the testimony of others does not lead them to a mistaken conclusion. In the eyes of almost all contemporary adults, that testimony has led them to a sound conclusion.

The situation is intriguingly different with respect to the origin of species. Children in different communities in the USA do not converge on a single agreed set of beliefs. For better or worse, they typically go along with the views of their community. Here, we begin to see Rousseau's point more acutely. Few children in either community appear to be thinking for themselves. If they were, we would scarcely see such clear-cut parallels in each community between the views of the adults and the views of the children.

The second part of this chapter begins to unpack this continuity across generations. Human culture is rich, complicated, and in many ways cumulative, as ideas are passed on and reshaped from one generation to the next. Despite Rousseau's admonition, children cannot reconstruct for themselves the accumulated wisdom of their culture. If anything, nature appears to have designed children to be unthinkingly contemporary or "modern"—to accept the beliefs and practices they see around them, no matter what their provenance or history. To the extent that children choose among their informants, they are likely to accept the claims of people who are familiar to them, who have a record of cognitive reliability, and whose views are endorsed in the larger community. These biases are practically guaranteed to produce children who think in much the same ways as the adults around them.

Finally, even when they could easily check a disconcerting claim— one that runs counter to their basic intuitions—children often fail to do so. But perhaps we should not be so surprised at this lack of empiricism. As we saw at the beginning of the chapter, children are not alone in this respect—many adults are just as trusting.

10
Do children believe in magic?
Magic and miracles

Anthropologists have long worried about how to identify religious beliefs. When observing a traditional culture that is relatively isolated from the main religions of the world, it is not easy to decide what aspect of the belief system of that culture should be characterized as religion. Living among the Azande, the social anthropologist, Evans-Pritchard wryly pointed out that after a long period of fieldwork, he found he was comfortable enough regulating his life—as the Azande did—by reference to oracles and witches. Was he beginning to subscribe to a new religion? Had he undergone a kind of conversion? Perhaps in his case the answer ought to be no. He was simply acting out a set of beliefs and practices that made his everyday life among the Azande manageable, but he had not undergone any fundamental change of heart. On his return to England, he continued to practice Catholicism and he wrote of the beliefs of the Azande with anthropological detachment, describing, in magisterial prose, the coherence of those beliefs but scarcely insisting that they were true. Still, the Azande—as Evans-Pritchard was at pains to show—took the existence of witches for granted. So, should we conceive of their belief in witchcraft as a form of religion?

From our contemporary standpoint, that seems to collapse together two very different types of thinking: religious thinking, founded as it is on faith in an Almighty Deity, and superstitious thinking, in which a whole panoply of suspect magical powers is invoked. Yet we do not need to delve very deep into the history of Western Christianity to find it sitting comfortably alongside a complex set of witchcraft beliefs. Both in England and in New England, those accused of witchcraft were tried and sometimes put to death. At the time, the established church did not condemn these practices as mere superstition, even if a broad consensus eventually emerged—backed up by changes in the legal framework—that a belief in witchcraft was untenable and not part of the Christian religion. That narrowing of the canon of religious belief was accompanied by the rejection of a variety of allegedly magical practices and superstitions.

At the very least, these historical changes underscore the important point that the boundary between religion and magic is not permanently fixed. At one time, a belief in witchcraft was not regarded as superstition, even if it is so regarded today in most of the Western world. Given that the boundary is not fixed, it may not be as conceptually clear and self-evident as we are inclined to think. Consider these issues from the perspective of a young child. Confronted by any particular assertion—that Santa Claus or angels or witches or God exist—how does the child figure out what should be believed as a matter of religious conviction and what can be dismissed as mere superstition? Does the child make any kind of discrimination among these various special beings, and if so how?

In this chapter, I do two apparently contradictory things. I argue that young children are commonsensical. Even if they listen to fairy stories, become totally absorbed by Harry Potter, and enjoy Batman movies, they understand that the extraordinary events taking place in these narratives are not part of ordinary life. Such events may happen in stories or at the movies, but they do not happen in reality. In that respect, children are "modern". They do not believe in witchcraft or magic, even if they find them to be wonderful ingredients for a story. At the same time, the majority of children growing up in the West are exposed to monotheism, believe in God, and attribute to God some superhuman powers. We might sum up by saying that children are skeptical about magic but believe in miracles. Figuring out how they manage this balancing act will be the goal of the final section of this chapter. I argue that children's success is only surprising when viewed from a distant standpoint—one in which their conflicting views are surveyed in a single comprehensive glance. From closer up, and notably from the point of view of children themselves, I doubt there is any perceived contradiction: they think that witches and magic belong to one domain and that God belongs to another. But I will also argue that such balancing acts are not confined to children. Adults are also prone to a mix of skepticism about magic combined with faith in the miraculous. Consider our thinking about the afterlife. Most twenty-first-century Western adults are dubious about those who claim to have any communication with the dead. At the same time, most Western adults believe in the miracle of the afterlife. Why does our contemporary religious framework balk at the former but embrace the latter?

Do children believe in magic?

In 1927, Piaget visited Cambridge, England where he presented a paper to the Cambridge Education Society. He described his research suggesting that young children have only a "primitive" notion of causality. Rather than thinking of natural phenomena as having their own autonomous causal properties, Piaget argued that young children think of them as designed for, and dedicated to, human ends. For example, children think that clouds and rivers move to suit human purposes, not by virtue of independent physical laws. Granted this interpenetration of the human world and the natural world, Piaget also claimed that young children are prone to magical thinking—to believe that they have the power to move objects by their own magical gestures (Piaget, 1928).

During his visit to Cambridge, Piaget was a welcome visitor at the Malting House School, a progressive school run by Susan Isaacs—an admirer of Piaget but skeptical about his ideas on the primitive thinking of young children. In her book *The Intellectual Growth of Young Children*, Isaacs records an exchange that took place between Piaget and one of her pupils: "During a visit of Professor Piaget to the school, he had been remarking to me that he had found that the appreciation of mechanical causality does not normally occur until eight or nine years of age . . . He asked how our children stood in this respect. At that moment, Dan, a 5-year-old, happened to be sitting on a tricycle in the garden, back-pedaling." Isaacs goes on to explain that Dan gave a good account of how the tricycle worked in response to her questioning, one scarcely consonant with Piaget's negative characterization. "How does it go forward when it does?" she asked Dan. "Oh well", he replied, "your feet press the pedals, that turns the crank around, and the cranks turn that round" (pointing to the cog-wheel), "and that makes the chain go round, and the chain turns the hub round, and then the wheels go round—and there you are!" (Isaacs, 1930, Note 1, p. 44).

Sometime after his visit, Piaget wrote a long, thoughtful, and mostly laudatory review of Isaacs' book in which this exchange had been recorded (Piaget, 1931). Noting Dan's lucid explanation of the tricycle's forward movement and its inconsistency with his portrait of young children's notions of causality, Piaget points out (p. 141) that Dan was a very intelligent child with a measured IQ of 142. By implication, Dan's explanation of tricycle mechanics was as cogent as the account that an 8- or 9-year-old might produce, but was not representative of 5-year-olds.

Dan's intellectual precocity is certainly one possible explanation for his lack of magical thinking. However, in line with the school's philosophy of encouraging children to learn from their own active observation and experimentation, it is also worth emphasizing that the pupils at Malting House were given all sorts of things that they could experiment with and take apart. Conceivably, such hands-on tinkering, rather than his native cognitive ability, might also account for Dan's sensitivity to the workings of his tricycle.

But in any case, data gathered on the other side of the globe soon showed that magical thinking is not a hallmark of young children's causal explanations. In the course of her fieldwork in New Guinea on Manus, one of the Admiralty Islands, Margaret Mead interviewed children about familiar misfortunes and mishaps, such as a canoe going adrift (Mead, 1932). Among the adults of Manus, a belief in sorcery as a cause of misfortune was widespread. Mead wondered if the children of Manus would echo their parents' magical beliefs. In fact, contrary to what Piaget would have expected, she found that Manus children offered straightforward naturalistic explanations not magical ones—perhaps the canoe had not been fastened properly in the first place, they suggested. In a radical challenge to Piagetian theorizing, Mead concluded that young children mostly invoke plausible mechanical or physical explanations. It is only later—when they are socialized into the adult web of sorcery beliefs—that they have recourse to magical explanations. On this account, magical thinking does not come naturally to young children. It is something they acquire later—depending on the culture that they grow up in.

In a similar effort to probe young children's causal explanations, the Chinese psychologist Huang gave 4- to 10-year-olds a variety of puzzling phenomena to explain (Huang, 1930). For example, children were shown a tube that contained water. When a piece of paper was placed over the mouth of the tube and the tube was turned upside down, the paper remained in place and the water did not pour out. Children came up with various ingenious, albeit incorrect explanations, for example, "'Cause the paper is so thick and it sticks", but, like the Manus children, they almost invariably restricted themselves to physical explanations. Despite being puzzled by what they saw, they did not invoke magic. Based on his own findings, together with a subsequent review of various other studies of causal thinking, Huang came down firmly on the side of Mead rather than Piaget. Young children show no obvious predisposition toward magical thinking (Huang, 1930; 1943). That conclusion has been reinforced in subsequent decades, which has widened the range of phenomena presented to children. In general, even if their explanations are not always correct, they offer the appropriate type of natural explanation for a given phenomenon—biological explanations for biological outcomes, physical explanations for physical outcomes, and so forth (Wellman & Gelman, 1998).

Still, it is important to note that even if young children rarely invoke magic as an explanation, they do grasp what actions would count as magic if they ever occurred. In particular, when asked about an outcome that defies their standard causal picture of the world, they are prepared to ascribe it to magic. For example, having been told about two make-believe characters—Jack who does lots of ordinary things and Magic Fairy who never bothers with the ordinary way to do things, preferring to use magic instead—3- and 4-year-olds readily figured out which character might have done what. Asked who had pushed a toy car across the floor, they pointed to Jack. Asked who had made a toy car go across the floor all by itself, they pointed to Magic Fairy (Johnson & Harris, 1994). Similarly, although 4- and 5-year-olds recognized that, ordinarily, animals can grow bigger but not smaller, they acknowledged that a magician would be able to produce both types of change (Rosengren et al., 1994).

More generally, young children have a clear appreciation of the difference between what can happen in the ordinary world and what is impossible. Indeed, they are more conservative about what can actually happen than are older children and adults. When asked about events that could occur but are highly improbable—for example, finding an alligator under your bed when you wake up in the morning—preschoolers dismiss these as impossible. Effectively, they make little distinction between an outcome that is downright impossible and one that is highly improbable but possible (Shtulman & Carey, 2007)—they regard both as extraordinary events that cannot happen in the real world.

Children's differentiation between the ordinary and the magical is also evident in research on their ideas about fairy tales. In an influential—but muddled—analysis, the psychoanalyst Bruno Bettelheim argued that young children are attracted to fairy tales because they think that fairy tale magic is actually possible (Bettelheim, 1991). In fact, the evidence presented so far suggests precisely the opposite—fairy tales are attractive because they conjure up what children know to be impossible in reality. Even preschoolers realize that it is impossible to pass through solid barriers, travel back in time, or change people into frogs. For example, when 4- and 5-year-olds were asked about whether such transformations could really happen, almost all of them said no. Yet they agreed that such things could happen in a fairy tale (Subbotsky, 1994). Similarly, when

3-, 4-, and 5-year-olds were asked about fantastical events, such as a boy winning a fight with a monster, and regular events, such as a girl being called to dinner by her mother, children said that the regular events but not the fantastical events could happen in real life (Woolley & Cox, 2007).

To sum up, even before they go to school, young children are commonsensical. They rarely invoke magic as an explanation—even if adults in their community regularly do so. They deny that anything extraordinary can happen in real life. They think of magical or fantastical events as belonging to the world of fairy stories and not to real life. Still, as I will argue in the next section, this portrait of young children as sure-footed skeptics is one-sided. They are dubious about magic, but they have faith in miracles.

Conceptions of God

Anthropologists have pointed out that when we think about special beings—for example, when we think about God or indeed about supernatural beings such as witches or the Ancestors—we often think of them in terms of two sets of features. On the one hand, the special being is thought of as quasi-human: he or she can observe human affairs, feel disappointment, punish, forgive, and so forth. At the same time, the special being is thought of as possessing superhuman powers. The Christian God, for example, is regarded as omniscient, immortal, omnipresent, and omnipotent. Witches and the Ancestors are credited with malevolent powers—to cast spells and bring down misfortune on a victim.

What do children think about special beings? If the conclusions set out in the preceding section are correct, children ought to deny that God has superhuman powers. After all, such powers are essentially magical and the evidence reviewed in the preceding section shows that children are skeptical about the existence of magic, at least outside the world of fairy tales. On the other hand, everyday observation suggests that children readily believe in special beings with special powers, especially God. Indeed, recent experimental evidence confirms that children not only believe in the existence of special beings, but also accept that they have superhuman powers. For example, as discussed in Chapter 5, most 4- and 5-year-olds realize that human beings are prone to make mistakes. They understand that if someone is presented with a closed container, he or she cannot know its contents without taking a look inside or being told. In a clever experiment, Justin Barrett and his colleagues asked whether children think that God is subject to the same restrictions. What if God were shown a closed container? Would he know its contents? Four- and five-year-olds asserted that he would know—even though they acknowledged that ordinary mortals, including their mother, would not (Barrett et al., 2001). Comparable results emerged in a follow-up with Spanish children. Not only did children grant that God has privileged access to hidden information, but also they explicitly attributed that access to God's special powers. Similarly, when children were questioned about the lifecycle, they acknowledged that a friend would get older as time passed and eventually die, whereas they claimed that God would never age or die (Giménez-Dasí et al., 2005).

Apparently, even if children are broadly skeptical about magic—thinking of it as belonging to fiction rather than real life—they are still willing to entertain the miraculous with respect to God. One possible interpretation of these findings, consistent with the idea that children are mostly commonsensical, is that they think of religious assertions about God as a kind of transcendental fairy story, not as straightforwardly true. Just as they acknowledge that magic is possible in the special world of fairy stories but not in the real world, they might think that extraordinary powers are possible in the special place that God inhabits—wherever that might be—but not in the real world. However, various pieces of evidence argue against this conclusion. First, it implies that young children think of God's special powers as excluded from the everyday world of reality—just as magic is excluded from real life. Indeed, in their study of preschoolers, Woolley and Cox (2007) found that they made a sharp distinction between regular events that can happen in real life and fantastical or magical events that cannot. However, when these same children were asked to make a judgment about miraculous events—for example, God saving a man from the lions—5-year-olds thought of them as regular events. They classified them as possible in real life. By implication, young children do not think of miracles as belonging to a fairy tale world—they connect them to the real world.

Similar findings were obtained by Corriveau and colleagues (2015). They gave children three different types of stories—realistic stories that included no implausible events, quasi-fairy stories that included magical phenomena (e.g., seeds that make you live forever), and quasi-biblical stories that included miraculous phenomena (e.g., the parting of the seas or of the mountains). For each story, children were asked to say whether the central character was a real person or a made-up person. They typically said that the central character in realistic stories was a real person, whereas the central character in quasi-fairy stories was only a made-up person. Children's reactions to quasi-biblical stories depended on their education and upbringing. Secular children—who had not received any kind of religious instruction—said that the central character was a made-up person. They effectively treated the stories as if they were fairy stories. By contrast, religious children who had received some form of faith-based instruction—by attending a parochial school, or by going to religious services with their family, or both—said that the central character was a real person, not a fictional character. Similar results have emerged in follow-up studies in the USA, Iran, and China. When religious children are presented with a narrative involving an extraordinary outcome brought about by divine intervention, they are prone to think of it as describing something that actually happened. By contrast, children with no religious education think of it as fictional (Cui, 2021; Davoodi et al., 2022; Payir et al., 2021s).

Evidence that children connect God to the real world also comes from their developing ideas about prayer as compared to making a wish. Both prayer and wish-making are special in the sense that they involve a mental act aimed at securing a desired outcome via extraordinary means, rather than via ordinary instrumental activity.

Younger preschoolers are inclined to believe in the efficacy of wish-making, but by the age of 5 or 6 years they acknowledge that it does not really work (Woolley et al., 1999). The developmental pattern is very different for prayer. The majority of younger preschoolers believe in the efficacy of prayer, but among 6- to 8-year-olds, this belief is even more widespread (Woolley & Phelps, 2001). In short, children increasingly acknowledge that wish-making is ineffective, but increasingly claim that prayer is effective. Here, we have a miniature illustration—but a telling one, given the parallels between the two practices—of the difference between children's attitude toward magic as compared to miracles.

To summarize the conclusions so far, children are skeptical about magic—they claim that it only takes place in fairy tales, not in real life. On the other hand, children are not necessarily systematic or coherent in their skepticism toward events that defy ordinary causality. They accept that a special being, notably God, can perform miracles and they believe that prayers are answered. Yet children do not come to believe in such miracles because of a natural disposition toward religious belief. They only do so if they have received a religious education or upbringing. In the next section, we take a closer at children's belief in the miraculous.

Understanding death

The standard psychological approach to children's ideas about death has focused on when and how they come to understand its biological aspects—the fact that it is an inevitable and irreversible terminal point for all bodily and mental processes and for all living creatures. A solid body of research shows that children gradually construct such a biological understanding, typically in the course of their early school years. However, this line of research has routinely ignored the possibility that children also adopt a religious conception of death, a conception that defies or ignores the constraints imposed by biology.

To compare these two conceptions, Spanish children aged 7 and 11 years were given two parallel interviews that probed both their biological and their religious ideas about death

(Harris & Giménez, 2005). Before one interview, children listened to a short narrative about Juan's grandfather. They were told that at the end of his life, Juan's grandfather became very ill and was admitted to hospital. However, there was no cure and the doctor came to Juan to talk about what had happened, explaining that his grandfather was now dead. After hearing the narrative, children were asked a series of questions about whether or not the bodily and mental processes of Juan's grandfather continued to function. For example, a question about bodily processes focused on the eyes ("Have his eyes stopped working?") and a question about mental processes focused on the experience of seeing ("Can he still see?"). Children answered a parallel set of questions after hearing a narrative about Marta's grandmother. The cues in this narrative were different in that after her grandmother's death, a priest came to talk to Marta, explaining that her grandmother was now with God.

The two narratives led children to give a different pattern of answers. When the death was placed in a biomedical framework, as in the case of Juan's grandfather, children mostly said that bodily and mental processes had stopped and justified their answers by referring to a global cessation of all biological processes: for example, "He has been eaten by worms, he has no body. He just has bones" or "If he is dead, nothing can work." By contrast, when the death was placed in a religious framework, as in the case of Marta's grandmother, children were likely to claim that some processes would still continue, and they offered a religious explanation: for example, "In Heaven, everything can work even if she is dead" or "The soul keeps working."

These results were striking because the same child often reached different conclusions depending on the narrative they had just heard: for example, claiming that Juan's grandfather could no longer see but insisting that Marta's grandmother could still see. It might be argued that such conflicting judgments are atypical. Perhaps the children felt compelled to defer to the cues that the adult interviewer had included in each narrative—to talk about death from a biomedical perspective or from a religious perspective, depending on whether it was a doctor or a priest who spoke to the bereaved grandchild. To explore this possibility and to find out whether this conflicting conception of death is widespread, a further study was conducted in Madagascar among the Vezo people living in the village of Betania (Astuti & Harris, 2008). The Vezo, like many traditional groups in Madagascar, worship their ancestors—but not without anxiety, because a failure to do so in the prescribed ritualistic fashion can bring down illness and misfortune on the living descendants.

The procedure was similar to that used in Spain save that the stories were suitably adapted. For example, a biomedical story about Rampy described his serious malaria attack, the injections he received at the hospital, and his failure to recover. A "religious" story about Rapeto described his "good" death, surrounded by his descendants, and the proper preparation of his burial tomb by his children and grandchildren. Again, these different narratives triggered a different pattern of replies. In the context of the medical story, nearly half the participants claimed that all processes, mental as well as bodily, had stopped. In the context of the religious story, by contrast, such replies were rare. Instead, the majority claimed that certain processes, especially mental processes, would continue. This pattern emerged for adults as well as children, and so the inclination to both deny and assert that death is terminal cannot be explained by young children's deference to adult authority—it is also found among mature adults. In addition, it is not confined to cultures with a strong Christian tradition.

These results from Spain and Madagascar—together with similar findings from Mexico (Gutiérrez et al., 2020) and Vanuatu (Watson-Jones et al., 2017)—show that children and adults have two conceptions of death. They have a biological conception of death as an endpoint but also a quasi-miraculous conception in which death marks the beginning of an afterlife. These two conceptions are not regarded as mutually exclusive. Children and adults alike switch between them depending on whether the death is framed as a biological event that terminates mortal existence or as the beginning of a different form of life—with God or among the Ancestors. That beginning is regarded as a departure from this secular world for another place but not as the complete cessation of life (Harris, 2018).

Conclusions

Pascal Boyer describes a thought-provoking exchange that took place while he was doing postdoctoral research at Cambridge University (Boyer, 2002). Invited to talk about his work at a college dinner, he explained that he was a social anthropologist interested in supernatural beliefs and went on to describe the belief system of the Fang with whom he had done his fieldwork in Cameroon: "Witches have an extra internal animal-like organ that flies away at night and ruins other people's crops or poisons their blood. It is also said that these witches sometimes assemble for huge banquets, where they will devour their victims and plan future attacks. Many will tell you that a friend of a friend actually saw witches flying over the village at night, sitting on a banana leaf and throwing magical darts at various unsuspecting victims." A Cambridge theologian listening to this description of Fang beliefs commented: "This is what makes anthropology so fascinating and so difficult too. You have to explain how people can believe such nonsense."

As Richard Dawkins drily remarks of this exchange in *The God Delusion*, the theologian's remark suggests that he made a sharp distinction between the apparently irrational beliefs of the Fang and his own Christian beliefs (Dawkins, 2006). Yet the theologian's own beliefs were likely to include, amongst other things, a belief in the Virgin birth, the resurrection of Jesus, God's ability to hear our prayers, and the possibility of spending eternity with God in Heaven. It is tempting to agree with Dawkins and to dismiss the theologian's remark about the allegedly nonsensical beliefs of the Fang as uncharitable or insular. But from a psychological perspective, we should probably avoid such snap judgments. The interesting question is how the theologian—like so many of us—believes in miracles but finds it odd that anyone should believe in what he or she regards as mere superstition. More generally, how is it that we often find the supernatural beliefs of our own community to be understandable and even credible, whereas we find the supernatural beliefs of another community to be exotic and irrational?

Whatever the exact psychological explanation for that differentiation, it is clear that its seeds are planted in childhood. Children doubt whether ordinary causal constraints can really be defied by magic powers. Yet they routinely attribute miraculous powers to God and, thanks to God, they believe that human beings will enjoy an afterlife. Granted that children—and indeed adults—differentiate between magic and miracles, what is the ultimate basis for that distinction? My own suspicion is that, despite appearances to the contrary—and despite the likely protests of the Cambridge theologian mentioned earlier—there is no deep or principled distinction between the two realms. By that I mean that children come into a particular community, which designates certain phenomena as magical and others as miraculous. Children learn from their community where to draw the line between the two, but they are not offered, and nor do they ever arrive at, any fundamental conceptual rule for deciding which is which. In much the same way, they will come to regard some plants as weeds and others as flowers, or some animals as fit for human consumption and others not—but on the basis of tradition and community say-so rather than any principled distinction.

A compelling piece of evidence in favor of this possibility emerges when we adopt an historical perspective. As discussed at the beginning of the chapter, the line between magic and miracles was radically redrawn in Western civilization over the four centuries between approximately 1400 and 1800. The accusation and punishment of witches gradually abated and the Christian church slowly came to regard a belief in witchcraft as superstition. By implication, if we could test children growing up in the fourteenth century with the help of a time machine, we would find that the power of magic and witchcraft would be classified along with miracles: as an extraordinary but credible part of reality. It would certainly not be rejected as the kind of fantasy that is confined to fairy tales or best-selling fiction for children. By contrast, the same tests repeated with Western children of the twentieth and twenty-first centuries should indicate that they—in line with the prevailing Christian doctrine—differentiate between miracles and witchcraft. Similarly, many adults in the USA and Europe will pray for the recovery of a sick person and sincerely believe that prayer will be efficacious, but they will rarely explain the sickness, or seek to remedy it, by invoking witchcraft.

11

Is developmental psychology ethnocentric?

Cross-cultural differences in ways of thinking

Findings in developmental psychology are overwhelmingly based on children growing up in the West, especially the towns and cities of North America and Western Europe. How far can we generalize those findings to children growing up elsewhere—in the Amazonian rain forest, a village in Nepal, or the Australian outback? When we do find differences, they can often be attributed to marked variation in access to the various accoutrements of modernity—schools, books, a market economy, urbanization, industrialization, and so forth. However, some psychologists have argued that beyond any differences in access to modernity and its institutions, there are also fundamental differences in psychological functioning that can be attributed to long-standing differences in cultural practices and assumptions. In this chapter, I highlight cultural differences in cognitive and emotional style between East and West, focusing initially on adults and then turning to children and their development.

Looking at the history and practice of medicine in the West as compared to Asia, Richard Nisbett and his colleagues argued for a profound difference in causal and analytic thinking (Nisbett et al., 2001). Western medicine frequently analyzes illness in terms of the malfunctioning of a discrete organ; an intervention directed at that organ is a standard remedy. Eastern medicine, by contrast, emphasizes the importance of harmony among various bodily forces, rather than the functioning—or malfunctioning—of a particular organ. More broadly, Nisbett and his colleagues argued for two different orientations to science. In the Western analytic tradition, traceable back to the Greeks, there is an emphasis on the misleading nature of appearances, the power of reasoning, and the elimination of contradiction. By contrast, in the Eastern and especially the Chinese tradition, there is an emphasis on the importance of observation, the power of holistic thinking, and the reconciliation of apparently contradictory claims rather than the elimination of one or the other. According to the Western tradition, objects—including bodily organs such as the heart or the liver—are best understood in terms of their own particular and essential properties. According to the Eastern tradition, objects are best understood in terms of their interrelations with other objects. This dichotomy between analytic and holistic thinking raises the possibility that various cognitive strategies that have been frequently identified in Western psychology might be less than universal. They might be widespread among Westerners but not among Asians.

Consider the way that we perceive and interpret a person's behavior. We may take as an example the behavior of the all-too-obedient participants in Milgram's experiments as described in Chapter 8. In interpreting his findings, Milgram emphasized the situational factors that affected their behavior: for example, he pointed out how the physical proximity of the white-coated scientist made obedience more likely, whereas the proximity of the apparently suffering learner made obedience less likely. Interestingly, the obedient participants tended to see things in much the same way as Milgram himself. When interviewed at the end of the experiment and invited to think about how they might have acted otherwise, they called attention to the situation they found themselves in, especially the scientist giving them instructions: "I wanted to stop but he wouldn't let me."

But when we first learn about these experiments, it is tempting to focus instead on the personality of the obedient subjects—to wonder what feature of their upbringing or temperament made them so disinclined to take responsibility upon themselves for deciding whether to continue delivering the electric shocks. Similarly, if we think about the prison guards in Abu Ghraib who tortured and humiliated their prisoners in the wake of 9/11, it is tempting to look to their personalities for an explanation of their behavior, even if the guards themselves sought to exonerate themselves in court—unsuccessfully in most cases—by claiming that they were acting under orders.

Our reactions to these cases highlight an asymmetry in the way that we explain other people's behavior as compared to our own behavior. When we think about someone else's behavior—the behavior of the obedient subjects in Milgram's studies or the prison guards in Abu Ghraib—we are inclined to attribute their behavior to their individual make-up rather than to the situational forces that are acting upon them. We speculate that other individuals, ourselves included, would have behaved differently in such circumstances. By contrast, the individuals who are actually placed in these situations attribute their behavior to external forces—to the instructions delivered by the white-coated scientist or to the orders handed down by superior officers in the US military.

Our tendency to focus on internal forces when explaining other people's behavior can lure us into error—as illustrated by the classic experiment of Edward Jones and Victor Harris (1967). Adult participants read an essay defending a controversial issue: for example, the legalization of marijuana. Subsequently, they were told that the person who had written the essay had been obliged to write it in the context of learning how to debate. Despite that information, however, participants often persisted in thinking that the person who had written the essay actually held those views about marijuana: they were prone to attribute the writer's statement to inner conviction rather than external circumstances—even if they were manifestly wrong in doing so, granted the set-up of the experiment.

Following various replications of this basic result, social psychologists dubbed it "the fundamental attribution error". They argued that there is a natural human disposition to explain other people's behavior in terms of their dispositions and characteristics rather than the situational pressures they face. But this is where the proposals by Nisbett and his colleagues raise important questions. They argue that the tendency to see the behavior of others as due to their own internal dispositions, even when a plausible situational explanation is available, may be widespread in Western culture but is less evident in Asia. In line with their more holistic mode of thinking, Asians lend greater weight to external situational factors, not to an individual's distinctive make-up.

For example, Choi and his colleagues (1999) tested Koreans and Americans in a repeat of the Jones and Harris experiment. In an initial study, participants of both nationalities were likely to misjudge the true attitudes of a target person. However, when given an opportunity to experience for themselves the same situational constraints as the target person, Americans still went on making the error, whereas Koreans almost never did so. By implication, Koreans could be easily alerted to the impact of situational constraints—Americans less so.

Peng and Nisbett (1999) examined another potential East–West difference—reactions to conflicting statements. Do adults try to find a way to reconcile them or are they inclined to assume that one of the two statements must be wrong? Peng and Nisbett gave students at the University of Michigan and at Beijing University pairs of opposing statements, each purporting to be brief descriptions of findings from research studies. One statement from a pair about prison overcrowding was as follows: "*A survey found that older inmates are more likely to be ones who are serving long sentences because they have committed severely violent crimes. The authors concluded that they should be held in prison even in the case of a prison population crisis.*" However, the other statement offered an opposing view: "*A report on the prison overcrowding issue suggests that older inmates are less likely to commit new crimes. Therefore, if there is a prison population crisis they should be released first.*"

When asked to evaluate each of these two statements separately, the Chinese and the American students drew similar conclusions about their relative plausibility. Both groups tended to judge the first statement, associating older inmates with more severe crime, as more plausible. The pattern was different when students were given both statements together. The Chinese students tended to moderate their judgments of each statement—they ended up judging the initially more plausible statement as less plausible and the initially less plausible statement as more plausible. They effectively showed a "spirit of compromise"—seeking the middle way between the two opposing statements. By contrast, when the American students were given both statements, they differentiated more sharply between them, ending up with an even firmer sense of the correctness of the initially more plausible claim.

Other research also points to the more "conciliatory" disposition of Asians. In a classic paradigm in social psychology, American students took part in what appeared to be an experiment on visual perception (Asch, 1956). When they arrived in the classroom, they found themselves to be part of a group of six or seven others. The experimenter presented a series of card pairs—with one card containing three vertical lines and the other containing a single vertical line. The students were asked to say which of the three lines matched the single line in length. They were also told that, for convenience, they would be tested in groups and that each person in the group would be called on in turn to state his judgment aloud. Unbeknownst to the real subject, the remaining members of the small group were accomplices of the experimenter. On several trials, these accomplices all indicated the same incorrect line, so that when it came to the real subject's turn—near the end of the row—he was faced with a dilemma. Should he pronounce his own judgment or go along with the preceding consensus? Asch found that students went along with the consensus about one-third of the time. In explaining his findings, Asch envisaged two competing forces. On the one hand, individuals could readily see which line was correct. Indeed, left to their own devices, they were able to do so on trial after trial. On the other hand, having heard several other people agree on a different line, there was the countervailing pressure of that consensus. Faced with this conflict, students sometimes went along with the consensus. According to Asch, they displayed a disturbing tendency to conform.

Subsequent research with the Asch paradigm has upheld the initial findings but pointed to a different interpretation. In a thorough review of many subsequent replication studies, Bond and Smith (1996) confirmed that the tendency to agree with the consensus is a robust phenomenon. As might be expected, conformity is more common when the force emanating from the group is potent: for example, when the size of the majority is greater, or when the majority consists of people known to the subject rather than strangers. Conversely, conformity is reduced when the force arising from the individual's own judgment is stronger: for example, when the differences among the lines are perceptually obvious.

But the result that is most relevant for present purposes is the pattern of cross-cultural variation that emerged from the review. To compare across studies carried out in different countries, Bond and Smith looked back at prior analyses of cross-national survey data. One such large-scale survey was carried out by Hofstede (1991), who argued that national cultures can be ordered along several different dimensions, including the collectivist–individualist dimension. In individualist cultures, the self is conceived as distinct from society as a whole and one's personal identity is primarily determined by individual achievement. By contrast, in collectivist cultures, self and identity are conceived in terms of group membership and the position of the group in the larger society. Group decisions are valued over individual decisions.

Bond and Smith asked whether the degree of conformity displayed in the Asch paradigm in any particular country was correlated with the level of collectivism reported in Hofstede's survey. A robust relationship emerged. In other words, participants in studies conducted in countries where collectivism is pronounced display a stronger tendency toward conformist responses as compared to the level reported by Asch and subsequent investigators in the USA. More specifically, consistent with the analysis offered by Nisbett and his colleagues, studies conducted in Asian cultures such as Hong Kong and Japan, where collectivism is prominent, reveal a greater conformist bias in the Asch paradigm than do studies conducted in the USA.

This intriguing outcome warrants further reflection. The fact that the tendency to conform is robust across different cultures, and indeed even stronger in some, suggests that the interpretation offered by Asch might need rethinking. He saw conformity as a regrettable lapse—a failure to honestly report one's own independent judgment. But there is another way to think about the findings. In many perceptual situations, our own judgment is likely to be quite accurate—judgments about which two lines are equal in length generally fall into that category, but if we are asked to say just how long a single line is in inches or centimeters, we might have less confidence in our own judgment. Indeed, hearing a majority give an estimate that exceeds our own, we might revise our initial judgment upward. Sticking to our original judgment might, in these circumstances, reveal our inflexibility rather than our independence. So, a less negative interpretation of the behavior of participants in Asch's studies, as well as subsequent replications, is that individuals and cultures vary in the way that they weigh two potentially important sources of information—judgments arrived at by the self and judgments arrived at by several other people—especially when they are in conflict with each other. The findings reported by Bond and Smith can be interpreted as showing that members of Asian cultures give more weight to a group consensus than do members of Western cultures.

One final intriguing cultural difference reported by Nisbett and his colleagues is worth describing. When adults concentrate on what is happening in one part of the visual field, they are prone to neglect what is taking place in some adjacent part of the visual field. Even when something quite dramatic appears in the adjacent visual field, it can often be overlooked. In one compelling illustration, adults watched a film in which they had to keep track of team members passing a ball to one another. When someone dressed up in a gorilla suit passed among the team members, adults were often so busy monitoring the ball and its travels that they failed to notice the gorilla (Simons & Chabris, 1999).

Applying these ideas to cultural differences, Masuda and Nisbett (2006) gave Japanese and American adults various scenic photographs to look at. Sometimes a change was introduced to objects in the foreground and sometimes to objects in the background. In general, American adults detected more changes in the foreground than Japanese adults and Japanese adults detected more changes in the background than American adults. By implication, the Americans looked at the scenes in a narrower or more targeted fashion, whereas the Japanese looked at them in a broader, more holistic fashion—a conclusion borne out by a broad range of studies examining cross-cultural differences in attention (Masuda, 2017).

The origins of cross-cultural variation

To explain these various cognitive and perceptual differences, Nisbett and his colleagues point to centuries-old differences in the intellectual traditions of Asia as compared to the West, referring back to Confucius and Aristotle among others. A plausible implication of their analysis is that the differences that they find in the various student populations under scrutiny are connected to long-standing differences in educational priorities. On this argument, Asian and American students differ because the intellectual values that they encounter are different. For example, American students might learn to debate opposing points of view and seek out flaws in an opponent's arguments. By contrast, Asian students might learn how to synthesize apparently conflicting points of view.

However, there is a different possibility. Perhaps the East–West differences observed by Nisbett and his colleagues—even if they are linked to different intellectual traditions, reaching back many centuries—are habits of mind that pervade social encounters well beyond the classroom or the lecture theater. Maybe they are also found in the context of everyday social interactions and not just in educational settings. Later, we will explore the intriguing possibility that these different habits of mind show up even in early interactions between caregivers and young children and are thereby transmitted from one generation to the next.

Talking and thinking

A recurrent feature of the Western intellectual tradition is thinking via dialogue. This Socratic approach is exemplified in the writings of Plato and we see it put to brilliant use by Galileo. Philosophers routinely acknowledge that they try out their ideas in the context of dialogue with fellow philosophers. In some universities, the tutorial exchange between teacher and student is a major pedagogic vehicle. A government-appointed inspector, seeking to assess the caliber of the teaching at the Oxford philosophy department, once ventured to ask the assembled faculty if any new teaching methods had been introduced in recent years. "Nothing since Plato" was the laconic reply. An emphasis on thinking through dialogue is less evident in East Asian cultures. Indeed, in both the Buddhist and Taoist tradition, the importance of silent reflection is stressed.

Asian students studying in Western universities sometimes evoke concern from their professors because they are less inclined to engage in classroom dialogue. But this may reflect a fundamentally different orientation toward learning, rather than reticence about public speaking or discussion. To explore this possibility, Kühnen and van Egmond (2018) asked German and Chinese students to think about various classroom dilemmas. For example, they were asked to think about a student who is taking a history course and finds that he doesn't agree with the professor on certain ideas. Should he interrupt the professor and discuss it with him in class? Similarly, students were asked to think about a student attending a psychology lecture. The professor is explaining one of the classic theories in the field. The student has doubts about that theory. Should he express his doubts openly or first make sure that he fully understands the theory?

As compared to the German students, the Chinese students were more likely to favor silence. They said that the students in the vignettes should not immediately voice disagreement or doubt but first ensure their understanding of the material. This pattern emerged even in interviews with Chinese students studying at a German university. Despite the faculty expectation that international students should also engage in classroom discussion—and indeed despite being graded for such participation—the Chinese students continued to advocate a more Confucian stance in which discussion should take place after mastery of the material, rather than being seen as a way to attain mastery.

Kim (2002) speculated that these distinctive cultural ideas about the relationship between thinking and talking might be linked not just to different assumptions about what helps thinking, but to variation in the process of thinking itself. More specifically, Asian students might actually think better if they think silently. Conversely, Western students might gain some cognitive benefit from talking. To examine these possibilities, Kim tested two groups of Stanford students—East-Asian Americans and European Americans—on a set of problems taken from the Advanced Raven's Progressive Matrices. Each of these problems consisted of a 3×3 matrix of patterns, with the pattern in the lower right cell missing. Participants had to select the pattern for the missing cell on the basis of the rules governing the patterns in the other eight cells. The test is a test of intelligence and is often regarded as relatively culture fair because it does not presume familiarity with material that is obviously more frequent or available in one culture than another.

All the students were asked to solve the first 10 problems in silence. For the next 10 problems they were asked to think aloud. Overall, across the two assignments, the two groups solved approximately the same number of problems, but the East-Asian students solved more when they worked in silence, whereas the European Americans solved just as many if not more problems when they thought aloud (Kim, 2002, Study 2). The students also completed a questionnaire in which they were asked to indicate their beliefs, family practices, and orientation with respect to thinking versus talking. As compared to the European-American students, the East-Asian students were less likely to believe that, for example, talking clarifies one's ideas, less likely to report stating their opinions—even to their parents—and more likely to report engaging in silent, non-verbal thinking as opposed to verbal thinking.

Kim's findings fit nicely with those described by Kühnen and van Egmond (2018) but go beyond them in two key respects. First, the East-Asians studying at Stanford were not new arrivals in the USA— they had grown up in the USA. Thus, unlike the Chinese students questioned in German universities, they had not gone to school in Asia. By implication, they acquired their orientation toward silent thinking from their migrant parents, or perhaps from the immigrant community in which they had grown up. Apparently, the family, or immigrant community, can successfully transmit an orientation to learning that is different from that of the majority culture. Second, the difference in learning orientation not only manifests itself in terms of perceived norms—ideas and values about what is appropriate versus inappropriate student behavior in the classroom—but also penetrates the process of thought itself. It is evident when students are alone, trying to solve a problem.

To probe the possible developmental origin of these deep-seated differences, it is helpful to take a closer look at cross-cultural differences in child-rearing practices, especially differences between the USA and Europe on the one hand and East Asia on the other.

Symbiotic harmony?

In two provocative papers, Fred Rothbaum and his colleagues (Rothbaum et al., 2000a; 2000b) argued that Asian and Western parents bring different assumptions about human relationships to the task of child rearing. In the West, there is the expectation that early emotional security will lay the foundations for feelings of independence. Think back to Ainsworth's influential concept of the secure base described in Chapter 1. According to the secure base metaphor, the child refuels emotionally either beside or in contact with the mother, but then strikes out independently to explore the world. Security enables the child to move away from the mother. However, independence is not an inevitable consequence of security. According to Rothbaum and his colleagues, Asian child-rearing practices are aimed at the nurturance of secure interdependence rather than secure independence. They review a variety of findings on early child rearing, especially in Japan, to support this contention.

Observing mothers interacting with their 13-month-olds, Bornstein and colleagues (1992a) divided mothers' vocalizations into those that were affective, including greetings (e.g., "Hello there"), recitations (e.g., "Peek-a-boo"), onomatopoeia (e.g., "Meow, meow"), and endearments ("Sweetie"), versus those vocalizations that were more information-oriented, including direct statements (e.g., "Try one more time"), questions (e.g., "What does that toy do?"), and reports (e.g., "You sure do like your blocks, don't you?"). They found that Japanese mothers used more affective as opposed to information-oriented vocalizations, whereas the reverse was true for American mothers.

A parallel difference emerged for the amount of contact and proximity. Japanese parents were likely to co-sleep with their infants, often held or carried them, and limited non-maternal care to approximately 2 hours per week, whereas American parents rarely co-slept, tended to promote independent mobility, and arranged non-maternal care for approximately 23 hours per week (Barratt et al., 1993). In short, Japanese babies spent more of their time in close proximity to their mothers than American babies did.

When Bornstein and his colleagues observed mothers interacting with their 5-month-olds, few differences emerged in the way that the infants behaved. For example, both Japanese and American babies were more likely to vocalize in a non-distressed fashion than to either cry or whimper. They were also more likely to attend to objects outside the dyad than to direct their attention within the dyad. Despite this stability across the babies, the mothers behaved differently. Unlike American mothers, Japanese mothers were more likely to respond when the baby paid attention to what was going on within rather than beyond the dyad, again suggesting a cultural difference in the accent placed on interconnectedness as opposed to outward exploration (Bornstein et al., 1992b).

Parallel differences were seen when Japanese and American mothers read a picture book to their infants, ranging from 6 to 18 months (Senzaki & Shimizu, 2020). The picture book contained a series of pages that depicted an ever-decreasing number of ladybugs together with various other creatures—bees, caterpillars—in the background. Whereas American mothers directed most of their comments to the ladybugs (e.g., "Look at these little ladybugs" or "There are nine ladybugs") rather than the creatures in the background, Japanese mothers divided their comments more evenly. Indeed, as compared to the American mothers, the Japanese mothers made twice as many comments about interactions between the background creatures and the ladybugs (e.g., "The caterpillar is looking at the ladybugs" or "Do you think bees will share the honey with the ladybugs?"). In sum, American mothers mainly focused on the central protagonists, the ladybugs, whereas Japanese mothers were more inclined to highlight social connections between them and the other creatures.

Further differences between Japanese and American mothers emerged in a study of how their 12-month-old infants reacted in the Strange Situation that was described in Chapter 1 (Takahashi, 1990). When the mother left her infant alone, almost all of the Japanese babies immediately started to cry, whereas less than half of the American babies did so. Indeed, most of the Japanese babies were still crying at the end of the separation period, whereas just over half of the American babies did so. Not surprisingly, the distress of the Japanese babies impinged on their behavior during the separation. Few of them engaged in any exploration, whereas more than half of the American babies did so. Moreover, when the mother returned, less than half of the Japanese babies played with the available toys, whereas more than three-quarters of the American babies did so.

One might reasonably ask whether these differences in the pattern of responding means that the Strange Situation is potentially misleading as an index of the degree to which babies are securely attached (Takahashi, 1990). Without returning to that debate, we may certainly infer—not so surprisingly in light of the findings on child rearing described earlier—that Japanese babies are less used to being left alone and more prone to distress when they are left alone. Having learned to expect that their mother will be at hand most of the time, their distress when she is unavailable is predictable. It is also consistent with the larger claim made by Rothbaum and his colleagues (2000a; 2000b) that Japanese babies are less disposed to independent exploration than their American peers.

These cultural differences continue into later childhood. Hess and his colleagues asked Japanese and American mothers to say at what age they expected their child to display various desirable characteristics. The two groups of mothers proved to have different priorities. Japanese mothers expected their children to be able to accommodate to other people before expressing their independence. American mothers, by contrast, believed that children should learn how to express their independence before learning to accommodate to other people (Hess et al., 1980). Moving on to somewhat older children, Mitchell and his colleagues found that as they got older, both Japanese and British children were increasingly likely to assert that they knew themselves better than did the adults around them. However, this tendency to have more confidence in one's own self-knowledge emerged earlier among the British children. Seven-year-old British children were more likely to have confidence in their own self-judgment than were 7-year-old Japanese children, both in terms of knowing themselves and in terms of knowing their own mind (Mitchell et al., 2010).

Pulling these various findings together, we can make somewhat speculative use of the idea of a "working model" introduced in Chapter 1. According to Bowlby, toddlers form a mental schema—an internal working model or blueprint—of how interactions with a caregiver typically play out. For example, the child can mentally represent the self in distress and the caregiver being responsive—or not. Bowlby advanced this concept as a way to explain the different expectations that secure as compared to insecure toddlers bring to caregiving interactions—interactions with their mother and indeed other potential caregivers. However, there is no reason why we cannot borrow the concept to think about cross-cultural variation in infants' expectations. More specifically, it is plausible that the Japanese baby is more likely to create a mental model in which the self is conceived as being in more or less constant proximity to a significant other—after all, this reflects reality. By contrast, the American baby is more likely to conceive of the self as sometimes acting autonomously—again this is likely to be a simple reflection of reality. To the extent that these primordial mental schemas serve as a starting point for the conceptualization of relationships in general, Japanese babies, and more generally East-Asian babies, will be disposed to perceive and expect interconnections between self and others, whereas American babies will be more likely to perceive and expect the self—and indeed other individuals—to be semi-independent agents.

This analysis makes an intriguing prediction. As discussed earlier, the different patterns of thought in East and West described by Nisbett and his colleagues might be linked to long-standing differences in patterns of scholarship, scientific investigation, and intellectual orientation. On that interpretation, those patterns of thought are likely to be transmitted from one generation to the next via the various institutions and media displaying those distinct intellectual orientations—schools and colleges, as well as books and newspapers. By implication, the longer and more sustained any given individual's exposure to those institutions and media, the greater the likelihood that he or she will adopt and endorse that distinct orientation. Based on this interpretation, we would not expect a child who has never been to school and cannot read to show the imprint of these long-standing historical differences in intellectual orientation—they should only emerge in the course of schooling. On the other hand, if those cultural differences are embedded in modes of early caregiving within the family, we can expect that young children will display them even before they have been exposed to formal schooling and literacy.

Four sets of findings lend support to this latter expectation. Corriveau and Harris (2010) gave preschoolers in Boston a child-friendly variant of the Asch task in which children had to select the biggest of three lines. Children did this without error when left to their own devices. However, if three adults preceded them and picked out a different line, children were prone to defer to this adult judgment—not always, but on about 25% of the trials. Moreover, children who deferred in this fashion were more likely than non-deferential children to say that the adults were good at judging the lines, and indeed to misremember which line the adults had pointed to, wrongly claiming that the adults had been correct in pointing to the biggest line. This pattern of behavior can reasonably be seen not

as simple compliance or conformity, but as respectful deference—
the deferential children seemed to have respectfully concluded that
the adults were better judges of the lines than they were.

Especially important for present purposes is the finding that the
rate of such respectful deference was greater among Asian-American
preschoolers than among European-American preschoolers (Corriveau & Harris, 2010). Moreover, a follow-up study confirmed that
it is only first-generation Asian-American not second-generation
children that differ from their American peers—suggesting that,
in the course of assimilation, Asian immigrants increasingly shift
toward the culture of the USA in their child-rearing practices (Corriveau et al., 2013; Harris & Corriveau, 2013).

Differences have also been found with respect to the distribution
of attention. Chen and Harris (2007) gave children a perceptual task
that probed how far they focused on the foreground as compared to
the background. Children were shown a series of photographs each
depicting a different bird against a distinctive background. Next,
children were shown test pairs of pictures. Both pictures in each pair
depicted a bird against a background, but only one of each pair had
been in the initial series—the other served as a foil. Children were
asked to say which of the two pictures they had seen before. Sometimes, the foil depicted a previously shown bird in the foreground
but with a different background, and sometimes the foil depicted a
previously shown background but with a different bird in the foreground. In general, young children in both Boston and Shanghai
were quite good at recognizing which of the pictures in any given
pair they had seen before. However, the pattern of performance
differed depending on the foil. If the foil included a change to the
background, the Chinese children performed better than American
children. By implication, when initially presented with the pictures,
the Chinese children had paid more attention to the background and
subsequently spotted any departures from what they had seen. By
contrast, if the foil included a change to the bird in the foreground,
American children performed better than Chinese children, suggesting that American children had initially paid more attention to
the foreground.

A similar crossover pattern was reported by Kuwabara and Smith (2012) in their studies of American and Japanese 4-year-olds. When the children were asked to find and point to a particular object, for example, a dog located somewhere in a richly detailed picture of a city, the American children were faster than the Japanese children, suggesting that the Japanese children were slowed by their broader attention to the urban scene. Indeed, they were just as fast as the American children once this rich background was replaced by a simpler background of randomly placed objects. Conversely, in a task where children were asked to match pictures on the basis of the spatial relations among the objects within each picture, the Japanese children performed better than the American children.

Finally, research on the child's theory of mind has uncovered an intriguing, cross-cultural difference in children's developing ideas about knowledge and belief. As discussed in Chapter 5, preschoolers typically solve the classic narrative-based, false-belief task at around 4 years of age (Wellman et al., 2001). But before that, at around 3 years of age, children understand two simpler aspects of knowledge and belief. They realize that one person might know a true fact—for example, what particular toy is inside a box—whereas another person might not know that fact. They also realize that when neither person knows what is actually in the box, they might well disagree in their opinions about its contents. It turns out that children in Western Europe and North America grasp the latter notion first: they first understand that two individuals might hold different opinions and then they understand that one individual might be knowledgeable and the other ignorant. But in China, the developmental pattern is reversed: children understand individual differences in knowledge versus ignorance before they recognize individual differences in opinion. So, echoing the proposals made by Nisbett et al. (2001), Western children appear more attuned to the possibility that individuals can hold conflicting opinions, whereas Asian children appear more attuned to what is known and who knows it (Wellman, 2018).

Conclusions

Research with adults reveals differences in the way that information is analyzed by East Asians as compared to Americans and Europeans. East Asians are more sensitive to the matrix in which a given claim or perceptual judgment is situated. At the intellectual level, they are more receptive to counter-arguments and more deferential toward countervailing judgments. At the perceptual level, their attention appears to be more distributed over a wider field. By contrast, Westerners appear to be more targeted in their apprehension of the world—less swayed by contrary arguments or judgments—and at the perceptual level more focused on a given object of attention.

A speculative but not implausible interpretation of these differences is that they have their origins in the types of social relationships that children encounter in their early years. There is evidence that babies in Asia come to think of themselves as regularly embedded in a social network, whereas babies in the USA and Europe are encouraged to think of themselves as having a secure base from which they can make autonomous explorations. More broadly, Asian babies are disposed to think of persons in relational terms, and by extension they are likely to see various entities in the world as interconnected. By contrast, Western babies are disposed to think of persons as autonomous agents, and they readily see entities in the world as separate.

Finally, it is important to qualify these already speculative ideas with a cautionary note. It is tempting to think about these variations—both among children and adults—in terms of an East–West contrast or dichotomy. Indeed, this is the main thrust of the research by Nisbett and his colleagues. However, it is important to keep in mind a different and more radical possibility. Arguably, from a global perspective, the USA and parts of Western Europe have a quite distinct and unusual set of values—one that is rare in most other parts of the world—whereas a focus on personal interrelatedness may be widespread. Further research should reveal, then, whether we should think in terms of a dichotomy or should instead regard the USA and much of Western Europe as outliers on an extended continuum (Henrich, 2020; Henrich et al., 2010).

12
What have we learned?

Children's minds

As noted in the Introduction, psychological research on children is a recent enterprise. The early giants of science—Copernicus, Galileo, and Newton—gazed outward and upward to read nature's book. If there were any children nearby, they were overlooked. The writings of Locke and Rousseau could be seen as the beginnings of psychological enquiry into children's thinking, but they were composed primarily with educational goals in mind. As mentioned in Chapter 7, Darwin was one of the first to approach the young child from a more empirical and psychological perspective, employing his characteristically meticulous observational methods—against the backdrop of big evolutionary thinking. Even so, it took another half century for a cross-national academic framework for research on child development to be established, primarily in the colleges and universities of Europe, Russia, and the USA.

What have we learned? Stepping back from the specifics of the previous chapters, can we draw any overarching conclusions about children's minds? Rather than clear-cut findings or prescriptions, three somewhat paradoxical lessons strike me as worth highlighting: the simultaneously biological and cultural nature of children's mental development; their capacity for stubborn independence as well as wide-ranging deference; and their lack of consistency across different measures and different contexts. Below, I discuss these three paradoxes, drawing on earlier chapters and adding further illustrations.

Biological universals and cultural variation

Early in the twentieth century, developmental psychology was blessed in having two towering figures—Piaget and Vygotsky—lay down some foundational ideas, but the two men were quite different in their background, intellectual orientation, and conception of development. Piaget was trained as a biologist and attuned to questions of adaptation. He approached development primarily in terms of the active adaptation of the species to the surrounding natural environment, whether it be the lake mollusks that he studied early in his career as a biologist or the human children that preoccupied him for the rest of his life (Morgan & Harris, 2015). Note that the specific environment in which children grow up was not Piaget's focus—at most, that environment remained an unwavering backdrop for development. Indeed, it is probably no coincidence that during his own intellectual development in neutral Switzerland—during the first two decades of the twentieth century—Piaget enjoyed an environment of comparative stability and tranquility, untouched by the slaughter and revolution taking place elsewhere on the European Continent (Harris, 1997).

In later years, Piaget did occasionally raise the possibility that particular cultural environments might slow or speed children's conceptual development. Even so, he tended to assume that no matter where they lived, children's progress in understanding the natural world was necessarily an advance, whether slow or rapid, along the same universal highway. A great deal of research on cognitive development in the middle decades of the twentieth century was inspired by this alluring vision of progress and of ever-increasing intellectual equilibrium. Developmental psychologists conducted hundreds of studies on, for example, children's developing understanding of the permanence of an object despite its movement and occlusion, the conservation of a given quantity (be it number, or weight, or volume) across changes in its appearance, or the transitivity of relationships across various types of comparison. In this steady proliferation of studies, with some exceptions, little attention was paid to the possible impact of cultural variation on children's thinking. Indeed, in important respects, that neglect of cultural variation makes good sense. The particular insights that Piaget studied are not likely to be culture-bound. Objects can be conceptualized as permanent, quantities as invariant, and transitive inferences as valid whether children are growing up in Switzerland, Singapore, or Suriname.

Does Piaget's vision of universal development, especially in the cognitive domain, still frame contemporary research? I think it does—and in a positive fashion. As noted, Piaget focused primarily on children's growing understanding of the physical world, but we can reasonably ask if Piaget's approach can be extended to their understanding of the human world. Indeed, just as children gradually construct more or less universal insights into recurrent features of the physical world, they are able to do the same with respect to recurrent aspects of the human world. Cultures clearly differ from each other, but nevertheless they all depend on the availability of certain key components: the use of language, a more or less complex technology, recourse to group rituals, and, crucially, of course, the engagement of human beings across successive generations, all born with approximately the same biological equipment and social dispositions. Not surprisingly, children everywhere appear to arrive at similar conclusions about these human capacities.

Research on the child's emerging understanding of mind and emotion provides persuasive examples of such universal insights. In Chapter 5, I described children's understanding of false beliefs because that understanding has fueled so much developmental research, but there are other aspects of the mind that children come to appreciate. In particular, they rapidly come to understand and talk about the guiding role of desires and of knowledge in human behavior (Bartsch & Wellman, 1995; Wellman, 2018). Children also construct an increasingly sophisticated understanding of emotion, as discussed in Chapter 7. They come to realize, for example, that a person's emotions can be hidden from others or redirected by entertaining particular thoughts (Harris, 1989). In each of these domains, we see intriguing echoes of the classic Piagetian account of development. With age, children build up an increasingly sophisticated understanding, using earlier insights as stepping-stones toward later advances. Moreover, the direction that they take as they move forward is similar across disparate cultures, as Piaget would have expected.

This has meant that it has been possible to devise simple, easy-to-administer tests to figure out how far children have traveled in their understanding of mind (Wellman, 2018; Wellman & Liu, 2004) and emotion (Harris & Cheng, 2022; Pons & Harris, 2005; Pons et al., 2004). Importantly, in each case, whether we interview children in the USA, in different countries within Europe, in Iran, China, or Australia, the sequence of conceptual stepping-stones is quite similar. In other words, even if children are receptive to the distinctive practices and ways of thinking that they encounter in their own culture—as discussed more extensively below—that does not mean that they lack a common set of conceptual tools, especially when thinking about something as critical to everyday life and mutual understanding as the nature of mind and emotion. By implication, it is not only the natural or physical world, but also the human world that lends itself to a common understanding—one that can be shared by children and adults from radically different cultural backgrounds. In that respect, Piaget's optimistic vision of children everywhere constructing an increasingly rich, elaborate, and valid set of concepts lives on in developmental psychology.

Vygotsky, in contrast to Piaget, lived in a challenging and uncertain environment. He experienced the Russian revolution and its vast repercussions for the Soviet Union. Trained as a humanist, Vygotsky was a student of Shakespeare and Tolstoy rather than of biology, a dedicated Marxist, and sympathetic to the communist regime. Unlike Piaget, he was impressed by the ways in which history and technology can radically transform psychological processes. One of his later research projects is especially revealing in this respect. In collaboration with Alexander Luria, he designed a multifactorial study to examine the impact of the communist reforms on the psychology of the peasants in a distant corner of the Soviet Union—Uzbekistan (Harris, 2000). The goal was to compare the thought processes of those hitherto landless peasants who had already been impacted by the Soviet agricultural reforms by receiving a basic education in literacy and numeracy and working on a collective farm with the thought processes of the uneducated and illiterate peasants not yet touched by those radical reforms. The findings revealed major differences between the two groups in their mode of thinking, especially in their willingness to reason about matters lying outside their everyday empirical experience. The "reformed" peasants were willing to draw new logical implications from claims about such unknown matters, whereas the "unreformed" peasants were leery of any conclusion that was not grounded in what they knew from their day-to-day lives. Subsequent research showed that a key driver of this shift—from experience-bound thinking to inferential reasoning on the basis of novel claims—is education (Scribner & Cole, 1981). After all, when they sit in a classroom, children are told about, and invited to contemplate, times, places, and possibilities that are remote from their own lives. Their first-hand experience is likely to prove an inadequate guide when they are asked to conceptualize unseen possibilities, removed from their immediate surroundings.

Not surprisingly, students of human development aiming to study cultural influences, especially children's incorporation of the intellectual habits and tools afforded by the surrounding culture, have typically turned to Vygotskian rather than Piagetian theory for inspiration. As described in Chapters 3 and 6, Vygotsky's influence can be detected in studies of the way that language is gradually internalized and then recruited in the context of private thinking, in the way that the structure of joint reminiscence is gradually internalized and then deployed in the context of individual recollection, and in the way that external number systems are steadily internalized and then put to use in individual enumeration and calculation.

Despite the continuing and valuable influence of Piaget and Vygotsky, it is important to highlight aspects of development not easily addressed by either theoretical framework. Two themes strike me as especially important—themes that are receiving greater attention in this century than they did in the last. The first concerns the basic notion of development, especially in the cognitive domain. In their different ways, Piaget and Vygotsky adopted a progressivist interpretation of children's cognitive development. Just as Whiggish historians have viewed human history as tending toward progress, justice, and enlightenment, so there has been a strong temptation, endorsed by Piaget and Vygotsky, albeit in their different ways, to view children as making intellectual progress as they get older (Harris, 2009). But there are domains of human belief and thought where the notion of progress seems inapposite. Religion offers one obvious example. Admittedly, some writers have concluded that there is a direction or momentum in the history of religious thinking—but direction and momentum are not in themselves clear indices of progress. When we study the development of children's religious thinking, it is challenging to know what might be expected of an older as compared to a younger child. No doubt, children will increasingly understand the specific doctrines of their community, whether they are Christian, Islamic, Buddhist, or atheistic. But it is not obvious that the older child who has assimilated those beliefs has made a conceptual advance on the thinking of his or her younger self. Moreover—and here the discrepancy from the domains explored by Piaget and by post-Piagetian researchers is vivid—children end up with radically different and sometimes contradictory beliefs, depending on what they learn from their culture about for example, the forgiveness of sin, differences between men and women, the origins of human life, what happens when we die, or the second coming.

We can draw two implications: first, developmental psychology in the twentieth century, especially in the domain of cognitive development, was a somewhat blinkered but optimistic enterprise. By focusing on those rationalist domains in which conceptual progress could be uncontroversially assessed across different cultures, it neglected or downplayed the centrality of other domains of belief, of which religion is an obvious example. Second, that neglect is not intellectually defensible. Just because there is no handy epistemic yardstick by which cognitive progress can be assessed, research is still feasible. Religious belief is as consequential for human life as any other domain of thought and its acquisition calls for serious study. Indeed, research on children's religious cognition is flourishing (Harris, 2021b). That said, we know a good deal more about the development of the Christian child growing up in the USA and Europe than, for example, the Muslim child growing up in Iran, the Buddhist child growing up in Thailand, or the (predominantly) secular child growing up in China. But I expect that to change in the coming decades.

Also not adequately addressed by either Piaget or Vygotsky is the fact that, as a species, human children are quite distinctive in the power of their cultural learning. To a greater extent than their primate cousins, they are biologically designed to turn to, and learn from, others when acquiring new skills (Hermann et al., 2007). Moreover, unlike their primate cousins, children can learn from what other people tell them (Harris, 2012). Indeed, as we saw in Chapter 3, they actively seek out such testimony by asking a lot of questions. But beyond their tendency to seek guidance and information from others, children are also biologically designed to be become members of their *local* culture—to construct ways of thinking and talking that are locally valid and acceptable. Moreover, as emphasized above, this type of transmission takes place even when those ways of thinking have little connection to objective reality or secular reward: the cross-generational transmission of beliefs in witchcraft, magic, miracles, and the afterlife exemplify this receptivity.

Importantly, children do not learn from just anyone. They are selective, favoring familiar informants and those who belong to their own culture, rather than informants or models belonging to an outgroup. Indeed, even young children are surprisingly good at spotting people whose claims and opinions are part of a consensus, and they prefer to learn from those endorsed individuals rather than from dissenters and deviants. As a result of these learning biases, ideas that are approved and received within the child's particular community have a selective advantage over more marginal ideas with respect to their perpetuation from one generation to the next. Children tend to internalize and endorse the presuppositions of the particular culture—or cultures—in which they are raised. In that respect, they are not naturally disposed to become citizens of the entire world, but of particular places and times.

In sum, children display an intimate intertwining of biological capacity and selective cultural learning. They are equipped to notice and conceptualize universals in both the physical and the human world. At the same time, it is advantageous for them to be gifted cultural apprentices, astutely deferring to the way that their own culture thinks and acts. Children's cultural receptivity and their ready incorporation of a set of cultural tools and beliefs is not something over and above their biological endowment or a magnifier of that endowment—it is a defining part of that endowment. The human species is biologically disposed to assimilate the practices and beliefs of the surrounding culture, and, for better or worse, it has flourished in increasing numbers as a result.

Independence and deference

In the course of the various chapters of this book, two different images of the child have intermittently come into view. We saw in Chapter 3 that, well before they go to school, children have their own intellectual agenda. They ask questions, often aimed at understanding why or how something has happened. If they fail to get a satisfactory answer from their conversation partner, they don't immediately give up. They pursue their enquiries, re-asking their original question, supply their own answer, or follow up with other questions. Admittedly, that cognitive agenda gets severely curtailed when children go to school. There, they will rarely have opportunities for a sustained dialogue with a teacher, guided by their own curiosity and puzzlement. Instead, it is the school board, the text-book, and the teacher that specify what children should interest themselves in. Still, the fount of question-asking seen in the preschool years attests to the fact that, in principle, children are independent scholars. Curiosity and puzzlement are not something that they need to be taught or rewarded for. They are autonomous dispositions, even if the standard school curriculum tends to overlook or stifle them (Engel, 2015).

As discussed in Chapter 8, children also display a considerable degree of autonomy in their moral reflection. They defend the continuing validity of certain basic moral principles—for example, not causing hurt or distress, not stealing or lying—even when invited to think about a world in which the moral authority of adults has been suspended. There are also some children who not only affirm these moral principles but also act on them when others do not. Despite growing up in meat-eating homes and living in a large and robust carnivorous culture, there are children who decide to become vegetarians, who stick with that decision for months and even years, and who articulate their reasons cogently in terms of animal suffering and well-being. Moreover, these children are surprisingly sensitive to the consequences that flow from an individual's assertion of a commitment to vegetarianism. Indeed, that same sensitivity is also shown by their meat-eating peers—somewhat surprisingly, they too recognize the way that an individual is bound by his or her chosen commitments, especially when those commitments have a moral component. By implication, even prior to adolescence, children have some appreciation of the fact that individuals can judge and act according to their own moral lights, and some children go right ahead and do just that.

Nevertheless, there is also plenty of evidence that children are prone to defer to those around them. First, although children's tenacious question-asking is, as just argued, an index of their cognitive autonomy, it is also an index of their ample willingness to seek information from other people and, more often than not, to trust the answers they are given. Admittedly, young children do sometimes point to flaws in the replies that they receive, or identify dubious implications, but their more typical response is trust in what they are told. Consider, for example, the study of children's thinking about the origin of species or, more precisely, the origin of dinosaurs, as discussed in Chapter 9. Margaret Evans (2000) found that children's views on evolution echoed those of the surrounding culture. So, although children growing up in a non-evangelical community did refer to the role of evolutionary processes, children growing up in an evangelical community almost never did so. Similarly, and in line with the theme of the previous section, children growing up in Madagascar believe in the ancestral afterlife, their Christian peers in the USA invoke Heaven, and their atheist peers in China are dubious about any form of afterlife. More generally, we know that children turn deferentially to other people for information about a vast range of information—the shape of the earth, the connections between mind and brain, and the existence of invisible germs and viruses (Harris & Koenig, 2006).

A plausible defense of children's deference across these various domains is that they rarely have other intellectual options. More specifically, they are in no position to do experiments on the origin of dinosaurs, the nature of the afterlife, the shape of the earth, linkages between mind and brain, or the existence of microscopic organisms. But children's deference sometimes goes further—faced with a consensus of other people who make a claim that goes against what they have observed for themselves, they will defer to that consensus. Also, given an opportunity to check out for themselves a claim that contradicts what they have just said, preschoolers rarely seize that opportunity, and indeed many older children also remain acquiescent. Told about miracles that defy known causal regularities, children raised in religious households take them to be true (Harris & Corriveau, 2019).

In summary, we end up with a contradictory picture—children are sometimes remarkably independent-minded and they even endorse and understand the notion of individual commitment in the moral domain. Yet, across a large range of intellectual matters, they defer to the testimony of other people. It is too early to see how best to resolve this tension, but two different interpretations seem feasible. One possibility is that children adopt different ways of thinking, depending on the particular domain under consideration. Perhaps they are more autonomous in the moral domain but more deferential in the factual domain. In support of that conclusion, there is evidence that children make an early start in distinguishing between the two domains. If they are invited to think about moral as compared to factual disagreements, they characterize them quite differently. In the case of moral disagreements, they judge disputants as right or wrong in light of principles to do with harm and fairness. In the case of factual disagreements, they judge disputants as right or wrong in light of relevant factual truths (Wainryb et al., 2004). So, we might speculate that in the moral domain, even before they begin formal schooling, children are confident about what moral principles to apply. They know, for example, that it's plain wrong to cause hurt and distress. By contrast, in the factual domain, children might have less confidence about the relevant facts. On this interpretation, children are prone to display what we might regard as an intellectual virtue in the domain of facts, namely humility and, sensing their own limited knowledge, turn to other people for guidance and accept what they are told. By contrast, in the moral domain, children might have conviction rather than humility—a conviction that can lead them to affirm and maintain their own judgment rather than consulting others for guidance.

But there is another possible explanation for children's differential stance toward moral and factual issues. Maybe they ultimately lack any deep-seated intuitions about the differences between two domains—they do not knowingly refer moral disputes to some internal moral compass and factual disputes to some external empirical adjudication. Rather, they pay close attention to the pattern of discussion surrounding particular issues and come to notice that moral and factual issues are talked about differently whether by older children or adults. More specifically, they notice that people are prone to express ignorance or uncertainty about a gamut of factual matters, sometimes acknowledging the need to seek further information. By contrast, they notice that adult people are more emphatic and confident, rarely voicing doubt or professing the need for expert guidance about most moral issues.

Such relatively subtle linguistic influences on young children's thinking might, at first, sound implausible: are they really such careful monitors of other people's comments and debates? In fact, there is emerging evidence that young children have surprisingly good antennae, especially when it is a question of gauging other people's uncertainty. For example, adults are prone to talk about many, ordinarily invisible, scientific phenomena—such as oxygen, germs, or vitamins—with greater certainty and fewer signs of doubt than ordinarily invisible religious or supernatural phenomena—such as the soul, God, or Heaven. In discussing such familiar scientific entities with their children, adults take their existence more or less for granted ("We need oxygen to breathe"), whereas in discussing religious entities, adults are prone to voice signs of doubt and uncertainty ("Some people think the soul is quite separate from the body"). Children soon pick up on these subtle linguistic cues, because they come to express more confidence in the existence of the scientific as compared to the religious entities (McLoughlin et al., 2021). An intriguing implication of these findings is that, by listening in on adult talk, children might arrive at more or less firm and settled views on some issues but less confident and more tractable views in others. Hence, children might display apparent autonomy on various moral issues because there is a relatively straightforward consensus and conviction about various basic moral truths—that it is plain wrong to cause hurt and distress, for example—but acknowledge more doubt, uncertainty, and deference in the domain of facts, whether about trivial practical matters, for example, whether a clean pair of socks is to be found in this drawer or that one, or more complicated issues, such as how bees make honey or fishes breathe underwater (Mills et al., 2001). In sum, by listening in on adult conversations, children might conclude that they need have few hesitations about what is right and wrong but should sometimes be ready to defer in the factual domain.

One recent social phenomenon offers a final striking example of the mix of autonomy and deference that young children display. In a series of pioneering studies, Gülgöz and her colleagues interviewed a large group of children ranging from 3 to 12 years of age who are identifying and living as a gender different from the one they were assigned on the basis of their biological characteristics at birth (Gülgöz et al., 2019). As important background to their findings, it is worth emphasizing that both children and adults typically think of gender in an "essentialist" fashion: they conceive of a person's gender as something inborn and stable, not as something that varies depending on a person's environment or that could readily change in the course of development. This stance is found among individuals living in a variety of countries. Indeed, as might be expected, both children and adults tend to be more essentialist in thinking about gender than in thinking about more obviously social categories such as religious affiliation, social class, or preferred sports team (Davoodi et al., 2020).

But the transgender children studied by Gülgöz et al. (2019) deviate from what might be expected on the basis of such essentialist thinking. They affirm that they belong to a different gender from the one that they were assigned at birth. Consistent with that affirmation—and supported by their parents—they adopt the clothing, hairstyle, and pronouns appropriate to that chosen gender. Note that the children included in these studies had not received any medical or hormonal intervention—although that may change as they get older.

A key question that we can ask about such children is how they came to affirm their new gender identity. Consider first the reasons why they might *not* do so. First, along with their cisgender peers—they may be prone to adopt an essentialist stance toward a person's natal gender including their own, i.e., to assume that whatever gender they were assigned at birth is an unalterable part of them—an essence that cannot be abandoned or changed. Such essentialist thinking is not likely to make it easy for them to contemplate and affirm a different gender identity. Second, they are likely to be raised with a wide-ranging set of social expectations about their preferences—with respect to clothing, toys, preferred activities, and comportment. Parents, siblings, peers, and family friends will often base those expectations on the child's natal gender rather than on the child's own preferences. In sum, whether children look "inward" at themselves—at their own bodies—or "outward" by attending to the routine expectations of those around them, it is unclear how they would ever come to affirm a gender different from the one they are assigned at birth.

The most plausible solution to this conundrum is to suppose that children have a powerful scam of independence. More specifically, no matter what signals they receive from their own bodies or from their social circle, it is feasible that children can and do monitor their own desires and feelings. Indeed, we saw in Chapters 5 and 7 that young children are capable of doing just that. Not only are they able to talk from the age of 2 about desires and feelings in general, they talk frequently about their own desires and feelings. Indeed, they sometimes distinguish explicitly between their own preferences and emotions and those of other people. Assuming that children are able to identify how they personally feel about various gendered activities, it is possible that some children discover, especially in the context of playing and interacting with their peers, that they feel more "themselves" when engaging in the activities associated with girls rather than boys, or vice versa. Based on this self-observation, they might increasingly gravitate to and feel comfortable with members of that other gender and eventually— provided they have support from their family—transition to that other gender, in terms of the key social indicators mentioned earlier: clothing, hairstyle, and preferred pronouns. In sum, the proposal is that young children have the ability to recognize their own gender orientation by taking due note of what they like and dislike. On this view, children may come to that recognition and engage in the associated behaviors even before they have made the transition in more public and recognizable terms.

How then do transgender children come to think about gender? In particular, do they hold onto the essentialist view espoused by the large majority of children, namely that gender is something that one is born with and that cannot be changed in the course of development? Alternatively, granted their own life experience, do they abandon a belief in the essentialist nature of gender and come to think of it as something more malleable, akin to membership of a religious group? One possibility is that children come to adopt both standpoints concurrently. They come to distinguish between the sex that they were assigned at birth and the gender that they ultimately identify with. That distinction is presumably difficult for the majority of children to make because these two aspects of their identity are so closely connected with each other. Transgender children, by contrast, learn that that connection is not inevitable—the gender they were assigned at birth does not correspond to the gender that they come to identify with. As a result, unlike cisgender children, transgender children are likely to claim that someone can change from being a boy to a girl or vice versa if they wish to. Indeed, the siblings of transgender children—who presumably get to observe changes—are similarly flexible (Gülgöz et al., 2021).

To review, there is a plethora of evidence that children's judgments and beliefs are often based on listening to and observing other people, especially in domains where children have difficulty in gathering any relevant evidence for themselves: for example, in the domains of history, science, and religion. At the same time, as almost all parents will concede, children can display "a mind of their own". They are aware of what puzzles them and ask a lot of questions in an effort to resolve those mysteries. They can make independent judgments about what is right and wrong and sometimes act on those independent judgments even when it means that their actions go against the habits and preferences of their family and the surrounding culture. Finally, they have an early awareness of their own desires and preferences—which they readily express in words from an early age. Arguably, that awareness of their own distinctive desires and preferences is so powerful that it can lead children to consider whether they want to remain identified with the gender that they were assigned at birth, and in some cases to affirm that they do not.

Consistency and inconsistency

At various junctures, developmental researchers are confronted by inconsistency. Children say something at one moment and the opposite a moment later. They say they should share but fail to do so when given the chance. They seem relatively naïve when assessed in one way but insightful when assessed in another.

What are we to make of such inconsistency? Is it something that disappears as children become older and wiser? Will researchers eventually discover some consistency underlying these surface contradictions? My guess is that neither of these possibilities is likely. Children do not outgrow inconsistency as they get older—indeed, inconsistency may increase with age as different conceptions jostle for priority. Nor does it seem feasible that researchers will eventually discover some deep shaft of coherence. Inconsistencies arise for different reasons, but they can often be seen as highlighting an important psychological characteristic of human beings: our mental lives are complicated, sometimes more so as we get older. Different soundings of our mental processes yield different and sometimes opposing conclusions. This is not simply because we are hypocritical or mendacious but because we can bring more than one psychological process to bear on the situations or dilemmas that we face. By way of illustration, it is helpful to look at two examples.

Psychological research has shown that adults are not coherent in their thinking about race. When explicitly asked about their attitudes toward different racial groups, White Americans profess no explicit preference for members of their ingroup—other White Americans—as compared to members of other groups, such as African Americans. The pattern is different, however, if their implicit rather than their explicit attitudes are measured by means of the Implicit Association Test (IAT). When invited to make quick decisions—for example, about whether a given photo is of a White person or a Black person or whether a given word (e.g., "flower" or "insect") has good or bad connotations—adults respond faster when the same key must be pressed for both White faces and good words than when the same key must be pressed for both Black faces and good words. Baldly stated, they find it easier to associate the positive with White faces than with Black faces. Effectively, there is a gap between the egalitarianism they profess explicitly and the bias they express implicitly via their reaction times.

Do young children display a similar gap between explicit and implicit attitudes? To find out, Baron and Banaji (2006) tested 6-year-olds, 10-year-olds, and adults from a mostly middle-class European community in the Boston area. Participants were asked about their explicit attitudes and their reaction times were measured via the IAT, suitably adapted for children as well as adults. The results were straightforward. All three age groups showed a bias on the IAT—and the strength of that bias remained stable across the three age groups. The 6-year-olds also showed an explicit bias—overtly expressing a preference for ingroup members—but to a greater extent than the 10-year-olds. So, here we have a case where inconsistency waxes rather than wanes with development. Young children express a similar bias both overtly and implicitly. As they get older, they learn, or at least profess, a more egalitarian stance, whereas their implicit bias remains potent throughout development and into adulthood. The gap between implicit and explicit attitudes emerges in the course of development but is absent in young children.

The finding that inconsistency increases with age can help us to figure out what is driving what. Three conclusions seem warranted. First, it appears that developmental changes in children's overt attitudes to outgroup members do not have any measurable impact on their implicit attitudes. If they did have such an impact, we would have expected to see an increase in implicit egalitarianism and not just an increase in overt egalitarianism. But we do not: implicit bias persists from childhood into adulthood despite changes in overt attitudes. Second, the dissociation between the explicit and the implicit points to the gloomy possibility that dialogue, overt reflection, and explicit affirmation—the focus of many workplace programs on diversity—may have benefits, but they are unlikely to remedy implicit bias. Third, the early appearance of implicit bias—and its persistence in the face of overtly professed egalitarianism—suggests that we should look for ways to forestall or attenuate its emergence in early childhood. To do that, however, we need to figure out why exactly young children are prone to an implicit ingroup bias from an early age.

It is too early to be sure but ongoing research strongly suggests that such a bias is not inevitable, because young children do not show it across the board. Admittedly, when young children from the majority group are assessed, whether in the USA, the UK, or Japan, they all show an implicit ingroup bias (Dunham et al., 2006; Rhodes & Baron, 2019; Rutland et al., 2005). Such stable results—across different countries—might appear to suggest that young children are naturally and inevitably biased against individuals belonging to an outgroup, but other research suggests that social forces are at work. When young Hispanic-American children are tested, they show no implicit bias when asked about outgroup members belonging to the White majority. By implication, bias against the outgroup does not stem from children's unthinking prejudice toward anyone who belongs to another group. It depends on the group. From a young age, children appear to pick up on where groups—and their members—stand in the larger social hierarchy (Dunham et al., 2007). In that case, interventions might reduce implicit bias if they could shift or offset children's assumptions about the social hierarchy and its divisions: for example, by presenting children with vivid examples of individuals who run counter to hierarchical assumptions (Gonzales et al., 2021) or by promoting children's ability to differentiate among individuals belonging to an outgroup (Qian et al., 2017, 2019). But it remains to be seen whether such psychological interventions in early childhood can have a stable and persistent impact into adolescence and adulthood, especially if the surrounding social hierarchy and its divisions remain unchanged.

In Chapter 10, I briefly referred to another telling example of inconsistency: our thinking about death. Children increasingly understand the biological nature of death—its irreversibility and the ensuing termination of bodily and mental processes. By the age of 10, and often earlier, most typically developing children have acquired this biological framework. However, alongside that framework, many children are introduced to another way of thinking about death—as a departure rather than a final state. In English, everyday talk about death frequently invokes the metaphor of life as a journey—a journey in which birth is an arrival and death is an exit, a departure, possibly for another form of life (Lakoff & Turner, 1989). So, after a bereavement, we might say that, "She is no longer with us" or that "He has left us." A destination is sometimes invoked: the deceased has "gone to a better place". Funereal rituals are viewed as a formal leave-taking, an opportunity to say "a final goodbye" to the "departed", but, in consequence, the bereaved are "left behind".

This extended metaphor of "death as departure" is not confined to English—it is found across disparate languages, including Polish, Spanish, Serbian, Turkish, and Mandarin. Nor is it confined to adults. When children are interviewed about a bereavement, they too call on the metaphor of departure: "I go to sleep fast so I won't think about his being gone" (a 7-year-old); "I don't want her to come back and be in such pain" (a 12-year-old) (Silverman et al., 1992). Amplifying that metaphor, children will, depending on the surrounding culture, learn about the final destination of the departed, whether it is Heaven or Hell or a place among the Ancestors.

Faced with these two conceptions of death—death as biological terminus and death as departure—how do children reply if they are invited to think about what happens when someone dies. Not surprisingly, as described in Chapter 10, they give inconsistent answers. If the death is presented to them within a biological framework, focusing, for example, on the illness leading up to the death and a doctor's explanation of what eventually happened, children are likely to claim that all living processes, and especially all bodily processes, have stopped. By contrast, if the death is presented to them within a religious framework, focusing on an explanation by a priest or on the ritual activity surrounding the death, children are likely to claim that some living process, particularly mental processes, continue even after death. Such inconsistency is not confined to children. Adults are also prone to shift, even within a single conversation, from one perspective to the other. Different ways of conceptualizing the same phenomenon seem to jockey for priority, depending on the context (Harris, 2018).

We should probably not despair. Emerson loftily dismissed consistency as the "hobgoblin of little minds, adored by little statesmen and philosophers and divines" (Emerson, 1949). He might take some comfort from psychological research. The hobgoblin of consistency is elusive and likely to remain so, whether we are talking about the minds of children or adults.

References

Adolph, K. E., Karasik, L. B. & Tamis-LeMonda, C. S. (2010). Using social information to guide action: Infants' locomotion over slippery slopes. *Neural Networks*, *23*, 1033–1042.

Ainsworth, M. D. S., Blehar, M. C., Waters, E. & Wall, S. (1978). *Patterns of attachment: A psychological study of the strange situation*. Oxford: Lawrence Erlbaum.

Ambady, N. & Rosenthal, R. (1992). Thin slices of expressive behavior as predictors of interpersonal consequences: A meta-analysis. *Psychological Bulletin*, *111*, 256–274.

Arend, R., Gove, F. L. & Sroufe, L. A (1979). Continuity of individual adaptation from infancy to kindergarten: A predictive study of ego-resiliency and curiosity in preschoolers. *Child Development*, *50*, 950–959.

Arsenio, W. F. & Kramer, R. (1992). Victimizers and emotions: Children's conceptions of the mixed emotional consequences of moral transgressions. *Child Development*, *63*, 915–927.

Asch, S. E. (1956). Studies of independence and conformity. A minority of one against a unanimous majority. *Psychological Monographs*, *70* (9, Whole no. 41), 1–70.

Astuti, R. & Harris, P. L. (2008). Understanding mortality and the life of the ancestors in Madagascar. *Cognitive Science*, *32*, 713–740.

Au, T.-K. (1986). Chinese and English counterfactuals: The Sapir-Whorf hypothesis revisited. *Cognition*, *15*, 155–187.

Avis, J. & Harris, P. L. (1991). Belief-desire reasoning among Baka children: Evidence for a universal conception of mind. *Child Development*, *62*, 460–467.

Bakermans-Kranenburg, M. J., van IJzendoorn, M. H. & Juffer, F. (2003). Less is more: Meta-analyses of sensitivity and attachment interventions in early childhood. *Psychological Bulletin*, *129*, 195–215.

Baldwin, D. (1991). Infants' contribution to the achievement of joint reference. *Child Development*, *62*, 875–890.

Baldwin, D. (1993). Early referential understanding: Infants' ability to recognize referential acts for what they are. *Developmental Psychology*, *29*, 832–843.

Baron, A. S. & Banaji, M. R. (2006). The development of implicit attitudes: Evidence of race evaluations from ages 6 and 10 and adulthood. *Psychological Science*, *17*, 53–58.

Baron-Cohen, S. (1991). Do people with autism understand what causes emotion? *Child Development*, *62*, 385–395.

Baron-Cohen, S., Leslie, A. M. & Frith, U. (1985). Does the autistic child have a "theory of mind"? *Cognition*, *21*, 7–46.

Baron-Cohen, S., Allen, J. & Gillberg, C. (1992). Can autism be detected at 18 months? The needle, the haystack, and the CHAT. *British Journal of Psychiatry*, *161*, 839–843.

Baron-Cohen, S., Baldwin, D. A. & Crowson, M. (1997a). Do children with autism use the speaker's direction of gaze strategy to crack the code of language? *Child Development*, *68*, 48–57.

Baron-Cohen, S., Jolliffe, T., Mortimore, C. & Robertson, M. (1997b). Another advanced test of theory of mind: evidence from very high functioning adults with autism or Asperger syndrome. *Journal of Child Psychology and Psychiatry*, *38*, 813–822.

Barratt, M. S., Negayama, K. & Minami, T. (1993). The social environment of early infancy in Japan and the United States. *Early Development and Parenting*, *2*, 51–64.

Barrett, J. L., Richert, R. A. & Driesenga, A. (2001). God's beliefs versus mother's: The development of non-human agent concepts. *Child Development*, *72*, 50–65.

Barrett, L. F., Mesquita, B. & Gendron, M. (2011). Context in emotion perception. *Current Directions in Psychological Science*, *20*, 286–290.

Bartsch, K. & Wellman, H. M. (1995). *Children talk about the mind*. New York: Oxford University Press.

Bechara, A., Damasio, A. R., Damasio, H. & Anderson, S. (1994). Insensitivity to future consequences following damage to prefrontal cortex. *Cognition*, *50*, 7–12.

Bechara, A., Damasio, H., Tranel, D. & Damasio, A. R. (1997). Deciding advantageously before knowing the advantageous strategy *Science*, *275*, 1293–1294.

Bettelheim, B. (1991). *The uses of enchantment: The meaning and importance of fairy tales*. London: Penguin. (Original work published 1975.)

Bloom, A. H. (1981). *The linguistic shaping of thought: A study in the impact of language on thinking in China and the West*. Hillsdale, NJ: Erlbaum Associates.

Boller, K., Rovee-Collier, C., Borovsky, D., O'Connor, J. & Shyi, G. (1990). Developmental changes in time-dependent nature of memory retrieval. *Developmental Psychology*, *26*, 770–779.

Bond, R. & Smith, P. B. (1996). Culture and conformity: A meta-analysis of studies using Asch's (1952b, 1956) line judgment task. *Psychological Bulletin*, *119*, 111–137.

Borke, H. (1971). Interpersonal perception of young children: Egocentrism or empathy? *Developmental Psychology*, *5*, 263–269.

Bornstein, M. H., Tal, J., Rahn, C., Galperín, C. Z., Pêcheux, M.-G., Lamour, M., Toda, S., Azuma, H., Ogino, M. & Tamis-LeMonda, C. S. (1992a). Functional analysis of the contents of maternal speech to infants of 5 and 13 months in four cultures: Argentina, France, Japan, and the United States. *Developmental Psychology*, *28*, 593–603.

Bornstein, M. H., Tamis-LeMonda, C., Tal, J., Ludemann, P., Toda, S., Rahn, C. W., Pêcheux, M.-G., Azuma, H. & Vardi, D. (1992b). Maternal responsiveness to infants in three societies: The US, France and Japan. *Child Development*, *63*, 808–921.

Boroditsky, L. (2001). Does language shape thought? Mandarin and English speakers' conceptions of time. *Cognitive Psychology*, *43*, 1–22.

Bowlby, J. (1953). *Childcare and the growth of love*. Baltimore, MD: Pelican Books.

Bowlby, J. (1969). *Attachment and loss: Volume I. Attachment*. London: Hogarth Press.

Bowlby, J. (1973). *Attachment and loss: Volume II. Separation*. London: Hogarth Press.

Bowlby, J. (1980). *Attachment and loss: Volume III. Loss*. London: Hogarth Press.

Boyer, P. (2002). *Religion explained*. New York: Basic Books.

Bradmetz, J. & Schneider, R. (1999). Is Little Red Riding Hood afraid of her grandmother? Cognitive vs. emotional response to a false belief. *British Journal of Developmental Psychology*, *17*, 501–514.

Brown, J. R. & Dunn, J. (1996). Continuities in emotion understanding from three to six years. *Child Development*, *67*, 789–802.

Brown, P. & Gaskins, S. (2014). Language acquisition and language socialization. In N. J. Enfield, P. Kockelman & J. Sidnell (Eds), *Cambridge handbook of linguistic anthropology* (pp. 187–226). Cambridge: Cambridge University Press.

Brown, R. (1973). *A first language: The early stages*. Cambridge, MA: Harvard University Press.

Brown, R. & Lenneberg, E. (1954). A study in language and cognition. *Journal of Abnormal and Social Psychology*, *49*, 454–462.

Brown, S. L., Nesse, R. M., House, J. S. & Utz, R. L. (2004). Religion and emotional compensation: Results from a prospective study of widowhood. *Journal of Personality and Social Psychology*, *30*, 1165–1174.

Cantril, H., Gaudet, H. & Herzog, H. (1940). *The invasion from Mars: A study in the psychology of panic with the complete script of the famous Orson Welles broadcast*. Princeton, NJ: Princeton University Press.

Carey, S. (1988). Lexical development—the Rockefeller years. In W. Hirst (Ed.), *The making of cognitive science: Essays in honor of George A. Miller*, Chapter 24. Cambridge: Cambridge University Press.

Casillas, M., Brown, P. & Levinson, S. C. (2020). Early language experience in a Tseltal Mayan village. *Child Development*, *91*, 1819–1835.

Ceci, S. J., Huffman, M. L. C, Smith, E. & Loftus, E. W. (1994). Repeatedly thinking about non-events: source misattributions among preschoolers. *Consciousness and Cognition*, *3*, 388–407.

Chen, D. (2009). *Culture, parent–child conversations and children's understanding of emotion*. Doctoral dissertation, Harvard Graduate School of Education.

Chen, D. & Harris, P. L. (2007). *How are modes of attention transmitted from generation to generation? Comparing American and Chinese children*. Unpublished paper, Harvard Graduate School of Education.

Choi, I., Nisbett, R. E. & Norenzayan, A. (1999). Causal attribution across cultures: Variation and universality. *Psychological Bulletin*, *125*, 47–63.

Chouinard, M. (2007). Children's questions: A mechanism for cognitive development. *Monographs of the Society for Research in Child Development*, *72* (1), vii–ix, 1–112; discussion 113–126.

Clarke, A. B. & Clarke, A. D. B. (1976). *Early experience: Myth and evidence*. London: Open Books.

Clément, F., Koenig, M. & Harris, P. L. (2004). The ontogenesis of trust in testimony. *Mind and Language, 19*, 360–379.

Coady, C. A. J. (1992). *Testimony: A philosophical study*. Oxford: Oxford University Press.

Colby, A., Kohlberg, L., Gibbs, J. & Lieberman, M. (1983). A longitudinal study of moral judgment. *Monographs of the Society for Research in Child Development, 48*, 1–124.

Corriveau, K. H. & Harris, P. L. (2009a). Choosing your informant: Weighing familiarity and recent accuracy. *Developmental Science, 12*, 426–437.

Corriveau, K. H. & Harris, P. L. (2009b). Preschoolers continue to trust a more accurate informant 1 week after exposure to accuracy information. *Developmental Science, 12*, 188–193.

Corriveau, K. H. & Harris, P. L. (2010). Preschoolers (sometimes) defer to the majority in making simple perceptual judgments. *Developmental Psychology, 46*, 437–445.

Corriveau, K. H., Harris, P. L., Meins, E., Fernyhough, C. Arnott, B., Elliott, L., Liddle, B., Hearn, S., Vittorini, L. & de Rosnay, M. (2009a). Young children's trust in their mother's claims: Longitudinal links with attachment security in infancy. *Child Development, 80*, 750–761.

Corriveau, K. H., Fusaro, M. & Harris, P. L. (2009b). Going with the flow: Preschoolers prefer non-dissenters as informants. *Psychological Science, 20*, 372–377.

Corriveau, K. H., Pickard, K. & Harris, P. L. (2011). Preschoolers trust particular informants when learning new names and new morphological forms. *British Journal of Developmental Psychology, 29*, 46–63.

Corriveau, K. H., Kim, E., Song, G. & Harris, P. L. (2013). Young children's deference to a consensus varies by culture and judgment setting. *Journal of Cognition and Culture, 13*, 367–381.

Corriveau, K. H., Chen, E. E. & Harris, P. L. (2015). Judgments about fact and fiction by children from religious and non-religious backgrounds. *Cognitive Science, 39*, 353–382.

Crystal, D. (2008). *Think on my words: Exploring Shakespeare's language*. Cambridge: Cambridge University Press.

Cui, Y. K. (2021). *Children's understanding of reality and possibility and its cultural transmission mechanisms*. PhD dissertation, Wheelock College of Human Development and Education, Boston University.

Damasio, A. R. (1994). *Descartes' error: Emotion, reason and the human brain*. New York: G.P. Putnam's Sons.

Darwin, C. (1877). A biographical sketch of an infant. *Mind, 2*, 285–294.

Darwin, C. (1998). *The expression of the emotions in man and animals*, 3rd edition. London: Harper Collins. (Original work published 1872.)

Davidson, P., Turiel, E. & Black, A. (1983). The effects of stimulus familiarity on the use of criteria and justifications in children's social reasoning. *British Journal of Developmental Psychology, 1,* 49–65.

Davoodi, T., Soley, G., Harris, P. L. & Blake, P. R. (2020). Essentialization of social categories across development in two cultures. *Child Development, 91,* 289–306.

Davoodi, T., Jamshidi-Sianaki, M., Payir, A., Cui, Y. K., Clegg, J., McLoughlin, N., Harris, P. L. & Corriveau, K. H. (2022). Miraculous, magical, or mundane? The development of beliefs about stories with divine, magical, or realistic causation. *Memory and Cognition* (accepted for publication; doi: 10.31219/osf.io/ev2wu).

Dawkins, R. (2006). *The God delusion.* New York: Houghton Mifflin.

De Rosnay, M., Pons, F., Harris, P. L. & Morrell, J. M. B. (2004). A lag between understanding false belief and emotion attribution in young children: relationships with linguistic ability and mothers' mental state language. *British Journal of Developmental Psychology, 22,* 197–218.

De Wolff, M. & van IJzendoorn, M. H. (1997). Sensitivity and attachment: A meta-analysis on parental antecedents of infant attachment. *Child Development, 68,* 571–591.

Dehaene, S., Izard, V., Spelke, E. & Pica, P. (2008). Log or linear? Distinct intuitions of the number scale in Western and Amazonian Indigene culture. *Science, 320,* 1217–1220.

Dunham, Y., Baron, A. S. & Banaji, M. (2006). From American city to Japanese village: a cross-cultural investigation of implicit race attitudes. *Child Development, 77,* 1268–1281.

Dunham, Y., Baron, A. S. & Banaji, M. (2007). Children and social groups: A developmental analysis of implicit consistency in Hispanic Americans. *Self and Identity, 6,* 238–255.

Dunn, J., Brown, J., Slomkowski, C., Tesla, C. & Youngblade, L. (1991). Young children's understanding of other people's feelings and beliefs: Individual differences and their antecedents. *Child Development, 62,* 1352–1366.

Eacott, M. & Crawley, R. A. (1998). The offset of childhood amnesia for events that occurred before age 3. *Journal of Experimental Psychology: General, 127,* 22–33.

Ekman, P. (1973). Cross-cultural studies of facial expression. In P. Ekman (Ed.), *Darwin and facial expression* (pp. 169–222). New York: Academic Press.

Elfenbein, H. A. & Ambady, N. (2002). On the universality and cultural specificity of emotion recognition: a meta-analysis. *Psychological Bulletin, 128,* 203—235.

Emerson, R. W. (1949). *Self-reliance.* Mount Vernon, NY: Peter Pauper Press. (Originally published 1841.)

Engel, S. (1986). *Learning to reminisce: A developmental study of how young children talk about the past.* Unpublished doctoral dissertation, City University of New York.

Engel, S. (2015). *The hungry mind: The origins of curiosity in childhood.* Cambridge, MA: Harvard University Press.

Evans, E. M. (2000). Beyond Scopes: Why Creationism is here to stay. In K. Rosengren, C. N. Johnson & P. L. Harris (Eds), *Imagining the impossible: The* development of magical scientific and religious thinking in contemporary society (pp. 305–333). Cambridge: Cambridge University Press.

Fabes, R. A., Eisenberg, N., Nyman, M. & Michaelieu, Q. (1991). Young children's appraisals of others' spontaneous emotional reactions. *Developmental Psychology, 27*, 858–866.

Fenson, L., Dale, P. Resnick, J. S., Bates, E., Thal, D. J. & Pethick, S. J. (1994). Variability in early communicative development. *Monographs for the Society for Research in Child Development, 58* (5, Serial No. 242), 1–173; discussion 174–185.

Fernald, A., Marchman, V. A. & Weisleder, A. (2013). SES differences in language processes skill and vocabulary are evident at 18 months. *Developmental Science, 16*, 234–248.

Fonagy, P., Steele, H. & Steele, M. (1991). Maternal representations of attachment during pregnancy predict the organization of infant–mother attachment at one year of age. *Child Development, 62*, 891–905.

Fraley, R. C. & Shaver, P. R. (2000). Adult romantic attachment: Theoretical developments, emerging controversies, and unanswered questions. *Review of General Psychology, 4*, 132–154.

Frazier, B. N., Gelman, S. A. & Wellman, H. M. (2009). Preschoolers' search for explanatory information within adult–child conversation. *Child Development, 80*, 1592–1611.

Freud, S. (1973). *Introductory lectures on psychoanalysis.* Harmondsworth: Penguin.

Fusaro, M. & Harris, P. L. (2008). Children assess informant reliability using bystanders' non-verbal cues. *Developmental Science, 11*, 781–787.

Galindo, J. H. & Harris, P. L. (2017). Mother knows best? How children weigh their first-hand memories against their mothers' reports. *Cognitive Development, 44*, 69–84.

Garner, P. W., Jones, D. C., Gaddy, G. & Rennie, K. M. (1997). Low-income mothers' conversations about emotions and their children's emotional competence. *Social Development, 6*, 37–52.

Gaskins, S. (2013). Pretend play as culturally constructed activity. In M. Taylor (Ed.), *The Oxford handbook of the development of the imagination* (pp. 224–247). New York: Oxford University Press.

Giménez-Dasí, M., Guerrero, S. & Harris, P. L. (2005). Intimations of immortality and omniscience in early childhood. *European Journal of Developmental Psychology, 2*, 285–297.

Gladwell, M. (2005). *Blink.* New York: Little Brown and Co.

Golding, W. (1954). *Lord of the flies.* London: Faber and Faber.

Golinkoff, R. M., Hoff, E., Rowe, M. L., Tamis-LeMonda, C. S. & Hirsh-Pasek, K. (2019). Language matters: Denying the existence of the 30-million-word gap has serious consequences. *Child Development, 90*, 985–982.

Gonzales, A. M., Steele, J. R., Chan, E. F., Lim, S. A. & Baron, A. S. (2021). Developmental differences in the malleability of implicit racial bias following exposure to counterstereotypical exemplars. *Developmental Psychology, 57*, 102–113.

Gopnik, A. & Astington, J. W. (1988). Children's understanding of representational change in its relation to the understanding of false belief and the appearance-reality distinction. *Child Development*, *59*, 26–37.

Gordon, P. (2004). Numerical cognition without words: Evidence from Amazonia. *Science*, *306*, 496–499.

Goy, C. & Harris, P. L. (1990). *The status of children's imaginary companions*. Unpublished manuscript, Department of Experimental Psychology, University of Oxford.

Granqvist, P. & Kirkpatrick, L. A. (2016). Attachment and religious representations and behavior. In J. Cassidy & P. R. Shaver (Eds), *Handbook of attachment: Theory, research, and clinical applications*, 3rd edition, pp. 906–933. New York: Guilford Press.

Granqvist, P., Sroufe, L. A., Dozier, M., Hesse, M. & Steele, M. (2017). Disorganized attachment in infancy: a review of the phenomenon and its implications for clinicians and policy makers. *Attachment and Human Development*, *19*, 534–558.

Granqvist, P., Mikulincer, M. & Shaver, P. R. (2020). An attachment theory perspective on religion and spirituality. In K. E. Vail III & C. Routledge (Eds), *The science of religion, spirituality, and existentialism* (pp. 175–186). London: Academic Press.

Greene, J. Sommerville, R. B., Nystrom, L. E., Darley, J. M. & Cohen, J. D. (2001). An fMRI investigation of emotional engagement in moral judgment. *Science*, *293*, 2105–2107.

Gülgöz, S., Glazier, J., Glazier, J. J., Enright, E. A., Alonso, D. J., Durwood, L. J., Fast, A. A., Lowe, R., Ji, C., Heer, J., Martin, C. L. & Olson, K. R. (2019). Similarity in transgender and cisgender children's gender development. *Proceedings of the National Academy of Sciences of the United States of America*, *116*, 24480–24485.

Gülgöz, S., Alonso, D. J., Olson, K. R. & Gelman, S. A. (2021). Transgender and cisgender children's essentialist beliefs about sex and gender identity. *Developmental Science*, *24* (6), e13115.

Gutiérrez, I, Menendez, D., Jiang, M. J., Hernandez, I. G., Miller, P. & Rosengren, K. S. (2020). Embracing death: Mexican parent and child perspectives on death. *Child Development*, *91*, e491–e511.

Haidt, J. (2001). The emotional dog and its rational tail: A social intuitionist approach to moral judgment. *Psychological Review*, *108*, 814–834.

Hamlin, J. K. (2013). Failed attempts to help and harm. Intention versus outcome in preverbal infants' social evaluations. *Cognition*, *128*, 451–474.

Hamlin, J. K., Wynn, K. & Bloom, P. (2007). Social evaluation in preverbal infants. *Nature*, *450* (7169), 557–559.

Happé, F. G. E. (1993). Communicative competence and theory of mind in autism: A test of relevance theory. *Cognition*, *48*, 101–119.

Happé, F. G. E. (1994). An advanced test of theory of mind: Understanding of story characters' thoughts and feelings by able autistic, mentally handicapped and normal children and adults. *Journal of Autism and Developmental Disorders*, *24*, 129–154.

Happé, F. G. E. (1995). The role of age and verbal ability in the theory-of-mind task performance of subjects with autism. *Child Development, 66*, 843–855.

Harlow, H. (1958). The nature of love. *American Psychologist, 13*, 573–685.

Harris, P. L. (1983). Children's understanding of the link between situation and emotion. *Journal of Experimental Child Psychology, 36*, 490–509.

Harris, P. L. (1989). *Children and emotion: The development of psychological understanding*. Oxford: Blackwell.

Harris, P. L. (1996). Desires, beliefs and language. In P. Carruthers & P.K. Smith (Eds), *Theories of theories of mind* (pp. 200–220). Cambridge: Cambridge University Press.

Harris, P. L. (1997). Piaget in Paris: From 'autism' to logic. *Human Development, 40*, 109–123.

Harris, P. L. (2000). *The work of the imagination*. Oxford: Blackwell.

Harris, P. L. (2005). Conversation, pretence, and theory of mind. In J. W. Astington and J. Baird (Eds). *Why language matters for theory of mind* (pp. 70–83). New York: Oxford University Press.

Harris, P. L. (2009). Piaget on causality: The Whig interpretation of cognitive development. *British Journal of Psychology, 100*, 229–232.

Harris, P. L. (2012). *Trusting what you're told: How children learn from others*. Cambridge, MA: Belknap Press/Harvard University Press.

Harris, P. L. (2018). Children's understanding of death: From biology to religion. *Philosophical Transactions of the Royal Society B, 373*: 20170266.

Harris, P. L. (2021a). Early constraints on the imagination: The realism of young children. *Child Development, 92*, 466–483.

Harris, P. L. (2021b). Omniscience, preexistence, doubt and misdeeds. *Journal of Cognition and Development, 22*, 418–425.

Harris, P. L. & Cheng, L. (2022). Evidence for similar conceptul progress across cultures in children's understanding of emotion. *International Journal of Behavioral Development*, 1–13.

Harris, P. L. & Corriveau, K. H. (2013). Respectful deference: Conformity revisited. In M. R. Banaji & S. A. Gelman (Eds), *Navigating the social world: What infants, children, and other species can teach us*, Chapter 4.6. New York: Oxford University Press.

Harris, P. L. & Corriveau, K. H. (2019). Some, but not all, children believe in miracles. *Journal for the Cognitive Science of Religion, 5*, 21–36.

Harris, P. L. & Corriveau, K. H. (2020). Beliefs of children and adults in religious and scientific phenomena. *Current Opinion in Psychology, 40*, 20–23.

Harris, P. L. & Giménez, M. (2005). Children's acceptance of conflicting testimony: The case of death. *Journal of Cognition and Culture, 5*, 143–164.

Harris, P. L. & Jalloul, M. (2013). Running on empty: Observing causal relationships of play and development. *American Journal of Play, 6*, 29–38.

Harris, P. L. & Kavanaugh, R. D. (1993). Young children's understanding of pretense. *Monographs of the Society for Research in Child Development, 58* (231), v–92.

Harris, P. L. & Koenig, M. (2006). Trust in testimony: How children learn about science and religion. *Child Development, 77*, 505–524.

Harris, P. L. & Núñez, M. (1996). Children's understanding of permission rules. *Child Development, 67,* 1572–1591.

Harris, P. L., Brown, E., Marriott, C., Whittall, S. & Harmer, S. (1991). Monsters, ghosts and witches: testing the limits of the fantasy–reality distinction. *British Journal of Developmental Psychology, 9,* 105–123.

Harris, P. L., German, T. & Mills, P. (1996). Children's use of counterfactual thinking in causal reasoning. *Cognition, 61,* 233–259.

Harris, P. L., de Rosnay, M. & Pons, F. (2005). Language and children's understanding of mental states. *Current Directions in Psychological Science, 14,* 69–73.

Harris, P. L., Pasquini, E. S., Duke, S., Asscher, J. J. & Pons, F. (2006). Germs and angels: The role of testimony in young children's ontology. *Developmental Science, 9,* 76–96.

Harris, P. L., de Rosnay, M. & Ronfard, S. (2014). The mysterious emotional life of Little Red Riding Hood. In K. H. Lagattuta (Ed.), *Children and emotion. New insights into developmental affective sciences* (pp. 106–118). Basel: Karger. Contributions to Human Development, *26.*

Harris, P. L., de Rosnay, M. & Pons, F. (2016). Understanding emotion. In L. Feldman Barrett, M. Lewis & J. Haviland-Jones (Eds), *Handbook of emotions,* 4th edition, pp. 293–306. New York: Guilford Press.

Harter, S. (1983). Children's understanding of multiple emotions: a cognitive-developmental approach. In W. F. Overton (Ed.), *The relationship between social and cognitive development,* Chapter 6. Hillsdale, NJ: Lawrence Erlbaum.

Harter, S. & Buddin, B. (1987). Children's understanding of the simultaneity of two emotions: A five-stage developmental acquisition sequence. *Developmental Psychology, 23,* 388–399.

Hartshorne, H., May, M. A. & Shuttleworth, F. K. (1930). *Studies in the organization of character.* Oxford: Macmillan.

Haslam, S. A., Reicher, S. D. & Birney, M. E. (2016). Questioning authority: new perspectives on Milgram's 'obedience' research and its implications for intergroup relations. *Current Opinion in Psychology, 11,* 6–9.

Hayiou-Thomas, M., Dale, P. S. & Plomin, R. (2012). The etiology of variation in language skills changes with development: a longitudinal twin study of language from 2 to 12 years. *Developmental Science, 15,* 233–249.

Hazan, C. & Shaver, P. (1987). Romantic love conceptualized as an attachment process. *Journal of Personality and Social Psychology, 52,* 511–524.

Heider, E. R. (1972). Universals in color naming and memory. *Journal of Experimental Psychology, 93,* 10–20.

Henrich, J. (2020). *The WEIRDest people in the world: How the West became psychologically peculiar and particularly prosperous.* New York: Farrar, Strauss and Giroux.

Henrich, J., Heine, S. & Norenzayan, A. (2010). The weirdest people in the world? *Behavioral and Brain Sciences, 33,* 61–83.

Hermann, E., Call, J., Hernández-Lloreda, M. V., Hare, B. & Tomasello, M. (2007). Humans have evolved specialized skills of social cognition: The cultural intelligence hypothesis. *Science, 317,* 1360–1366.

Hess, R. D., Kashiwagi, K. & Azuma, H. (1980). Maternal expectations for mastery of developmental tasks in Japan and the United States. *International Journal of Psychology, 15,* 259–271.

Hirsh-Pasek, K., Adamson, L., Bakeman, R., Owen, M. T., Golinkoff, R. M., Pace, A., Yust, P. K. S. & Suma, K. (2015). The contribution of early communication quality to low-income children's language success. *Psychological Science, 26,* 1071–1083.

Hofstede, G. (1991). *Cultures and organisations: Software of the mind.* London: McGraw-Hill

Huang, I. (1930). Children's explanations of strange phenomena. *Psychologische Forschung, 14,* 63–183.

Huang, I. (1943). Children's conception of physical causality: A critical summary. *Journal of Genetic Psychology, 63,* 71–121.

Hume, D. (1902). *An enquiry concerning human understanding* (L. A. Selby Bigge, Ed.). Oxford: Clarendon Press. (Original work published 1748.)

Hussar, K. M. & Harris, P. L. (2010). Children who choose not to eat meat: A demonstration of early moral decision-making. *Social Development, 19,* 627–641.

Huttenlocher, J., Haight, W., Bryk, A., Seltzer, M. & Lyons, M. (1991). Early vocabulary growth: Relation to language input and gender. *Developmental Psychology, 27,* 236–248.

Huttenlocher, J., Vasilyeva, M., Waterfall, H.R., Vevea, J. L. & Hedges, L. V. (2007). The varieties of speech to young children. *Developmental Psychology, 43,* 1062–1083.

Isaacs, S. (1930). *Intellectual growth in young children.* New York: Harcourt, Brace and Company.

Johnson, C. N. & Harris, P. L. (1994). Magic: special but not excluded. *British Journal of Developmental Psychology, 12,* 35–51.

Jones, E. E. & Harris, V. A. (1967). The attribution of attitudes. *Journal of Experimental Social Psychology, 3,* 1–24.

Kagan, J. (1995). On attachment. *Harvard Review of Psychiatry, 3,* 104–106.

Kanner, L. (1943). Autistic disturbances of affective contact. *Nervous Child, 2,* 217–250.

Katz, N., Baker, E. & Macnamara, J. (1974). What's in a name? A study of how children learn common and proper names. *Child Development, 45,* 469–473.

Kavanaugh, R. D. & Harris, P. L. (1994). Imagining the outcome of pretend transformations: Assessing the competence of normal and autistic children. *Developmental Psychology, 30,* 847–854.

Keller, H. (2018). Universality claim of attachment theory: Children's socioemotional development across cultures. *Proceedings of the National Academy of Sciences of the United States of America, 115* (45), 11414–11419.

Keller, H., Bard, K., Morelli, G., Chaudhary, N., Vicedo, M., Rosabal-Coto, M., Scheidecker, G., Murray, M. & Gottlieb, A. (2018). The myth of universal sensitive responsiveness: Comment on Mesman et al. (2017). *Child Development, 89*, 1921–1928.

Keller, M., Lourenço, O., Malti, T. & Saalbach, H. (2003). The multifaceted phenomenon of 'happy victimizers': A cross-cultural comparison of moral emotions. *British Journal of Developmental Psychology, 21*, 1–18.

Kellman, P. & Spelke, E. (1983). Perception of partly occluded objects in infancy. *Cognitive Psychology, 15*, 483–524.

Kim, H. S. (2002). We talk, therefore we think? A cultural analysis of the effect of talking on thinking. *Journal of Personality and Social Psychology, 83*, 828–842.

Klin, A., Jones, W., Schultz, R., Volkmar, F. & Cohen, D. (2002). Visual fixation patterns during viewing of naturalistic social situations as predictors of social competence in individuals with autism. *Archives of General Psychiatry, 9*, 809–816.

Koenig, M. & Harris, P. L. (2005). Preschoolers mistrust ignorant and inaccurate speakers. *Child Development, 76*, 1261–1277.

Koenig, M., Clément, F. & Harris, P. L. (2004). Trust in testimony: Children's use of true and false statements. *Psychological Science, 10*, 694–698.

Kohlberg, L. (1969). Stage and sequence. In D. A. Goslin (Ed.), *Handbook of socialization theory and research* (pp. 347–480). Chicago: Rand McNally.

Koriat, A., Melkman, R., Averill, J. R. & Lazarus, R. S. (1972). The self-control of emotional reactions to a stressful film. *Journal of Personality, 40*, 601–619.

Kühnen, U. & van Egmond, M. (2018). Learning: A cultural construct. In. J. Proust & M. Fortier (Eds), *Metacognitive diversity: An interdisciplinary approach* (pp. 245–264). Oxford: Oxford University Press.

Kulke, L., von Duhn, B., Schneider, D. & Rakoczy, H. (2018). Is implicit theory of mind a real and robust phenomenon? Results from a systematic replication study. *Psychological Science, 29*, 888–900.

Kuwabara, M. & Smith, L. B. (2012). Cross-cultural differences in cognitive development: Attention to relations and objects. *Journal of Experimental Child Psychology, 113*, 20–35.

Lagattuta, K. (2005). When you shouldn't do what you want to do: Young children's understanding of desires, rules, and emotions. *Child Development, 76*, 713–733.

Laible, D. (2004). Mother–child discourse surrounding a child's past behavior at 30-months: Links to emotional understanding and early conscience development at 36-months. *Merrill Palmer Quarterly, 50*, 159–189.

Lakoff, G. & Turner, M. (1989). *More than cool reason: a field guide to poetic metaphor*. Chicago: Chicago University Press.

Lang, P. J., Melamed, B. G. & Hart, J. D. (1970). A psychophysiological analysis of fear modification using an automated desensitization procedure. *Journal of Abnormal Psychology, 76*, 220–234.

Lang, P. J., Levin, D. N., Miller, G. A. & Kozak, M. J. (1983). Fear behavior, fear imagery, and the psychophysiology of emotion: The problem of affective response integration. *Journal of Abnormal Psychology, 92*, 276–306.

Latané, B. & Darley, J. (1970). *The unresponsive bystander: Why doesn't he help?* New York: Appleton-Century Crofts.

Lionetti, F., Pastore, M. & Barone, L. (2015). Attachment in institutionalized children: A review and meta-analysis. *Child Abuse and Neglect*, *42*, 135–145.

Loftus, E. F. (1993). The reality of repressed memories. *American Psychologist*, *48*, 518–537.

Luria, A. R. & Vygotsky, L. S. (1992). *Ape, primitive man and behavior: Essays in the history of behavior*. Orlando: Paul M. Deutsch Press.

Main, M. & Solomon, J. (1990). Procedures for identifying infants as disorganized/disoriented during the Ainsworth Strange Situation. In M. T. Greenberg, D. Cicchetti & E. M. Cummings (Eds), *Attachment in the preschool years: Theory, research, and intervention* (pp. 121–160). Chicago: University of Chicago Press.

Main, M., Kaplan, N. & Cassidy, J. (1985). Security in infancy, childhood, and adulthood: A move to the level of representation. *Monographs of the Society for Research in Child Development*, *50*, 66–104.

Markman, E. M. (1990). Constraints children place on word meanings. *Cognitive Science*, *14*, 57–77.

Markson, L. & Bloom, P. (1997). Evidence against a dedicated system for word learning in children. *Nature*, *385*, 813–815.

Masuda, T. (2017). Culture and attention: Recent empirical findings and new directions in cultural psychology. *Social and Personality Psychology Compass*, *11*, e12363.

Masuda, T. & Nisbett, R. E. (2006). Culture and change blindness. *Cognitive Science*, *30*, 381–399.

McLoughlin, N., Jacob, C., Samrow, P. & Corriveau, K. H. (2021). Beliefs about unobservable scientific and religious entities are transmitted via subtle linguistic cues in parental testimony. *Journal of Cognition and Development*, *22*, 379–397.

Mead, M. (1932). An investigation of the thought of primitive children, with special reference to animism. *Journal of the Royal Anthropological Institute*, *62*, 173–190.

Meehan, C. L. & Hawkes, S. (2013). Cooperative breeding and attachment among the Aka foragers. In N. Quinn & J. M. Mageo (Eds), *Attachment reconsidered: Cultural perspectives on a Western theory* (pp. 85–113). New York: Palgrave Macmillan.

Meerum Terwogt, M., Schene, J. & Harris, P. L. (1986). Self-control of emotional reactions by young children. *Journal of Child Psychology and Psychiatry*, *27*, 357–366.

Meins, E., Fernyhough, C., Fradley, E. & Tuckey, M. (2001). Rethinking maternal sensitivity: Mothers' comments on infants' mental processes predict security of attachment at 12 months. *Journal of Child Psychology and Psychiatry*, *42*, 637–648.

Meltzoff, A. N. (1988). Infant imitation and memory: Nine-month-olds in immediate and deferred tests. *Child Development*, *59*, 1221–1229.

Mesman, J., Van IJzendoorn, M. H. & Sagi-Schwartz, A. (2016). Cross-cultural patterns of attachment: Universal and contextual dimensions. In J. Cassidy &

P. R. Shaver (Eds), *Handbook of attachment: Theory, research, and clinical applications*, 3rd edition, Chapter 37. New York: Guilford Press.

Mesman, J, Mintner, T., Angnged, A., Cissé, I. A. H., Salali, G. D. & Migliani, A. B. (2018). Universality without uniformity: A culturally inclusive approach to sensitive responsiveness in infant caregiving. *Child Development, 89*, 837–850.

Milgram, S. (1963). Behavioral study of obedience. *Journal of Abnormal and Social Psychology, 67*, 371–378.

Milgram, S. (1974). *Obedience to authority: An experimental view*. New York: Harper & Row.

Milligan, K., Astington, J. W. & Dack, L. A. (2007). Language and theory of mind: Meta-analysis of the relation between language ability and false-belief understanding. *Child Development, 78*, 622–646.

Mills, C. M., Danovitch, J. H., Mugambi, V. N., Sands K. R. & Fox, C. P. (2021). "Why do dogs pant?": Characteristics of parental explanations about science predict children's knowledge. *Child Development* (online, doi.org/10.1111/cdev.13681).

Mitchell, P., Teucher, U., Kikuno, H. & Bennett, M. (2010). Cultural variations in developing a sense of knowing your own mind: A comparison between British and Japanese children. *International Journal of Behavioral Development, 34*, 248–258.

Morelli, G., Bard, K., Chaudhary, N., Gottlieb, A., Keller, H., Murray, M., Quinn, N., Rosabal-Coto, M., Scheidecker, G., Takada, A. & Vicedo, M. (2018). Bringing the real world into developmental science: A commentary on Weber, Fernald, and Diop (2017). *Child Development, 89* (6), e594–e603.

Morgan, T. J. H. & Harris, P. L. (2015). James Mark Baldwin and contemporary theories of culture and evolution. *European Journal of Developmental Psychology, 12*, 666–678.

Nelson, K. (1993). The psychological and social origins of autobiographical memory. *Psychological Science, 4*, 7–14.

Nisbett, R. E., Peng, K., Choi, I. & Norenzayan, A. (2001). Culture and systems of thought: Holistic versus analytic cognition. *Psychological Review, 108*, 291–310.

Nunner-Winkler, G. & Sodian, B. (1988). Children's understanding of moral emotions. *Child Development, 59*, 1323–1338.

O'Connor, T. G. & Rutter, M. (2000). Attachment disorder behavior following early severe deprivation: Extension and longitudinal follow-up. *Journal of the American Academy of Child and Adolescent Psychiatry, 39*, 703–712.

Onishi, K. H. & Baillargeon, R. (2005). Do 15-month-old infants understand false beliefs? *Science, 308*, 255–258.

Ozonoff, S., Pennington, B. F. & Rogers, S. J. (1991). Executive function deficits in high functioning autistic individuals: Relationship to theory of mind. *Journal of Child Psychology and Psychiatry, 32*, 1081–1105.

Pace, A., Alper, R., Burchinal, M. R., Golinkoff, R. M. & Hirsh-Pasek, K. (2019). Measuring success: Within and cross-domain predictors of academic and social trajectories in elementary school. *Early Childhood Research Quarterly, 46*, 112–125.

Pasquini, E. S., Corriveau, K. H., Koenig, M. & Harris, P. L. (2007). Preschoolers monitor the relative accuracy of informants. *Developmental Psychology*, 43, 1216–1226.

Payir, A., McLaughlin, N., Cui, Y. K., Davoodi, T., Clegg, J., Harris, P. L. & Corriveau, K. H. (2021). Children's ideas about what can really happen. The impact of age and religious background. *Cognitive Science*, 45 (1), e13054.

Peng, K. & Nisbett, R. E. (1999). Culture, dialectics, and reasoning about contradiction. *American Psychologist*, 54, 741–754.

Perner, J., Sprung, M., Zauner, P. & Haider, H. (2003). *Want that* is understood well before *say that, think that*, and false belief: A test of de Villiers's linguistic determinism on German-speaking children. *Child Development*, 74, 179–188.

Peterson, C. & Siegal, M. (2000). Insights into theory of mind from deafness and autism. *Mind and Language*, 15, 123–145.

Piaget, J. (1923a). *The language and thought of the child*. New York: Harcourt, Brace & World.

Piaget, J. (1923b). La pensée symbolique et la pensée de l'enfant. *Archives de Psychologie*, 18 (72), 275–304.

Piaget, J. (1928). La causalité chez l'enfant: Children's understanding of causality. *British Journal of Psychology*, 18, 276–301.

Piaget, J. (1931). Le développement intellectual chez les jeunes enfants. Étude critique. *Mind*, 40, 137–160.

Piaget, J. (1962). *Play, dreams and imitation*. New York: Norton.

Piaget, J. (1965a). *The child's conception of number*. New York: Norton.

Piaget, J. (1965b). *The moral judgment of the child*. New York: Free Press. (Original work published 1932.)

Pillemer, D. B. (1992). Preschool memories of personal circumstances: The fire alarm study. In E. Winograd & U. Neisser (Eds), *Affect and accuracy in recall: Studies of 'flashbulb' memories* (pp. 121–137). New York: Cambridge University Press.

Pillemer, D. B., Picariello, M. L. & Pruett, J. C. (1994). Very long-term memories of a salient preschool event. *Applied Cognitive Psychology*, 8, 95–106.

Pinker, S. (1994). *The language instinct*. New York: Morrow.

Plomin, R., Fulker, D. W. Corley, R. & DeFries, J. C. (1997). Nature, nurture, and cognitive development. *Psychological Science*, 8, 442–447.

Pons, F. & Harris, P. L. (2005). Longitudinal change and longitudinal stability of individual differences in children's emotion understanding. *Cognition and Emotion*, 19, 1158–1174.

Pons, F., Lawson, J., Harris, P. L. & de Rosnay, M. (2003). Individual differences in children's emotion understanding: Effects of age and language. *Scandinavian Journal of Psychology*, 44, 347–353.

Pons, F., Harris, P. L. & de Rosnay, M. (2004). Emotion comprehension between 3 and 11 years: Developmental periods and hierarchical organization. *European Journal of Developmental Psychology*, 1, 127–152.

Premack, D. & Woodruff, G. (1978). Does the chimpanzee have a theory of mind? *The Behavioral and Brain Sciences*, 1, 516–526.

Principe, G. F., Kanaya, T., Ceci, S. J. & Singh, M. (2006). Believing is seeing. How rumors can engender false memories in preschoolers. *Psychological Science, 17,* 243–248.

Qian, M. K., Quinn, P., Heyman, G., Pascalis, O., Fu, G. & Lee, K. (2017). Perceptual individuation training (but not mere exposure) reduces implicit racial bias in preschool children. *Developmental Psychology, 53,* 845–859.

Qian, M. K., Quinn, P., Heyman, G., Pascalis, O., Fu, G. & Lee, K. (2019). A long-term effect of perceptual individuation training on reducing implicit racial bias in preschool children. *Child Development, 90,* e290–e305.

Quine, W. V. (1960). *Word and object.* Cambridge, MA: Technology Press of the Massachusetts Institute of Technology.

Reese, E. & Newcombe, R. (2007). Training mothers in elaborative reminiscing enhances children's autobiographical memory and narrative. *Child Development, 78,* 1153–1170.

Reese, E., Haden, C. A. & Fivush, R. (1993). Mother–child conversations about the past: relationships of style and memory over time. *Cognitive Development, 8,* 403–430.

Rhodes, M. & Baron, A. (2019). The development of social categorization. *Annual Review of Developmental Psychology, 1,* 359–386.

Robertson, J. & Robertson, J. (1971). Young children in brief separation. *The Psychoanalytic Study of the Child, 26,* 264–315.

Roese, N. J. (1997). Counterfactual thinking. *Psychological Bulletin, 21,* 133–148.

Romeo, R. R., Leonard, J. A., Robinson, S. T., West, M. R., Mackey, A. P., Rowe, M. L. & Gabrieli, J. D. E. (2018). Beyond the 30-million-word gap: Children's conversational exposure is associated with language-related brain function. *Psychological Science, 29,* 700–710.

Ronfard, S., Chen, E. E. & Harris, P. L. (2018). The emergence of the empirical stance: Children's testing of counterintuitive claims. *Developmental Psychology, 54,* 482–493.

Ronfard, S., Ünlütabak, B., Bazhydai, M., Nicolopoulou, A. & Harris, P. L. (2020). Preschoolers in Belarus and Turkey accept an adult's counter-intuitive claim and do not spontaneously seek evidence to test that claim. *International Journal of Behavioral Development, 44,* 424–432.

Ronfard, S., Chen, E. E. & Harris, P. L. (2021). Testing what you're told: Young children's empirical investigation of a surprising claim. *Journal of Cognition and Development, 22,* 426–447.

Rosengren, K. S., Kalish, C. W., Hickling, A. K. & Gelman, S. A. (1994). Exploring the relation between preschool children's magical beliefs and causal thinking. *British Journal of Developmental Psychology, 12,* 69–82.

Rothbaum, F., Pott, M., Azuma, H., Miyake, K. & Weisz, J. (2000a). The development of close relationships in Japan and the United States: Paths of symbiotic harmony and generative tension. *Child Development, 71,* 1121–1142.

Rothbaum, F., Weisz, J., Pott, M., Miyake, K. & Morelli, G. (2000b). Attachment and culture. *American Psychologist, 55,* 1093–1104.

Rousseau, J.-J. (1999). *Emile*. Oeuvres Complètes, Volume IV. Paris: Gallimard, Bilbiothèque de La Pléiade. (Original work published 1762.)

Rowe, M. (2008). Child-directed speech: relation to socioeconomic status, knowledge of child development and child vocabulary skill. *Journal of Child Language*, 35, 185–205.

Rowe, M. L. & Leech, K. A. (2019). A parent intervention with a growth mindset approach improves children's early gesture and vocabulary development. *Developmental Science*, 22, e12792.

Rowe, M. L. & Weisleder, A. (2020). Language development in context. *Annual Review of Developmental Psychology*, 2, 201–223.

Rowe, M. L., Raudenbush, S. W. & Goldin-Meadow, S. (2012). The pace of vocabulary growth helps predict later vocabulary skill. *Child Development*, 83, 508–525.

Ruppenthal, G. C., Arling, G. L., Harlow, H. F., Sackett, G. P. & Suomi, S. J. (1976). A 10-year perspective of motherless-mother monkey behavior. *Journal of Abnormal Psychology*, 85, 341–349.

Rutland, A., Cameron, L., Milne, A. & McGeorge, P. (2005). Social norms and self-presentation: Children's implicit and explicit intergroup attitudes. *Child Development*, 76, 451–466.

Rutter, M. (1972). *Maternal deprivation reassessed*. Harmondsworth: Penguin.

Rutter, M., Colvert, E., Kreppner, L., Beckett, C., Castel, J., Groothues, C., Hawkins, A., O'Connor, T. G., Stevens, S. E. & Sonagu-Barke, E. J. S. (2007). Early adolescent outcomes for institutionally deprived and non-deprived adoptees. I: Disinhibited attachment. *Journal of Child Psychology and Psychiatry*, 48, 17–30.

Sak, R. (2020). Preschoolers' difficult questions and their teachers' responses. *Early Childhood Education Journal*, 48, 59–70.

Salvatore, J. E., Kuo, S. I.-C., Steele, R. D., Simpson, J. A. & Collins, W. A. (2011). Recovering from conflict in romantic relationships: A developmental perspective. *Psychological Science*, 22, 376–383.

Sanderson, C. A. (2020). *Why we act? Turning bystanders into moral rebels*. Cambridge, MA: Belknap Press/Harvard University Press.

Scarr, S. & McCartney, K. (1983). How people make their own environments: A theory of genotype → environment effects. *Child Development*, 54, 424–435.

Schneider, B. H., Atkinson, L. & Tardif, C. (2001). Child–parent attachment and children's peer relations: A quantitative review. *Developmental Psychology*, 37, 86–100.

Scribner, S. & Cole, M. (1981). *The psychology of literacy*. Cambridge, MA: Harvard University Press.

Senju, A., Southgate, V., White, V. & Frith, U. (2009). Mindblind eyes: An absence of spontaneous theory of mind in Asperger syndrome. *Science*, 325, 883–885.

Senju, A., Southgate, V., Snape, C., Leonard, M. & Csibra, G. (2011). Do 18-month-olds really attribute mental states to others: A critical test? *Psychological Science*, 22, 878–880.

Senzaki, S. & Shimizu, Y. (2020). Early learning environments for the development of attention: Maternal narratives in the United States and Japan. *Journal of Cross-Cultural Psychology*, *51*, 187–202.

Shtulman, A. & Carey, S. (2007). Improbable or impossible? How children reason about the possibility of extraordinary events. *Child Development*, *78*, 1015–1032.

Siegal, M., Butterworth, G. & Newcombe, P. A. (2004). Culture and children's cosmology. *Developmental Science*, *7*, 308–324.

Siegal, M. & Storey, R. M. (1985). Daycare and children's conceptions of moral and social rules. *Child Development*, *6*, 1001–1008.

Silverman, P. R., Nickman, S. & Worden, J. W. (1992). Detachment revisited: the child's reconstruction of a dead parent. *American Journal of Orthopsychiatry*, *62*, 494–503.

Simons, D. J. & Chabris, C. F. (1999). Gorillas in our midst: sustained inattentional blindness for dynamic events. *Perception*, *28*, 1059–1074.

Slade, A. (1987). Quality of attachment and early symbolic play. *Developmental Psychology*, *23*, 78–85.

Smetana, J. G. (1981). Preschool children's conception of moral and social rules. *Child Development*, *52*, 1333–1336.

Smetana, J. G. (1984). Toddler's social interactions regarding moral and conventional transgressions. *Child Development*, *55*, 1767–1776.

Smetana, J. G., Kelly, M. & Twentyman, C. T. (1984). Abused, neglected and nonmaltreated children's conceptions of moral and socio-conventional transgressions. *Child Development*, *55*, 277–287.

Smith, C. E., Chen, D. & Harris, P. L. (2010). When the happy victimizer says sorry: Children's understanding of apology and emotion. *British Journal of Developmental Psychology*, *28*, 727–746.

Smith, C. E., Blake, P. R. & Harris, P. L. (2013). I should but I won't: Why young children endorse norms of fair sharing but do not endorse them. *PLoS ONE*, *8* (3), e5910.

Smolak, L. & Weinraub, M. (1983). Maternal speech: Strategy or response? *Journal of Child Language*, *10*, 369–380.

Snarey, J. R. (1985). Cross-cultural universality of social-moral development: A critical review of Kohlbergian research. *Psychological Bulletin*, *97*, 202–232.

Snow, C. E., Burns, S. & Griffin, P. (1998). *Preventing reading difficulties in young children*. Washington, DC: National Academy Press.

Sodian, B. & Frith, U. (1992). Deception and sabotage in autistic, normal and retarded children. *Journal of Child Psychology and Psychiatry*, *33*, 591–605.

Southgate, V., Senju, A. & Csibra, G. (2007). Action anticipation through attribution of false belief by 2-year-olds. *Psychological Science*, *18*, 587–592.

Spaepen, E., Coppola, M., Spelke, E. S., Carey, S. E. & Goldin-Meadow, S. (2011). Number without a language model. *Proceedings of the National Academy of Sciences of the United States of America*, *108*, 3163–3168.

Sperry, D. E., Sperry, L. L. & Miller, P. J. (2019). Reexamining the verbal environments of children from different socioeconomic backgrounds. *Child Development*, *90*, 1303–1318.

Sroufe, L. A. (1983). Infant–caregiver attachment and patterns of adaptation in preschool. In M. Perlmutter (Ed.), *Minnesota Symposium on Child Psychology, 16*, 41–83. Hillsdale, NJ: Erlbaum.

Subbotsky, E. V. (1994). Early rationality and magical thinking in preschoolers: Space and time. *British Journal of Developmental Psychology, 12*, 97–108.

Sully, J. (2000). *Studies of childhood*. London: Free Association Books. (Original work published 1896.)

Surian, L., Caldi, S. & Sperber, D. (2007). Attribution of beliefs by 13-month-old infants. *Psychological Science, 18*, 580–586.

Tager-Flusberg, H. (1993). What language reveals about the understanding of minds in children with autism. In S. Baron-Cohen, H. Tager-Flusberg & D. J. Cohen (Eds), *Understanding other minds: Perspectives from autism* (pp. 138–157). Oxford: Oxford University Press.

Takahashi, K. (1990). Are the key assumptions of the 'Strange Situation' procedure universal? A view from Japanese research. *Human Development, 33*, 23–30.

Tan, E., Mikami, A. Y., Luzhanska, A. & Hamlin, J. K. (2021). The homogeneity and heterogeneity of moral functioning in preschool. *Child Development, 92*, 959–975.

Tardif, T. & Wellman, H. M. (2000). Acquisition of mental state language in Mandarin- and Cantonese-speaking children. *Developmental Psychology, 36*, 25–43.

Taumoepeau, M. & Ruffman, T. (2006). Mother and infant talk about mental states relates to desire language and emotion understanding. *Child Development, 77*, 465–481.

Taumoepeau, M. & Ruffman, T. (2008). Stepping-stones to others' minds: Maternal talk relates to child mental state language and emotion understanding at 15, 24, and 33 months. *Child Development, 79*, 284–302.

Taylor, M. (1999). *Imaginary companions and the children who create them*. New York: Oxford University Press.

Tizard, B. & Hughes, M. (1984). *Young children learning*. London: Fontana.

Tomasello, M. & Barton, M. E. (1994). Learning words in nonostensive contexts. *Developmental Psychology, 30*, 639–650.

Tong, Y., Wang, F. & Danovitch, J. (2020). The role of epistemic and social characteristics in children's selective trust: Three meta-analyses. *Developmental Science, 23*, e12895.

Tottenham, N., Tanaka, J. W., Leon, A. C., McCarry, T., Nurse, M., Hare, T. A., Marcus, D. J., Westerlund, A., Casey, B. J. & Nelson, C. (2009). The NimStim set of facial expressions: Judgments from untrained research participants. *Psychiatry Research, 168*, 242–249.

Trabasso, T., Stein, N. L. & Johnson, L. R. (1981). Children's knowledge of events: A causal analysis of story structure. In G. Bower (Ed.), *Learning and motivation* (Vol. 15, pp. 237–282). New York: Academic Press.

Trentacosta, C. J. & Fine, S. E. (2010). Emotion knowledge, social competence and behavior problems in childhood and adolescence: A meta-analytic review. *Social Development, 19*, 1–29.

Ursache, A., Gouley, K., Dawson-McClure, S., Calzada, E. J., Barajes-Gonzalez, R. G., Calzada, J., Goldfield, K. S. & Brotman, L. M. (2020). Early emotion knowledge and later academic achievement among children of color in historically disinvested neighborhoods. *Child Development*, *91*, e1249–e1266.

Usher, J. A. & Neisser, U. (1993). Childhood amnesia and the beginnings of memory for four early childhood life events. *Journal of Experimental Psychology: General*, *122*, 155–165.

Van Bergen, P., Salmon, K., Dadds, M. R. & Allen, J. (2009). The effects of mother training in emotion-rich, elaborative reminiscing on children's shared recall and emotion knowledge. *Journal of Cognition and Development*, *10*, 162–187.

Van de Vondervoort, J. W. & Hamlin, J. K. (2016). Evidence for intuitive morality: Preverbal infants make sociomoral evaluations. *Child Development Perspectives*, *10*, 143–148.

Van IJzendoorn, M. H. (1995). Adult attachment representations, parental responsiveness, and infant attachment: A meta-analysis on the predictive validity of the Adult Attachment interview. *Psychological Bulletin*, *117*, 387–403.

Van IJzendoorn, M. H., Schuengel, C. & Bakermans-Kranenburg, M. J. (1999). Disorganized attachment in early childhood: Meta-analysis of precursors, concomitants, and sequelae. *Development and Psychopathology*, *11*, 225–249.

Vygotsky, L. (1986). *Thought and language*. Cambridge, MA: Harvard University Press. (Original work published 1934.)

Wainryb, C., Shaw, L. A., Langley, M., Cottam, K. & Lewis, R. (2004). Children's thinking about diversity of belief in the early school years: Judgments of relativism, tolerance, and disagreeing persons. *Child Development*, 75, 687–703.

Waldinger, R. J. & Schulz, M. S. (2016). The long reach of nurturing family environments: Links with midlife emotion-regulatory styles and late-life security. *Psychological Science*, *27*, 1443–1450.

Wang, Q. (2001). Cultural effects on adults' earliest childhood recollection and self-description: Implications for the relation between memory and self. *Journal of Personality and Social Psychology*, *81*, 220–233.

Wang, Q. (2006). Earliest recollections of self and others in European American and Taiwanese young adults. *Psychological Science*, *17*, 708–714.

Wang, Q. (2021). Cultural pathways and outcomes of autobiographical memory development. *Child Development Perspectives*, *15*, 196–202.

Wang, Q. & Fivush, R. (2005). Mother–child conversations of emotionally salient events: Exploring the functions of emotional reminiscing in European-American and Chinese families. *Social Development*, *14*, 473–495.

Wang, Q. & Song, Q. (2018). He says, she says: Mothers and children remembering the same events. *Child Development*, *89*, 2215–2229.

Wang, Q., Shao, Y. & Li, Y. J. (2010). "My way or Mom's way?" The bilingual and bicultural self in Hong Kong Chinese children and adolescents. *Child Development*, *81*, 555–567.

Watson-Jones, R. E., Busch, J. T. A., Harris, P. L. & Legare, C. H. (2017). Does the body survive death? Cultural variation in beliefs about life everlasting. *Cognitive Science*, *41*, 455–476.

Weber, A., Fernald, A. & Diop, Y. (2017). When cultural norms discourage talking to babies: Effectiveness of a parenting program in rural Senegal. *Child Development*, *88*, 1513–1526.

Weisleder, A. & Fernald, A. (2013). Talking to children matters: Early language experience strengthens processing and builds vocabulary. *Psychological Science*, *24*, 2143–2152.

Wellman, H. M. (2018). Theory of mind: The state of the art. *European Journal of Developmental Psychology*, *15*, 728–755.

Wellman, H. M. & Gelman, S. A. (1998). Knowledge acquisition in foundational domains. In D. Kuhn & R. S. Siegler (Eds), *Handbook of child psychology: Vol. 2. Cognition, perception and language*, 4th edition (pp. 523–574). New York: John Wiley.

Wellman, H. M. & Liu, D. (2004). Scaling of theory-of-mind tasks. *Child Development*, *75*, 523–541.

Wellman, H. M., Harris, P. L., Banerjee, M. & Sinclair, A. (1995). Early understanding of emotion: Evidence from natural language. *Cognition and Emotion*, *9*, 117–149.

Wellman, H. M., Cross, D. & Watson, J. (2001). Meta-analysis of theory-of-mind development: The truth about false belief. *Child Development*, *72*, 655–684.

Wells, G. L. & Gavanski, I. (1989). Mental simulation and causality. *Journal of Personality and Social Psychology*, *56*, 161–169.

Wimmer, H. & Perner, J. (1983). Belief about beliefs: Representation and constraining function of wrong beliefs in young children's understanding of deception. *Cognition*, *13*, 103–128.

Winsler, A. & Naglieri, J. (2003). Overt and covert verbal problem-solving strategies: Developmental trends in use, awareness, and relations with task performance in children aged 5 to 17. *Child Development*, *74*, 659–678.

Wittgenstein, L. (1953). *Philosophical investigations*. Oxford: Blackwell.

Woodward, A. L. (1998). Infants selectively encode the goal object of an actor's reach. *Cognition*, *69*, 1–34.

Woolley, J. D. & Cox, V. (2007). Development of beliefs about storybook reality. *Developmental Science*, *10*, 681–693.

Woolley, J. D. & Phelps, K. E. (2001). The development of beliefs about prayer. *Journal of Cognition and Culture*, *1*, 139–167.

Woolley, J. D., Phelps, K. E., Davis, D. L. & Mandell, D. J. (1999). Where theories of mind meet magic: the development of children's beliefs about wishing. *Child Development*, *70*, 571–587.

Index